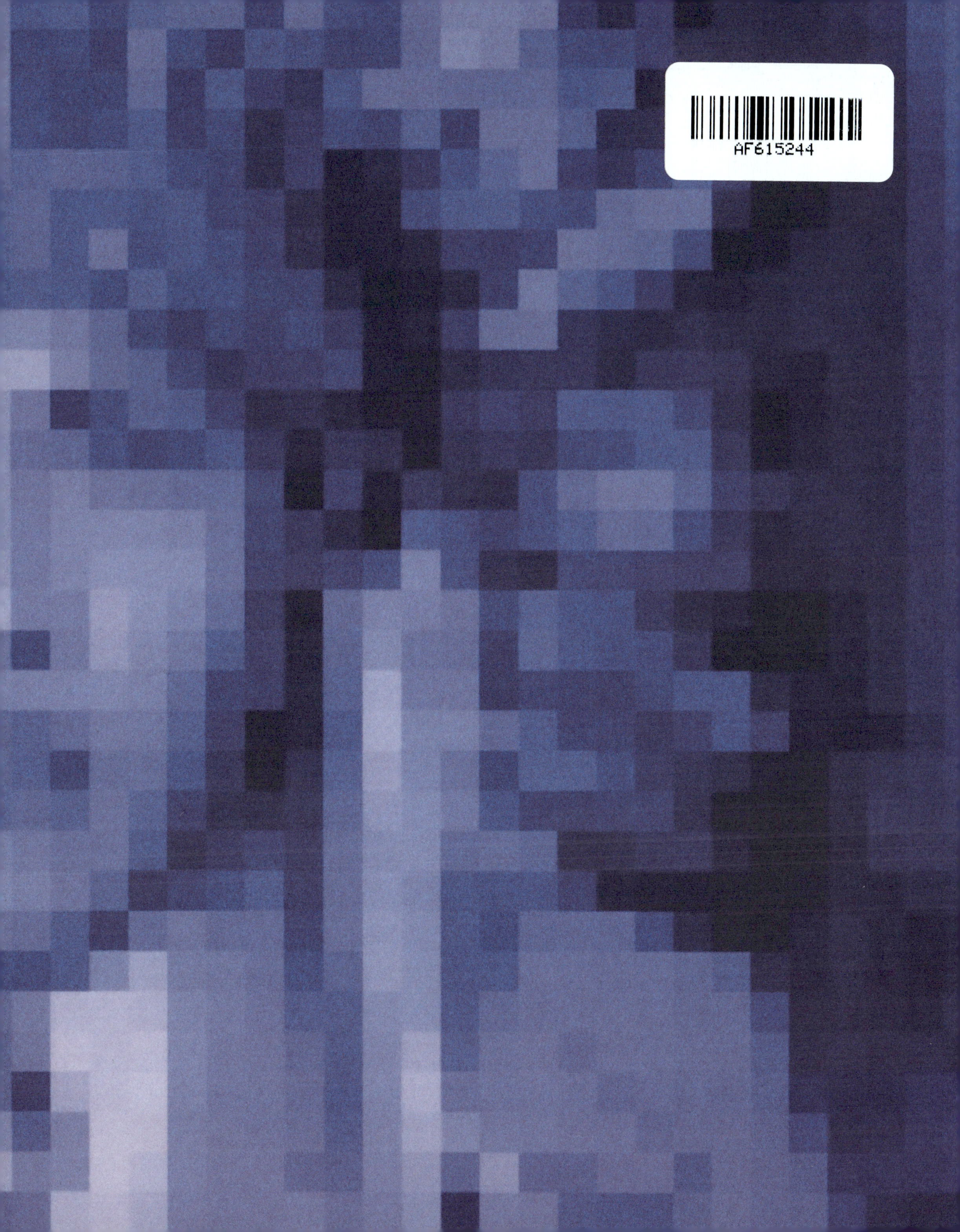

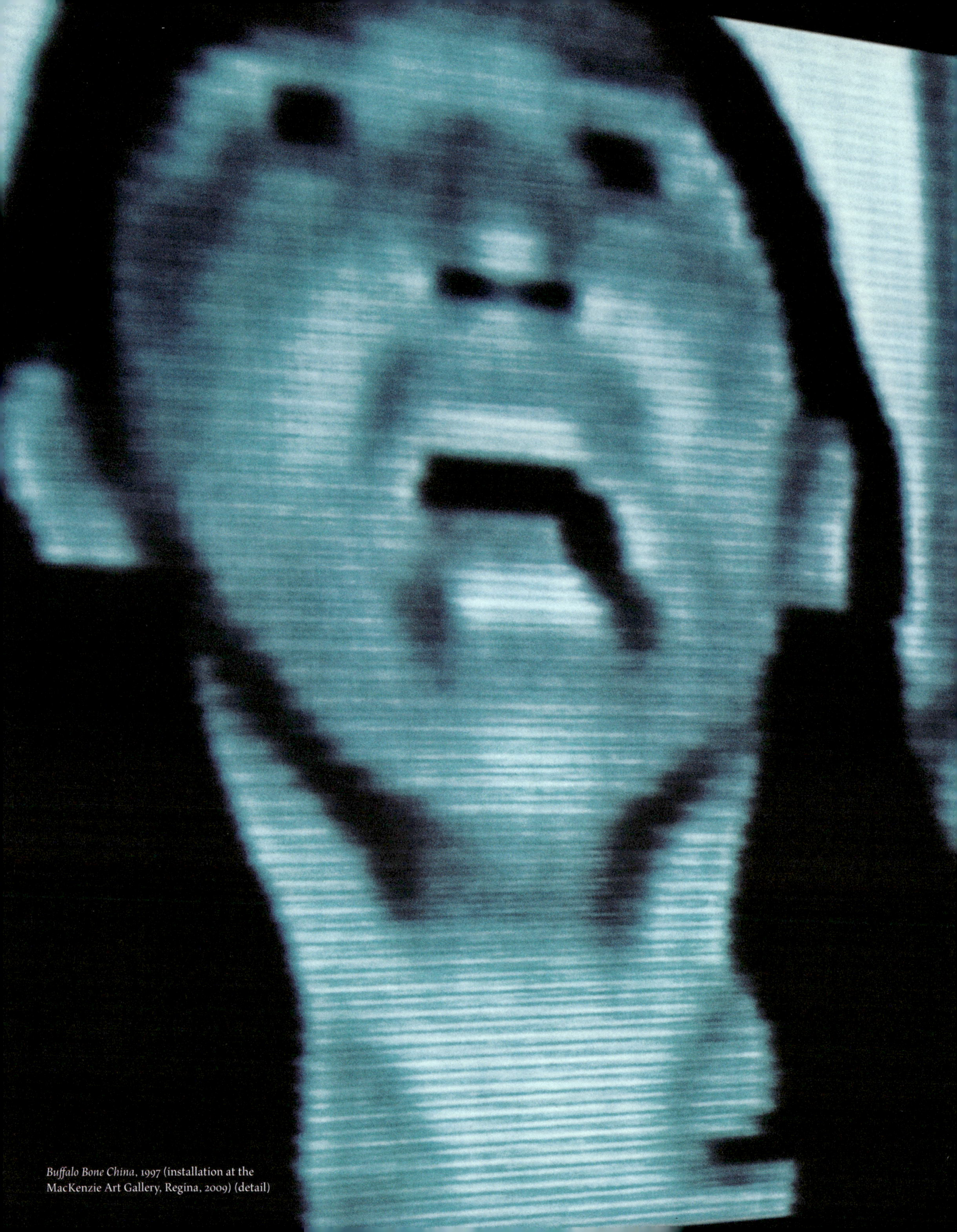

Buffalo Bone China, 1997 (installation at the MacKenzie Art Gallery, Regina, 2009) (detail)

DANA CLAXTON

FRINGING THE CUBE

Vancouver Artgallery

Figure.1

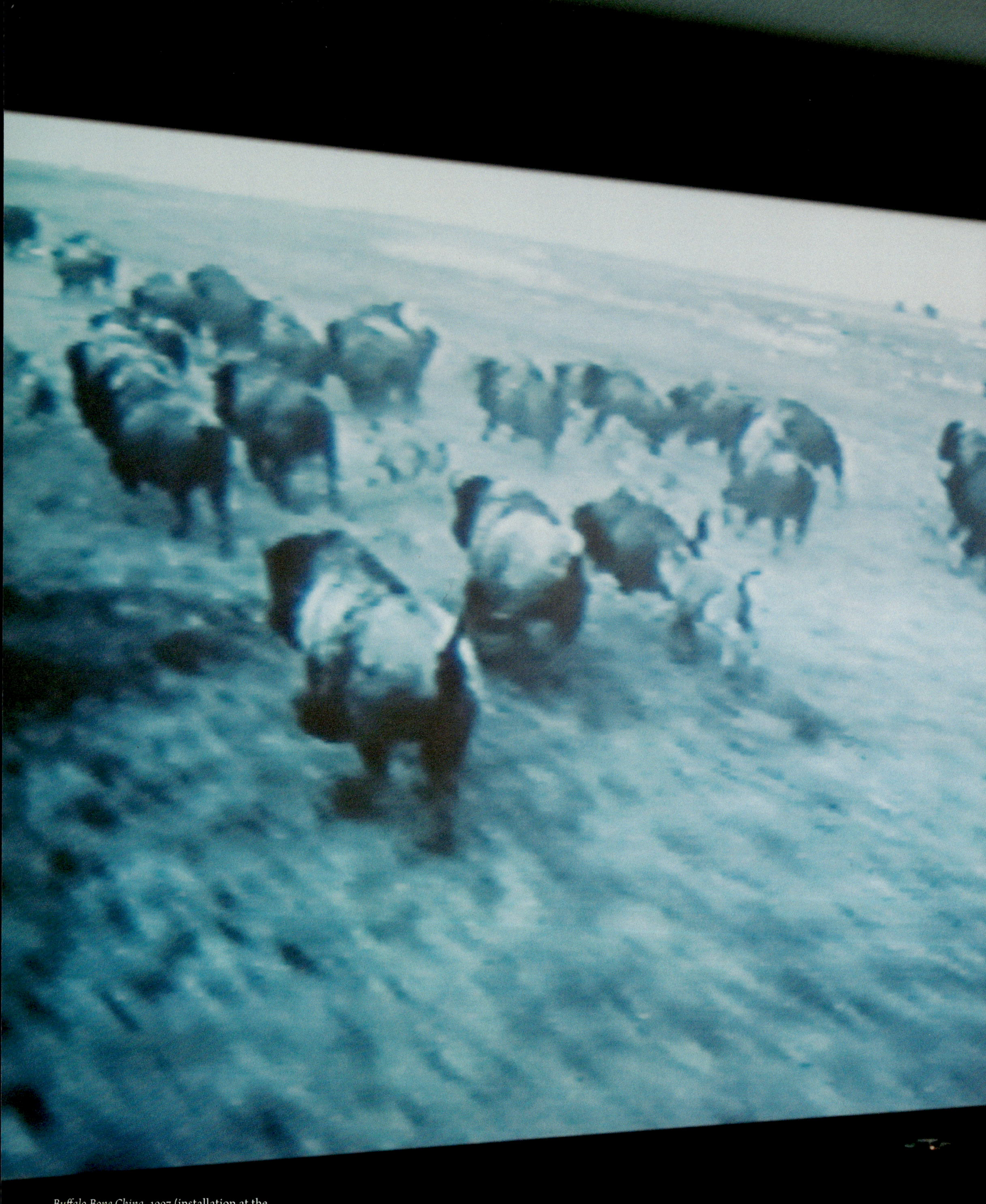

Buffalo Bone China, 1997 (installation at the MacKenzie Art Gallery, Regina, 2009) (detail)

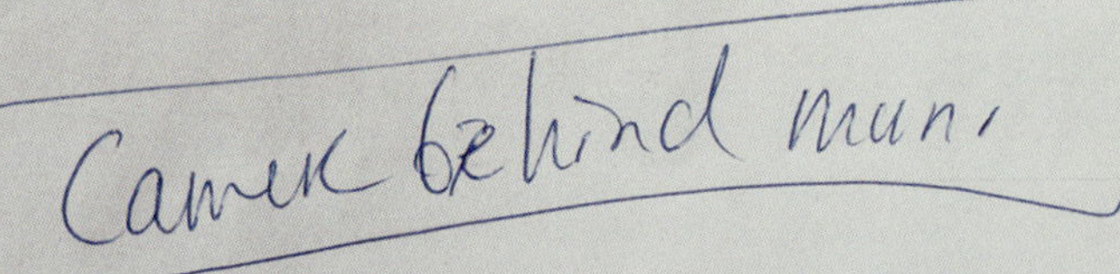

11 FADE IN: MAN SITS ALONE IN CHAIR IT IS DARK, WE HEAR HEEL STEPS, WINKET ENTERS FRAME, MAN MOTIONS HIS HEAD. 11

WINKET

THEY CANNOT TAKE AWAY OUR GODS
WHY DO THEY CONTINUE TO TRY.

MAN

I DID NOT KNOW. I DID NOT KNOW.
IRREVERENCE STANDS ALONE
AWAY FROM ME.

WINKET BEGINS TO WALK OVER TO MAN, AS HE GETS CLOSER MAN FALLS FROM HIS CHAIR ONTO FLOOR- WINKET SITS . FADE TO BLACK.

12 LONG SHOT OF WINKET IN HIS BEDROOM. HE WALKS UP THE LARGE MIRROR. SERVANTS ATTEND TO HIM. THEY TAKE OFF HIS CLOAK. UNDER
HIS CLOAK IS A BLACK LACY DRESSING GOWN.
HE WALKS OVER TO HIS LARGE DRAPED BED. HE CLIMBS INTO BED SLOW MOTION. HE FALLS A SLEEP. 12

DREAM LIKE EXTERIOR QUICK CUTS OF WINKET WALKING THRU GARDEN WITH COLONIAL BUILDINGS.

WINKET (VOICE OVER)

CONDEMNED TO EXILE
SENT OFF TO BE EXCOMMUNICATED
SPRINKLED, DIPPED AND BAPTIZED

MERCILESSLY

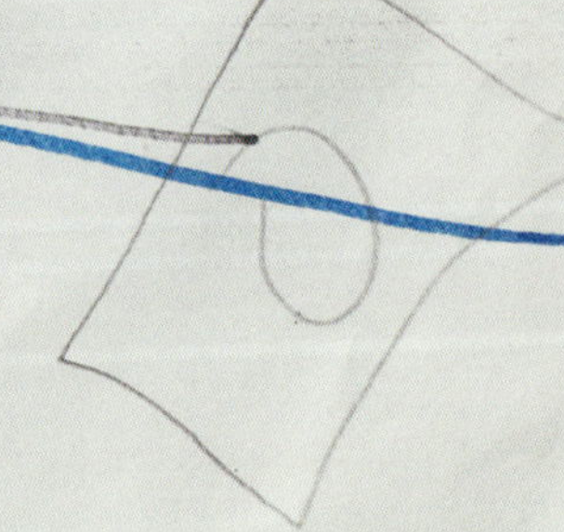

DIRECTOR'S FOREWORD

KATHLEEN S. BARTELS

Over the past three decades, the widely acclaimed Vancouver-based Hunkpapa Lakota artist Dana Claxton has developed an extraordinary and singular body of work in performance, video, film and photography. Through a powerful mix-meld-mash approach to art making that weaves together tradition, history and contemporary culture, Claxton forcefully expresses Indigenous cultural values and spirituality while challenging the persistent legacy of colonialism and the stereotypical representations of Indigenous people that circulate in art, literature and pop culture. Although Claxton's work has been exhibited widely in Canada, the United States and Europe, there has not been an exhibition or publication that addresses the remarkable breadth of her practice. The Vancouver Art Gallery is especially honoured to survey the full range and richness of Claxton's career over the past thirty years through the exhibition *Dana Claxton: Fringing the Cube* and this accompanying catalogue.

As indicated by the presentation of exhibitions such as *Susan Point: Spindle Whorl*; *We Come to Witness: Sonny Assu in Dialogue with Emily Carr*; *James Hart: The Dance Screen (The Scream Too)*; *Beat Nation: Art, Hip Hop and Aboriginal Culture* and *Charles Edenshaw*, the work of Indigenous artists plays a prominent role in the Gallery's programs and we are very pleased to extend our commitment to bring artwork that articulates Indigenous perspectives to the attention of a broad public through *Dana Claxton: Fringing the Cube*.

I am deeply grateful for financial assistance that has made this significant endeavour possible. Special recognition goes to Board Trustee Cathy Zuo for her major gift in support of this exhibition, and Trustee Larry Lunn along with his wife Maureen and son Miles, who provide support as our Visionary Partners for Photography Exhibitions. My thanks also extend to Vancity, our exhibition Supporting Sponsor, and to Trustee Bruce Munro Wright for his additional gift. This catalogue has been made possible with generous financial assistance from Gallery Trustee Pamela Richardson and her family, our Visionary Partners for Scholarship and Publications. I also would like to acknowledge funds from the Jack and Doris Shadbolt Endowment for Research and Publications.

My profound gratitude goes out to the Vancouver Art Gallery's Board of Trustees and staff for their high standards and commitment to the realization of the Gallery's programs. I greatly appreciate the many lenders to the exhibition who have made work from their collections available for this important project and to Figure 1 Publishing and Studio Blackwell for creating this handsome publication. I extend special thanks to Grant Arnold, Audain Curator of British Columbia Art at the Vancouver Art Gallery, for his excellent work on this exhibition and publication; Monika Kin Gagnon and Olivia Michiko Gagnon, David Garneau, Layli Long Soldier, Jaleh Mansoor and Siobhan McCracken Nixon for their insightful texts; and Pauline Petit for her indispensable assistance on this project. Most importantly, I offer my profound thanks to Dana Claxton for her exceptionally powerful and beautiful artwork and her remarkable generosity of spirit.

Script for *The Red Paper*, 1996

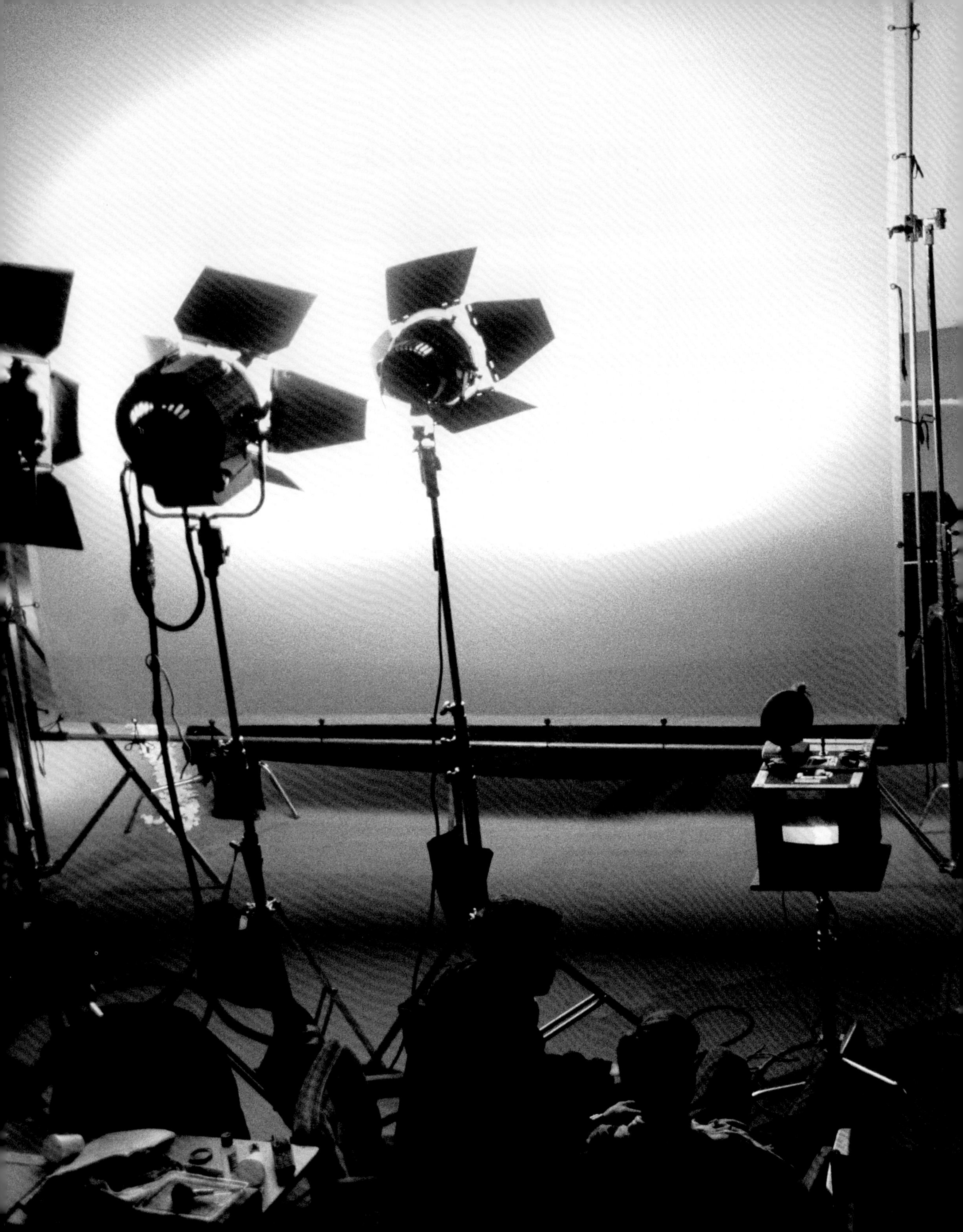

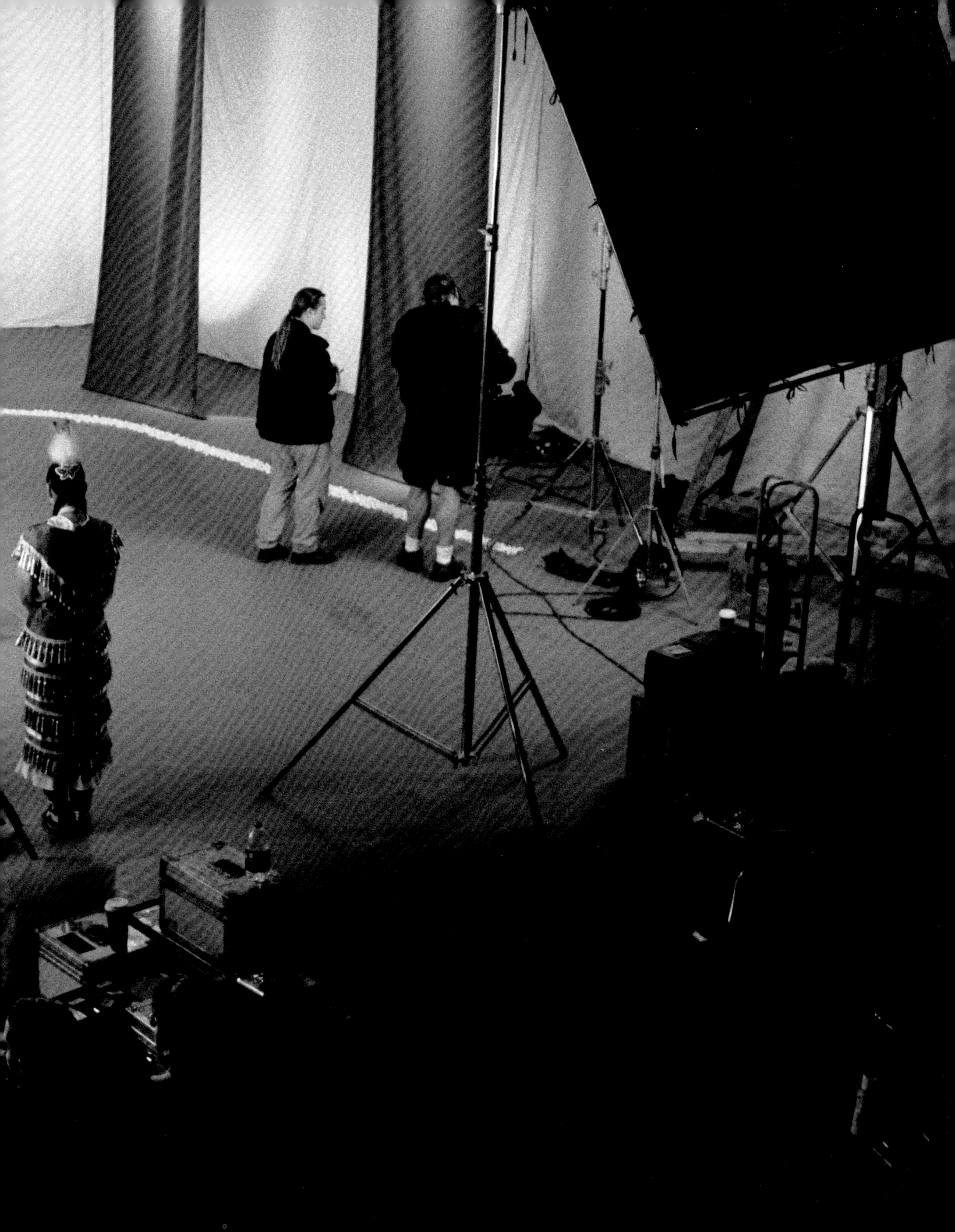

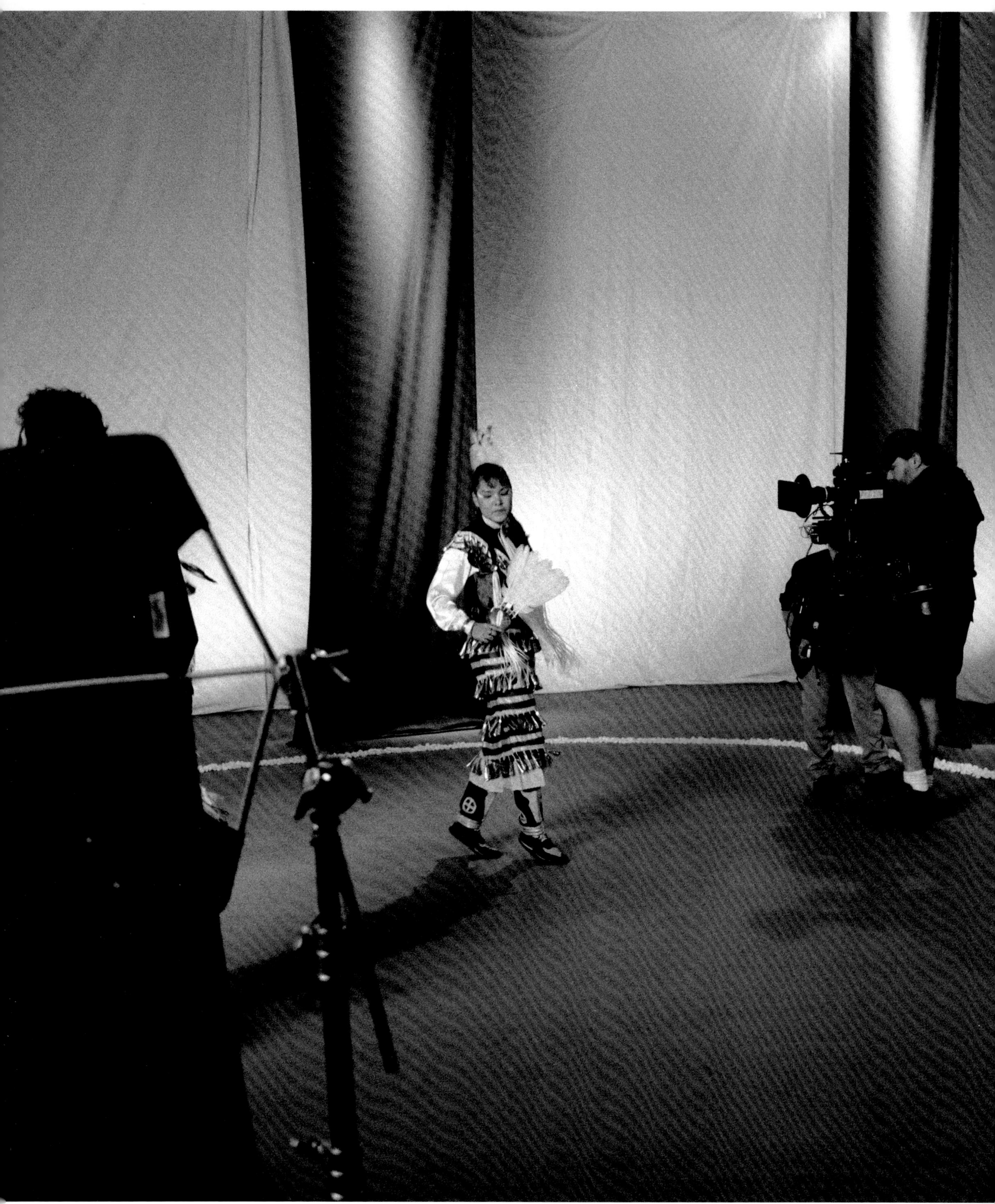

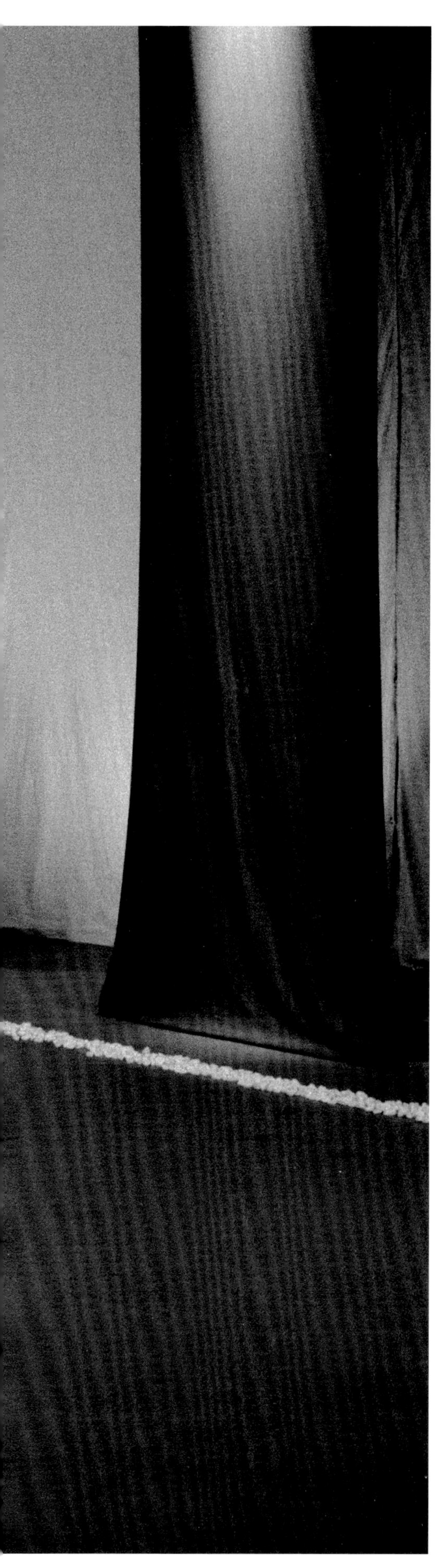

TRIBUTE TO DANA CLAXTON AND THE ART OF GENEROSITY

LAYLI LONG SOLDIER

Out of curiosity, I asked Dana Claxton to name qualities that have been central to her work over the years. Quickly, she emailed back, "My work has been about spirit-ancestors-NDN ways of knowing—Lakota teachings—generosity / wisdom / fortitude / courage / and more spirit / celebrating and honouring ourselves / and never surrendering / showing our NDN beauty." I couldn't help but smile and glow in reading her response. In this list of qualities and values, all are felt throughout her work, even to a novice viewer. But of all, what resonates most is, *generosity.*

I leaned back, thinking, *What does generosity mean, how does it work, in the making of art?* Further, *What does it mean for a Lakota artist?* In Lakhótiyapi, generosity is *cantéyuke*, and its meaning extends beyond the giving of things or possessions. It is seen in one's willingness to dig deep, to drop one's guard and to *feel*. Through generosity, we offer concern, sympathy, empathy, kindness, compassion, and most generous of all: forgiveness. It is to express one's emotion as a vulnerable act of connection, e.g. as a relative grieves, we are not content to offer a tissue and hold their hand. No. We lean in, hold our sister close and let our tears flow in grief with her. Generosity is an offering of time, and even further, it is a giving of labour—that is, to work selflessly for the well-being of others. Yet, in the workings of generosity, it is not the *what* that defines it—possessions, time, emotion—but it's the *how.* We recognize generosity because it is performed *beyond* what is moderate, expected, or easy. It is an act that is free of any expectation of return. With all this in mind, how does this apply to art?

I pause to remember that for generosity to exist, there must, first, exist a relationship. There must be an *other* with whom we are generous. And at its most sincere, we might even say that generosity is a giving *beyond* oneself to the, ultimate, giving *over* of oneself. That is to say, the painter gives herself over to the painting or the poet gives himself over to the poem, as offering to the viewer, the reader, and by extension, the world.

Dana Claxton is both an artist and an educator, and I see this *giving over* throughout her immense body of work. In an article

PREVIOUS: *Jingle Dress #1*, 1998–2011 OPPOSITE: *Jingle Dress #2*, 1998–2011 (detail)

written by Leah Collins for *CBC Arts*, Claxton is reported to have asked her students at the University of British Columbia, "When people think of indigenous women, what do they see? What's the stereotype?" Yet, Claxton doesn't ask this question for herself; she isn't waiting for an answer. "I'll tell them I don't want to know the answer, you just think about what yours is."[1] In letting go of a demand for answers, Claxton's question, thus, becomes a giving—perhaps doubly so, because as Claxton is an Indigenous woman herself, she is implicit to both the question and answer. Nonetheless, she allows her students to think a thing through, internally. There's selflessness and a particular kind of grace in this. It is a question to *raise questions* and, in turn, consciousness. Thus, it is a gift of liberation.

Still, the generosity in Claxton's art is not entirely "selfless," that is to say, it weaves the self as thread to the whole. In the same *CBC Arts* article, Claxton says, "Indigenous people have been structurally dehumanized in all facets of life in North America, whether it's through education, through the state, through the church. In some ways, my work has attempted to show us as human beings."[2] I reflect on Claxton's nod toward a collective *us,* how it is simultaneously inclusive (holding close), while reaching and radiating outward. Might I, just for a moment, remember that *Lakota* translates (generally) as "friend" or "ally." That is, to *be* Lakota is to be a friend or ally; it is an existence that cannot be understood as *I*, alone. Moreover, as a friend or ally, one stands with and, when necessary, *stands up* for others—is this fair to say? Turning to Claxton's visual work, I find affirmation of this principle. She has looked to our community and asked, what is it that *we* need? Claxton is included in this "we," though her concerns reach far beyond the personal. To shake structural dehumanization, Indigenous people *need* to be understood fully as human beings—surprising, complex, feeling. We are people from developed cultures and, all the more, evolving. To show this, Claxton's efforts are not reserved, moderate and expected. She works boldy. Generously! She gives us video, photographs, objects, interviews, voices, sounds, text, historical documents, faces, bodies, public interventions, installations, vivid colour and her pieces are sometimes, literally, as big as billboards. I come to her work with an overwhelming desire to say, *Thank you!...* as anyone receiving a generous gift, would.

Yet I must not forget the most important aspect of generosity: that is, *spirit*. It is the spirit in which a thing is made or given—this moving, breathing, intangible quality—that makes an act generous; and for the recipient, makes it valuable. I return to Claxton's list of essential qualities in her art making, seized by her profound sentence fragment "and more spirit." How easy it might be to skim over this, yet the word "more" sings to me. I think about a Lakota practice of giving something to a visitor in one's home before they leave; to always send a guest away with something to hold onto. That "something" can be anything, honestly—food, a piece of jewellery, a photograph, a little keepsake. Whether it's big or small, store bought, or handmade, consumable or a treasure, is not so important. What matters is the spirit in which it's given, the thought and intention. The usefulness, the medicine. The "more" of something.

So I consider two "somethings" that Dana generously gives all of us to hold onto—1) medicine and 2) a commitment to justice, both of which are braided together, inseparable in her work. In her curatorial essay for an online exhibition, *The Medicine Project*, we find these two somethings latent in Claxton's vision:

> We expect a great deal from art, and art gives us so much. Many contemporary Aboriginal artists offer their art to acknowledge and honour the ancestors and the way of life. In addition, the works have assisted with defining selfhood and locating the de-subjugated, decolonized self—the Aboriginal self. And through the dissemination of such works, there is hope that our inter-relatedness via public performances and the gallery space will allow for greater freedom of thought and a refusal of inequality.

> The works portray the Aboriginal experience and imperative in all its complexities. To locate medicine through the application of art-making is an enormous undertaking. These artworks have the considerable potential to shift contemporary consciousness toward support of Aboriginal justice.

Though Claxton wrote this as a curator, her statements equally translate as a treatise of her own work: defining of Aboriginal selfhood. A refusal of inequality. Medicine through the application of art making. Artwork with the potential to shift contemporary consciousness toward Aboriginal justice. I hold onto these ideas dearly. And my understanding of Dana Claxton's generosity shifts: her art is not simply a gift of the visual—but it is vital *action*. Provocation, disruption, reclamation, movement and resilience.

I remember the Lakota word for generosity is *cantéyuke*, which literally translates to "has a heart." So I regard how Claxton's art/action, this stem of generosity, slides into the world from the heart, first. The heart, pump and spark, light and engine of the body. The heart, our seat of feeling and intuition. So that to make art as an act of generosity, is "to have heart," thus it is to make art feelingly, alight with energy. In the heart, there lives no farce or pretense. One's art emerges from a home, safe and deep within the chest; birthed from pulse, beat, rhythm, force and command. And what I know about the heart—the *canté*—is that it is also the carrier of wound(s). Take for example Claxton's installation, *Buffalo Bone China*, in which we view black-and-white footage of a buffalo herd in motion, running in pounding rhythm. On the floor, under a spotlight, we see a pile of pieces, shards and white dust from broken bone china—a visual signifier of colonization and, in particular, colonizers; of the slaughter and erasure of vast buffalo herds from the Plains; and of the searing, capitalistic practice of collecting and shipping buffalo bones to be made into bone china. This dinnerware used to decoratively serve food on colonizers' tables was ironically (or, perversely!) the very spoils of oppression and starvation of Lakota people. This bone china, we can say, served up the dishes of submission, dependence, depression and heartbreak. This is a wound in the collective memory of Indigenous people of the Plains, yet Claxton's installation does not operate as a map of guilt and blame. Rather, it brings the wound to air and light. It is acknowledgement. It is restoration and balance. A leveling of the scale. It is elegant in its justice.

As a Lakota artist/writer myself, I find that Claxton has "rattled" and shaken something in my core—a sense of responsibility, a yearning—to work toward justice, but to do it from the heart with all of its latent, thundering energy. I want more from an art practice and I want more from myself. That is, I am driven to an insatiable desire to give myself over. What *more,* of anyone's art, could I ask?

ENDNOTES

1 Leah Collins, "Dana Claxton Wants to Change the Way You Think About Indigenous Women," *CBC Arts*, January 14, 2016, http://www.cbc.ca/arts/dana-claxton-wants-to-change-the-way-you-think-about-indigenouswomen-1.3403600.

2 Ibid.

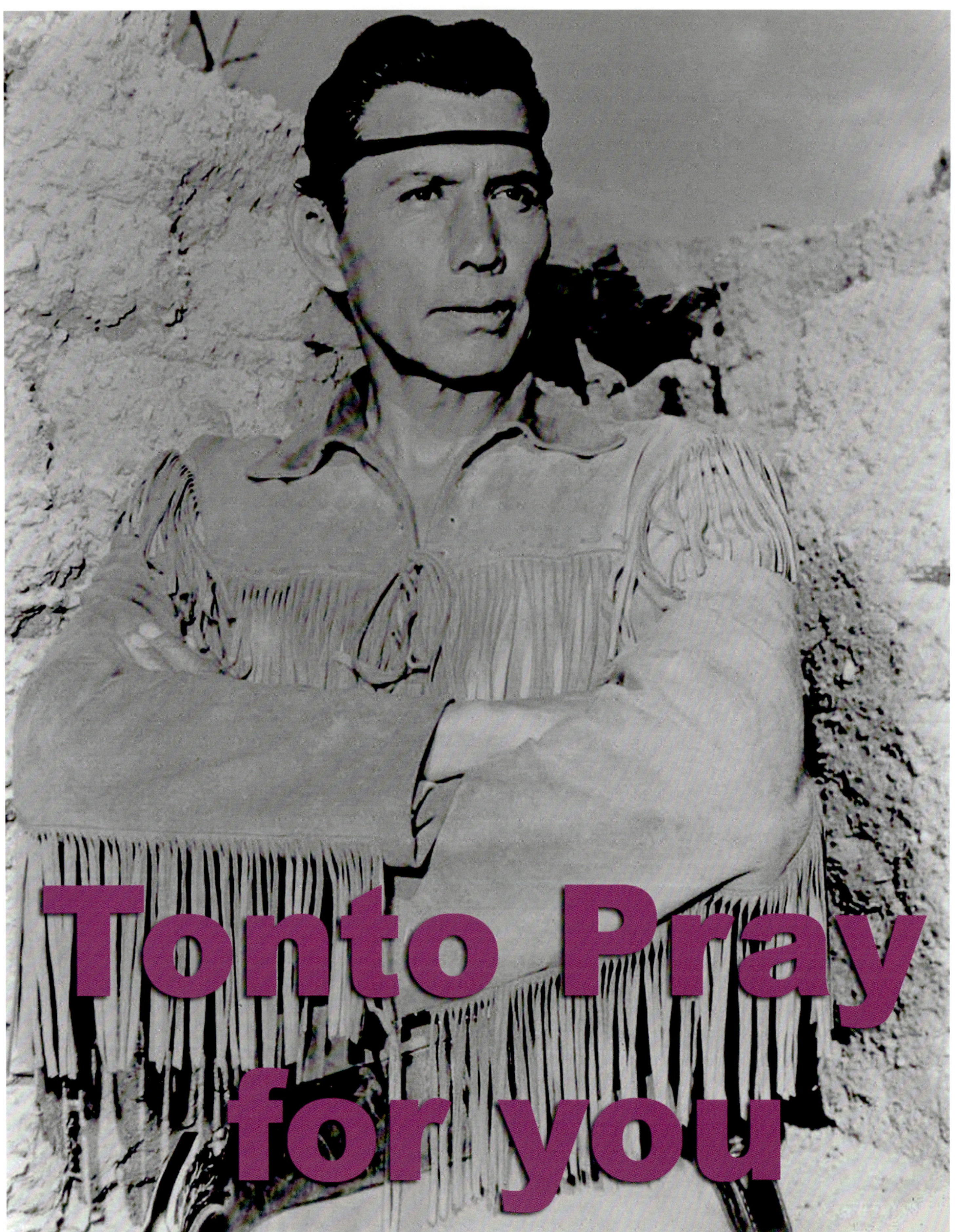
Tonto Pray
for you

THE ART OF DANA CLAXTON

A Prologue

GRANT ARNOLD

The indian *is a simulation, the absence of natives; the* indian *transposes the real, and simulation of the real has no referent, memories, or native stories. The* postindian *must waver over the aesthetic ruins of* indian *simulations.*
— GERALD VIZENOR[1]

Over the past three decades Dana Claxton has become widely known for an expansive multidisciplinary approach to art making that encompasses film, video, photography and performance and is informed by a remarkable family history and an extraordinarily cosmopolitan range of lived experience. More specifically, her work combines contemporary technologies and aesthetic strategies drawn from disparate idioms—from 1980s music videos to post-conceptual photography—with references to Indigenous cultures, particularly her own Lakota culture, to address the ongoing impact of colonialism on contemporary life while eloquently articulating Indigenous histories, world views and spirituality. To put it another way, her efforts to make space for the Indigenous subject in the gallery/museum system could be described as "fringing the cube"—an expression that draws upon the practical and metaphysical functions of fringe for the First Peoples of the Great Plains and the performative role Claxton has taken on to create that space.

Claxton's career as an artist began at a critical point in the struggle of First Nations for recognition of their claims to sovereignty by the Canadian state, a struggle in which the Oka crisis of 1990 remains as one of the most prominent episodes. Precipitated by plans to build a golf course on a traditional Kanien'kehá:ka (Mohawk) burial ground near the Québec town of Oka, a peaceful blockade of the site became a seventy-eight day armed standoff in which gunfire was exchanged, a Sûreté du Québec officer was killed and the province requisitioned assistance from the Canadian military. The crisis received extensive media coverage, which, although it tended to reflect a non-Indigenous perspective, sharply heightened awareness of the intense and deep divisions that separated First Nations peoples and the non-native public, especially in regard to questions of history and the ownership of land.

The Oka standoff corresponded roughly with a moment when contemporary Indigenous artists who were directly addressing the effects of colonialism—such as Joanne Cardinal-Schubert, Robert Houle, Carl Beam and Jane Ash Poitras—were making inroads into the country's predominantly Euro-Canadian art gallery/museum system. The crisis resonated intensely within the Canadian art world over the following years. It undoubtedly framed the organization of *INDIGENA* and *Land, Spirit, Power*, exhibitions mounted at the Canadian Museum of Civilization and the National Gallery of Canada respectively in 1992 to "decelebrate" the 500th anniversary of the arrival of Columbus in America. The programming that accompanied *Land, Spirit, Power*, for instance, included film footage shot during the crisis by the Abenaki filmmaker Alanis Obomsawin, which would later be used in her feature-length documentary *Kanehsatake: 270 Years of Resistance*. Commenting on the experience of watching footage "of nervous

Tonto Prayer (from *Indian Candy*), 2013

Canadian soldiers on the verge of hysteria because some eggs had been thrown at a tank, spliced with a scene of a badly beaten Mohawk," Scott Watson later wrote that "the film reminded us all of how close the Oka crisis came to utter disaster. It reminded us all that the veneer of civilization is very thin, and that Canadians are not exempt from the racism they love to accuse others of."[2]

The Oka crisis was galvanizing for Claxton. As she later put it, "I realized there was much work to be done. Aboriginal and non-Aboriginal communities were not communicating with each other. I asked myself: how could I facilitate this huge gap, in a meaningful way."[3] This led Claxton to make her first film, *Grant Her Restitution* (1991), with a secondhand Super 8 mm film camera, and curate two exhibitions of work by Indigenous artists—*Neo-Nativists* and *First Ladies*—for Vancouver's artist-run Pitt Gallery. An early indication of Claxton's longstanding interest in honouring the role of women in Indigenous cultures, *First Ladies* focused specifically on work by Indigenous women and included a star quilt by Kelly White and wigwas (birch bark bitings) by Angelique Levac, work that usually would have been seen as craft in an art museum context.

For Claxton the art world held out the potential to reconfigure the relationship between Aboriginal peoples and the dominant Euro-Canadian culture on at least two accounts. On one hand, recognition of the significance of work by Indigenous artists offered the possibility for a fundamental shift in the terms through which Aboriginal culture has been perceived; as she would later note, "the lens through which Western society viewed Aboriginal people resulted in the devaluation of Aboriginal art as a lower cultural form; the Aboriginal, it was believed, could never produce great art and therefore this lens was a critical part of the colonial rhetoric. The very idea that an Aboriginal could produce great art would erode the very underpinnings by which European colonizers and their descendants justified their destructive aims against Aboriginal civilizations."[4] Secondly, while the space of the gallery/museum is far from neutral and has often replicated conventional relationships between dominant and marginalized cultures, it is also a "site where the most radical and polemic critiques of Canadian society have taken place." And, although perhaps only through pressure from Indigenous artists, it was a space in which "the art community has helped lead the decolonization process."[5]

While *Fringing the Cube* might claim to survey Claxton's career as an artist, it is important to note that the artworks represented in this publication and the exhibition it accompanies are only one aspect of a broader project of reclaiming and redefining Indigenous culture she has taken on. Over the past thirty years she has scripted plays, produced and directed children's programs and documentary films for broadcast television, organized conferences, edited anthologies and written extensively on Indigenous art. She was a founding member of the board of directors of the Indigenous Media Arts Group and IASPA (Independent Aboriginal Screen Producers Association). She has curated exhibitions for traditional gallery spaces and the internet, participated in the Sitting Bull Sundance at Standing Rock, South Dakota, and actively supported the Standing Rock Lakota and Dakota in their opposition to the Dakota Access oil pipeline. She has taught at the School of Journalism at the University of Regina, the Department of Women's Studies at Simon Fraser University, the Emily Carr University of Art + Design, and the Department of Art History, Visual Art & Theory at the University of British Columbia, where she currently chairs the department. Community is central to her practice; her recent work *The Sioux Project—Tatanka Oyate*, which was exhibited at the MacKenzie Art Gallery in Regina in 2017, grew out of a number of workshops with Sioux youth from the Standing Buffalo and Whitecap First Nations and is presented in a video installation based on the form of a Sundance circle. Her work has been included in film festivals in Canada and the United States and her artwork has been presented in prestigious art

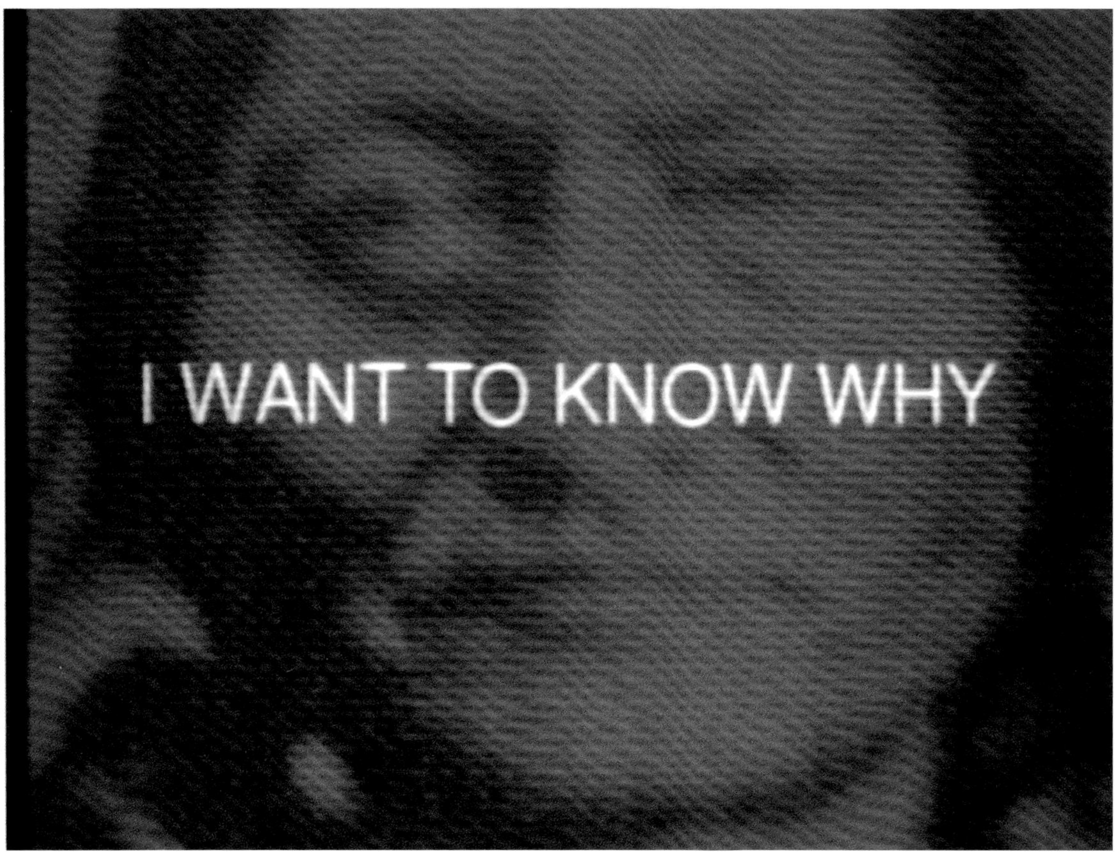

world venues such as the Metropolitan Museum of Art in New York and in spaces with a more direct connection to plains Indigenous cultures, such as the Wanuskewin Heritage Park in Saskatoon.

Claxton has employed a diverse set of strategies in her efforts to reclaim history and assert an Indigenous presence within it. Much of her early work is characterized by the disruption of imagery that might appear benignly familiar to a non-Indigenous audience through the deployment of specific tropes, references and formal devices. *I Want to Know Why* (1994)—a forcefully polemical work that dialogically addresses the events that brought Claxton's ancestors to Canada—deliberately mimics the look of an archival film in its gritty black and white character, while its fast-paced editing and use of a multiple-frames-within-a-frame format recalls the music videos that were a common sight in nightclubs and bars at the time the work was made. The almost banal images of the once ubiquitous Indian TV test pattern, drive-by views of the Statue of Liberty and architectural details that feature stereotypical representations of Native people are accompanied by a harrowing voice-over, in which Claxton demands to know why her great-grandmother had to walk, starving, to Canada and what led to the early death of her grandmother and mother. The only Indigenous presence in the work, Claxton's increasingly assertive voice contrasts sharply with the near-universal absence of an Indigenous subject position within popular culture, an absence signalled in the relentless repetition of clichéd images of Indian-ness and their juxtaposition with images of a colossal tourist attraction. Through the video's montage effects, the trauma of the history Claxton recounts and the rage that marks its telling, the Statue of Liberty is shifted from an emblem of the freedom and prosperity (however mythical these might be) the republic offered the dispossessed that arrived on its shores into a hollowed-out marker of the effacement of

I Want to Know Why, 1994 (video still)

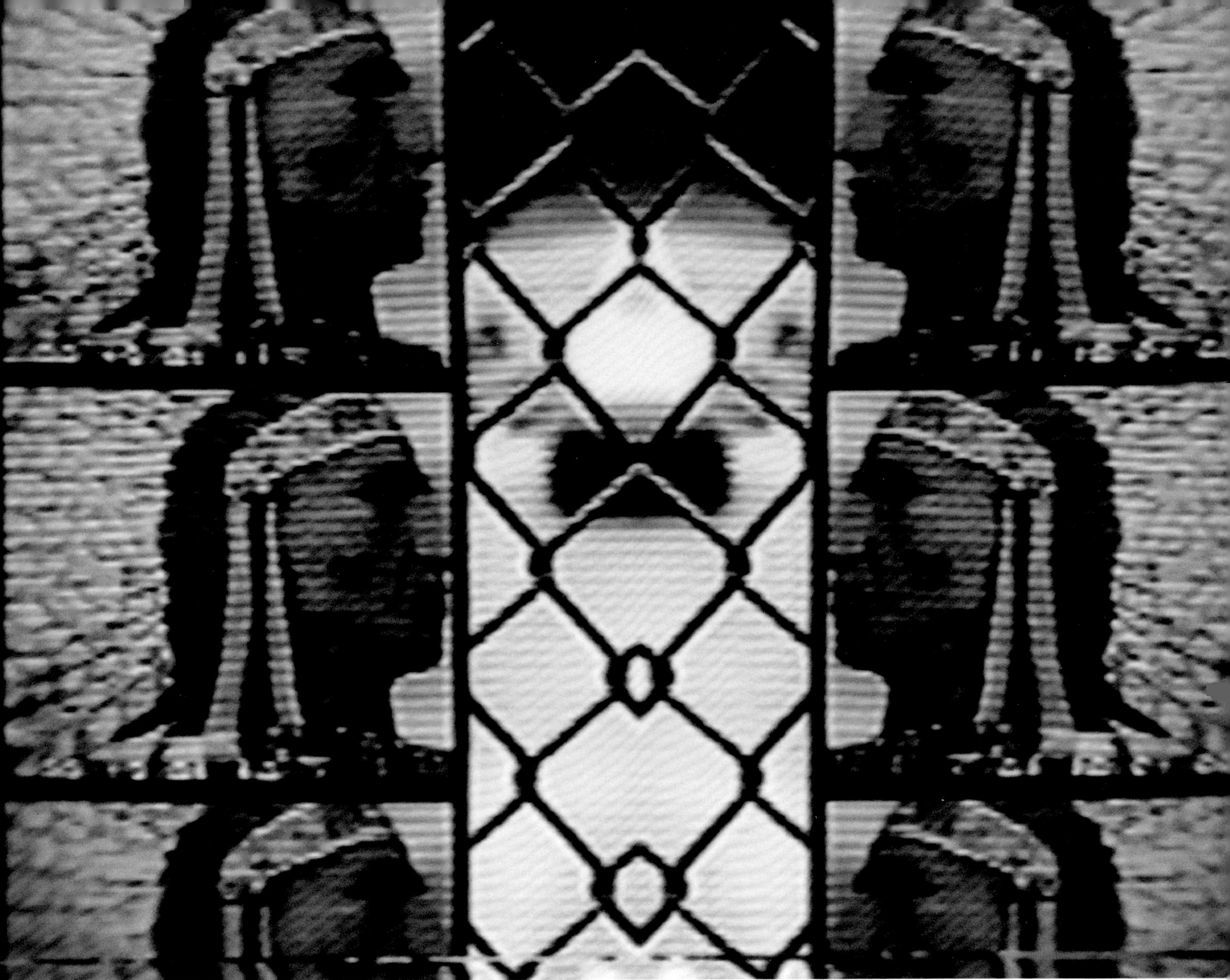

Indigenous identity and the loss of freedom and prosperity that was inflicted in the disasters that waves of European immigration brought to the inhabitants they displaced.

In contrast to *I Want to Know Why*, the single-channel video *10* (2003) and the photographs that comprise the *AIM* (2010) project are both made up of appropriated imagery. Drawn from three different feature films based on Agatha Christie's *Ten Little Indians*,[6] an immensely popular detective novel written in the late 1930s that took its title and narrative structure from a popular nursery rhyme, Claxton's *10* is composed of precisely chosen jump cuts presented as side-by-side images in a single frame. The genteelly ominous atmosphere of Christie's story, one of the principal templates for the modern detective novel, along with costumes, mannerisms and camera work that are clearly associated with particular eras in fashion and cinema are immediately familiar in the excerpts Claxton has assembled. As the video progresses though, any pleasure that might be associated with familiarity on the part of a non-Indigenous viewer is incrementally undercut through the repetition of the nursery rhyme's lyrics and the concurrent recognition of the connotations carried by the enduring popularity

I Want to Know Why, 1994 (video stills)

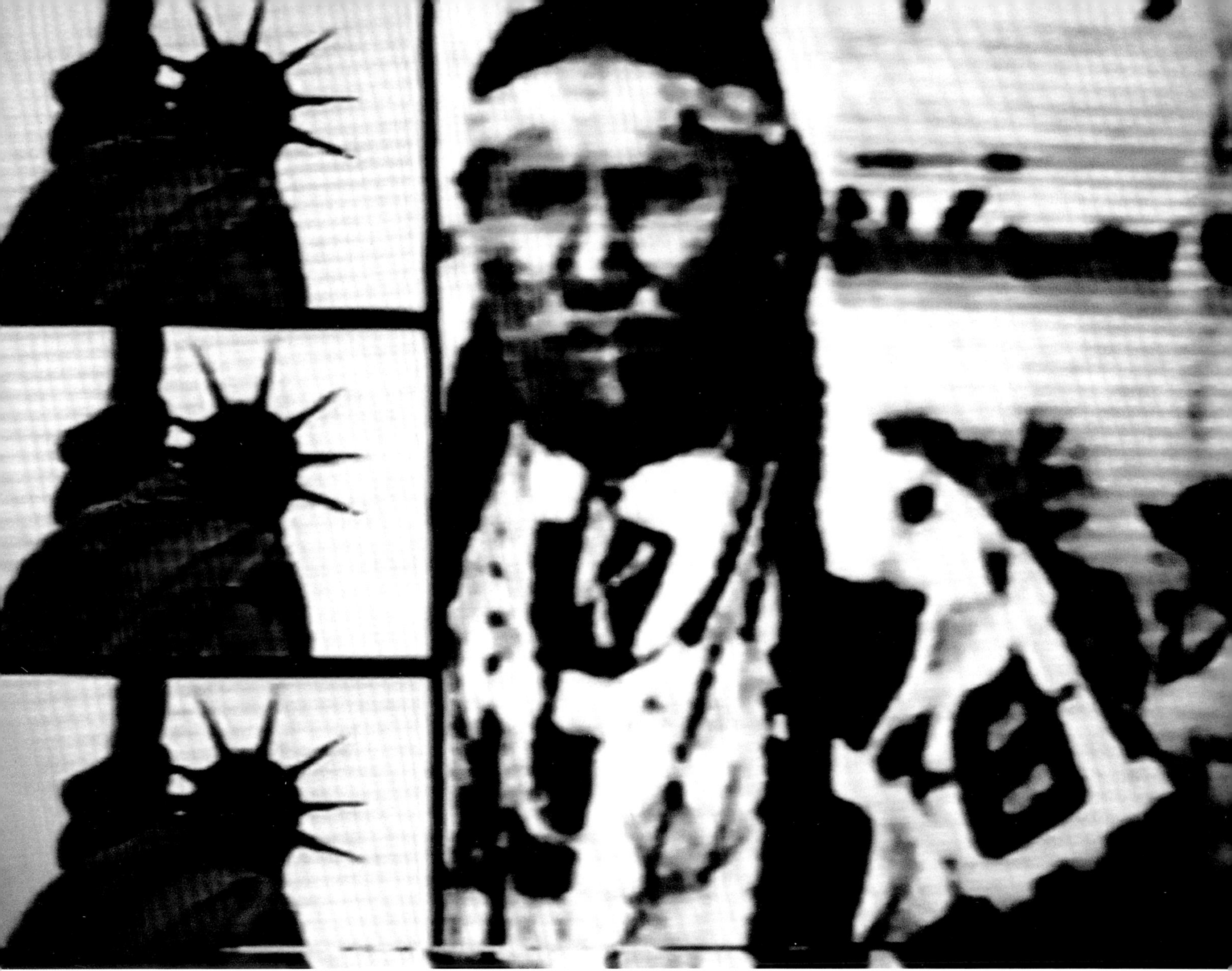

of a children's song that playfully describes the death of "little injuns," and the implications of its use as a conceit for plot development in popular entertainment.

The four black and white photographs of Claxton's *AIM* project are straightforward enlargements of declassified documents related to FBI surveillance of the American Indian Movement that Claxton found in the New York Public Library in the late 1980s. Founded in 1968, in Minneapolis, and given impetus by the American civil rights movement, AIM's objectives included the enforcement of existing treaties and recognition of sovereignty over their land. Their activities included an "anti-birthday party" on the top of Mount Rushmore (which is on Lakota territory), painting the Plymouth Rock red for Thanksgiving in 1970 and the 1973 occupation of the town of Wounded Knee, the site of an infamous 1890 massacre in which hundreds of Lakota men, women and children were killed by the 7th United States Cavalry. The confrontation between AIM and the FBI at Wounded Knee included an extended armed standoff in which a number of people were killed. The validity of the trials that followed has been called into question as the FBI has faced allegations of evidence tampering and withholding information.

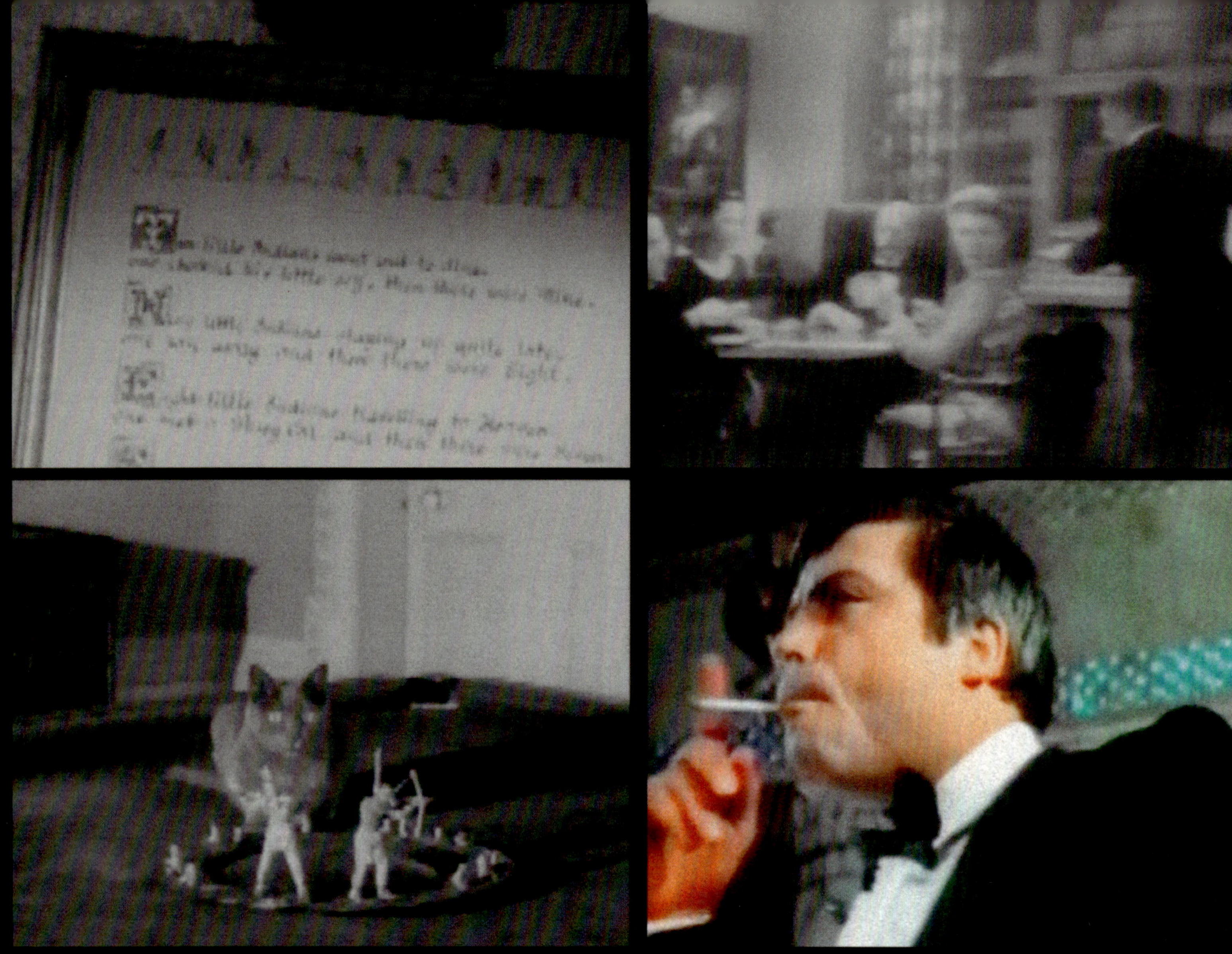

The documents Claxton has photographed are related to FBI reports on the activity of prominent AIM members, including Russell Means and Dennis Banks. The simple shift in scale from a letter-sized sheet of paper to a photograph five feet in height attaches a sense of violence to the enlarged, almost painterly gestures of the censor, which block out much of the text. We can see the names of the individuals under surveillance, but nothing on the historical context of AIM's actions, and nothing on the abrogation of the Treaty of Fort Laramie, which guaranteed title over the Black Hills of South Dakota to the Lakota and Dakota. The sense of erasure signified by the mute black areas metaphorically alludes to not only the suppression of history but the character of a state in which the enforcement of "order" can be linked to such a document.

Sitting Bull and the Moose Jaw Sioux (2004) can be seen as a companion to *I Want to Know Why*. A four-channel video commissioned by the Moose Jaw Museum & Art Gallery, *Sitting Bull and the Moose Jaw Sioux* traces the arrival of Sitting Bull and his people—including Claxton's maternal grandparents and great-grandparents—in the vicinity of Moose Jaw following the Battle of the Little Bighorn in 1876.

10, 2003 (video stills)

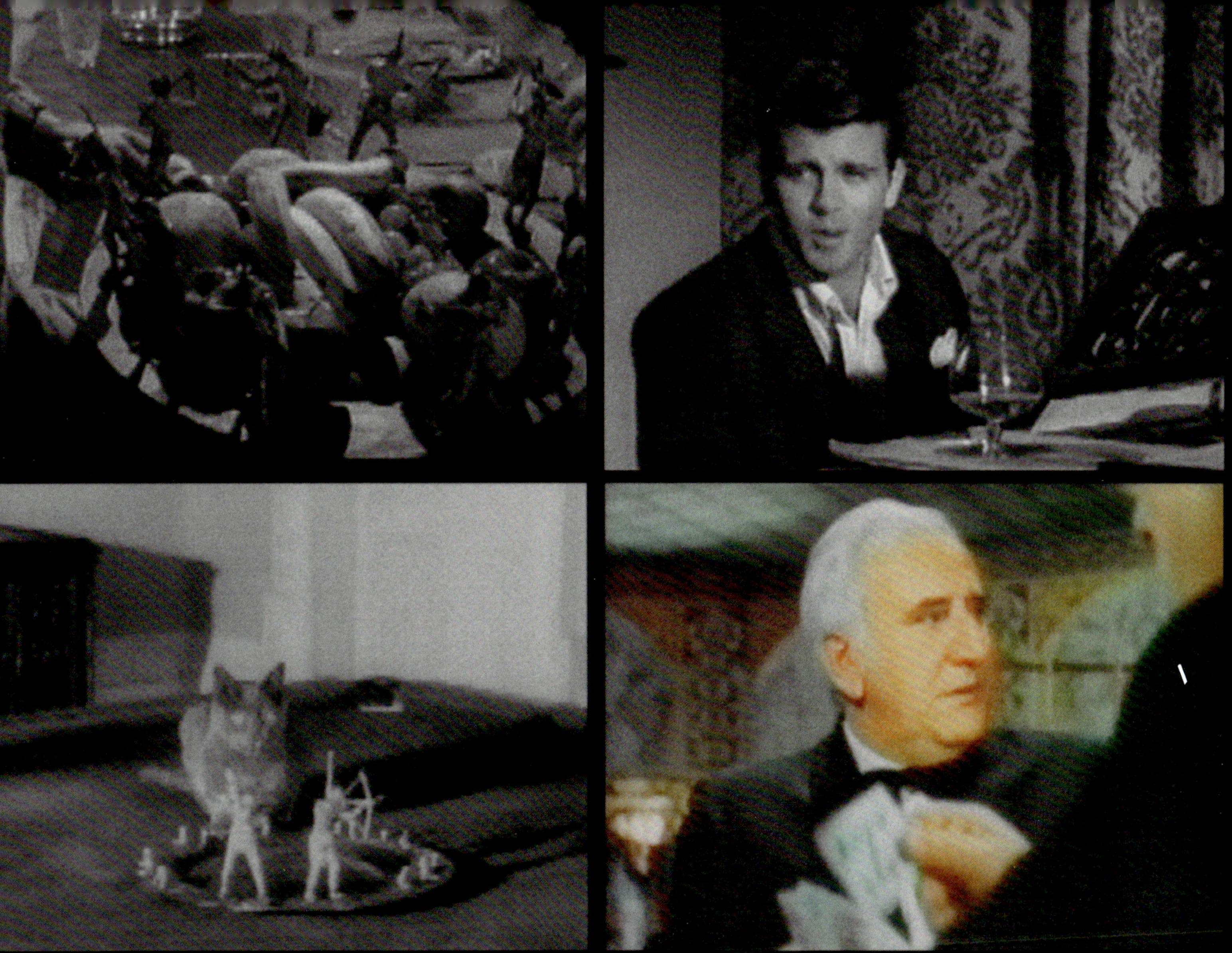

Three video channels, projected floor to ceiling and butted together side by side, present a constantly shifting collage comprised of images of Sitting Bull, portraits of the Lakota who remained after he returned to the United States, and ledger drawings depicting the Battle of the Little Bighorn, along with a scrolling translation of a conversation in Lakota between two elders—Francis and Hartland Goodtrack—who narrate episodes from the lives of their people over the past century, including their sometimes difficult but often cordial relationship with the Euro-Canadians who lived in the area and accounts of their ancestors sitting around campfires with warriors who had fought with Sitting Bull at the Battle of the Little Bighorn.

Projected on an adjacent wall, the fourth projection presents a series of views over a rolling prairie landscape under bright summer sunlight. Initially, the landscape seems pastoral and mundane, an idyllic place where nothing much happens beyond the passing of the seasons. However, as the narrative of Sitting Bull's exile unfolds through the installation's audio and scrolling text, the location is identified as the site of the primary Sioux encampment—which at one point included several hundred lodges—where Claxton's predecessors lived and her grandparents were married. The meaning of the scene shifts;

the undulating surface of the landscape becomes a metaphor for both the absence of Indigenous perspectives from the principal accounts of the country's history and the possibilities for locating suppressed narratives in the surfaces of the everyday.

While the work is marked by the artist's desire to connect with the past, it also implies a skepticism toward the conventional methods through which history is recounted. As David Garneau has noted, the narrative articulated in *Sitting Bull and the Moose Jaw Sioux*, "is layered rather than linear, dialogic rather than authoritarian, and open-ended rather than contained. At least four accounts unspool at any one time. While they always complement each other and advance the story, the gentle polyphony encourages repeated viewings and the sense that we can gather only glimpses and should not imagine ourselves completely informed."[7]

Claxton's engagement with questions of the absence and presence of Indigenous subjectivity finds parallels and intersections with the Anishinaabe novelist, poet and theorist Gerald Vizenor's notion of "survivance," a term that has become widely associated with the assertion of Indigenous identity in Canada and the United States over the past twenty years. Survivance is an archaic legal term that Vizenor has appropriated and, drawing upon Indigenous traditions of storytelling and the ideas of post-structural theorists such as Jacques Derrida and Jean Baudrillard, re-purposed to describe an Indigenous mode of address that is neither an ideology nor dissimulation but a form of practice that operates as "an active resistance and repudiation of dominance, obtrusive themes of dominance and tragedy, nihilism and victimry."[8] Survivance is a difficult term to define, one that deliberately avoids easy definition or translation, but is "invariably true and just...in native stories, natural reason, remembrance, traditions, and customs."[9] While survivance can assume many forms, its crucial feature is a sense of presence that emerges out of a rhetorical act to counter the historical absence and powerlessness established by and through the stereotypes and simulations of "Indian-ness" that circulate in the imagination of the colonizer. Survivance is not about memorializing the past but tracing continuity that extends from the past through the present to the future, and by doing so, it offers modes of personal and social renewal attained through "welcoming unpredictable cultural reorientations [that]...promise to radically transform current native life without requiring abandonment of the enduring value of their precontact cultural successes."[10]

For Vizenor, the term "Indian" is an accretion of simulations invented by European intruders to separate the Indigenous peoples of North America from their tribal traditions. It both reflects a fictive homogeneity that serves to contain Indigenous people within a false, racialized identity that has been "sustained in archives and lexicons as 'authentic' representations of indian cultures."[11] Vizenor proposes the term "postindian" as a more productive point of identification. The postindian, he argues, is knowingly bound in a relationship with the dominant culture's perceptions of Native people and therefore enters into discourse anticipating that the encounter with stereotypical simulation is inevitable. These simulations, however, aren't static but are open to alteration and replacement by new simulations that have the potential to upset the expectation of representation on which the stereotype is constructed. As Vizenor puts it, "the postindian warriors encounter their enemies with the same courage in literature as their ancestors once evinced on horses, and they create their stories with a new sense of survivance. The warriors bear the simulations of their time and counter the manifest manners of dominance."[12] Or, as Winfried Siemerling put it in his discussion of Vizenor's *The Heirs of Columbus,* "if access to subjectivity under dominance is mediated by this simulated other, one move towards healing leads through the creation of an other of this 'Indian' (or *indian*) other in language and stories."[13]

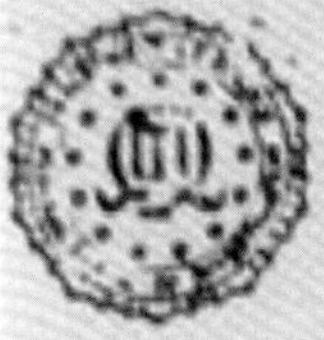

UNITED STATES DEPARTMENT OF JUSTICE
FEDERAL BUREAU OF INVESTIGATION

In Reply, Please Refer to
File No.

Denver, Colorado 80203
December 7, 1972

~~CONFIDENTIAL~~

AMERICAN INDIAN MOVEMENT
EXTREMIST MATTERS -
AMERICAN INDIAN AFFAIRS

ALL INFORMATION CONTAINED
HEREIN IS UNCLASSIFIED
DATE 12-29-83 SPS RJG/PNC

[redacted] a source, with whom contact has been insufficient to determine reliability, advised [redacted]

MEMBER OF SUBJECT ORGANIZATION

~~CONFIDENTIAL~~

Classified by [redacted]
Exempt from General Declassification
Schedule of Executive Order 11652
Exemption Category Number 2
Automatically Declassified On Indefinite

DECLASSIFIED BY 5886
ON 8/15/77

100-462483-89

ENCLOSURE

UNITED STATES DEPARTMENT OF JUSTICE

FEDERAL BUREAU OF INVESTIGATION

In Reply, Please Refer to File No.

San Francisco, California

July 19, 1973

AMERICAN INDIAN MOVEMENT

[redacted] unidentified American Indian Movement (AIM) members were among approximately two hundred persons who attended a social gathering in San Francisco June 16, 1973. [redacted] No specific information regarding the type of action or the dates was discussed.

> American Indian Movement is self-described as the shock troops of Indian sovereignty that intends to raise questions in the minds of Indians and non-Indians alike regarding Indian sovereignty, land and culture.

ALL INFORMATION CONTAINED HEREIN IS UNCLASSIFIED DATE 1-20-84 BY SPSRTG/pab

\- 1* -

This document contains neither recommendations nor conclusions of the FBI. It is the property of the FBI and is loaned to your agency; it and its contents are not to be distributed outside your agency.

ENCLOSURE

10- [illegible] -3 859

FBI

Date: 12/8/72

...mit the following in ________________
(Type in plaintext or code)

AIRTEL AIRMAIL
(Priority)

TO: ACTING DIRECTOR, FBI ATTN: DID

FROM: SAC, LOS ANGELES (157-8224) (P)

SUBJECT: AMERICAN INDIAN MOVEMENT (AIM)
EM - AMERICAN INDIAN AFFAIRS

Re Los Angeles teletype to Bureau dated 12/1/72, captioned, "AMERICAN INDIAN MOVEMENT, IS - INDIAN MATTERS."

On 12/8/72, [redacted] Bureau of Indian Affairs (BIA), Los Angeles, California, provided the names of the following AIM national leaders and their residences:

RUSSELL MEANS
Cleveland, Ohio

VERNON BELLECOURT
Denver, Colorado

CLYDE BELLECOURT
Minneapolis, Minnesota

DENNIS BANKS
Minneapolis, Minnesota

CALIF

ALL INFORMATION CONTAINED
HEREIN IS UNCLASSIFIED
DATE 12-29-83 BY SP5RJG/PMC

On 12/8/72, [redacted] Los Angeles County Sheriff's Office, Intelligence Division, Los Angeles, Californi[a] requested descriptive and background data concerning above individuals in order that they may be promptly identified in future visits to Los Angeles.

3 - Bureau (AM) (RM)
2 - Cleveland (AM) (RM)
2 - Denver (AM) (RM)
2 - Minneapolis (AM) (RM)
2 - Los Angeles

100-462483-

REC-70

DEC 13 1972

EX-101

[redacted] dmg
(11)

DEC 21 1972

Approved: ______ Sent ______ M Per ______
Special Agent in Charge

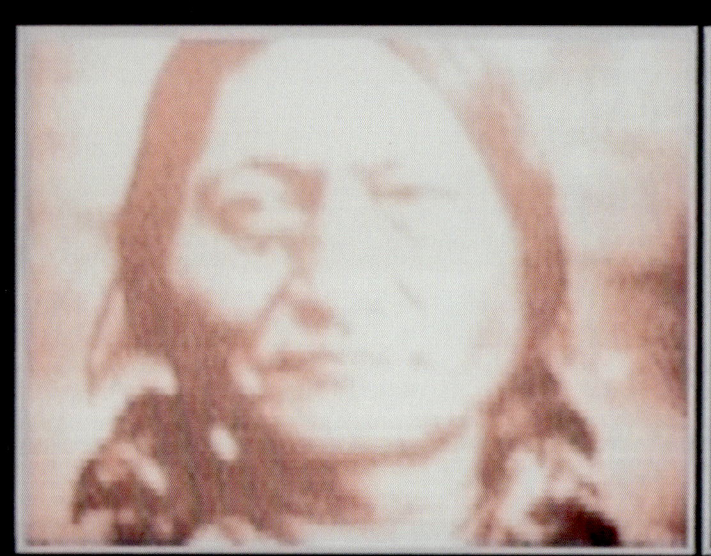

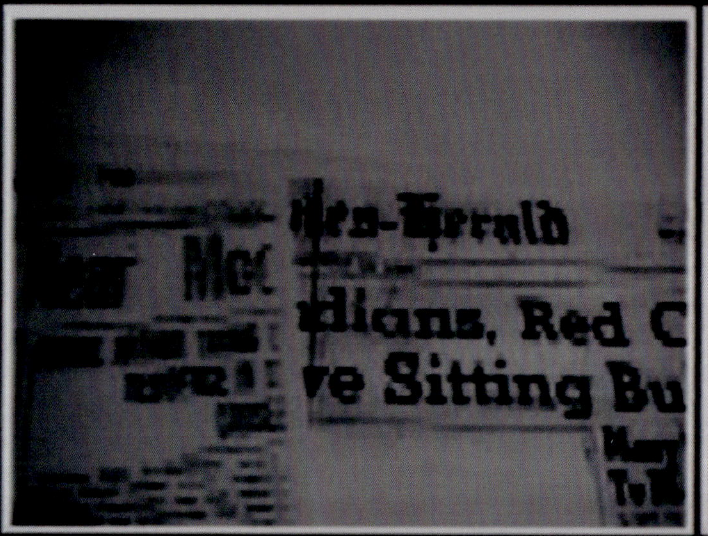

hey, sell flags, they got a lot of money, he said the

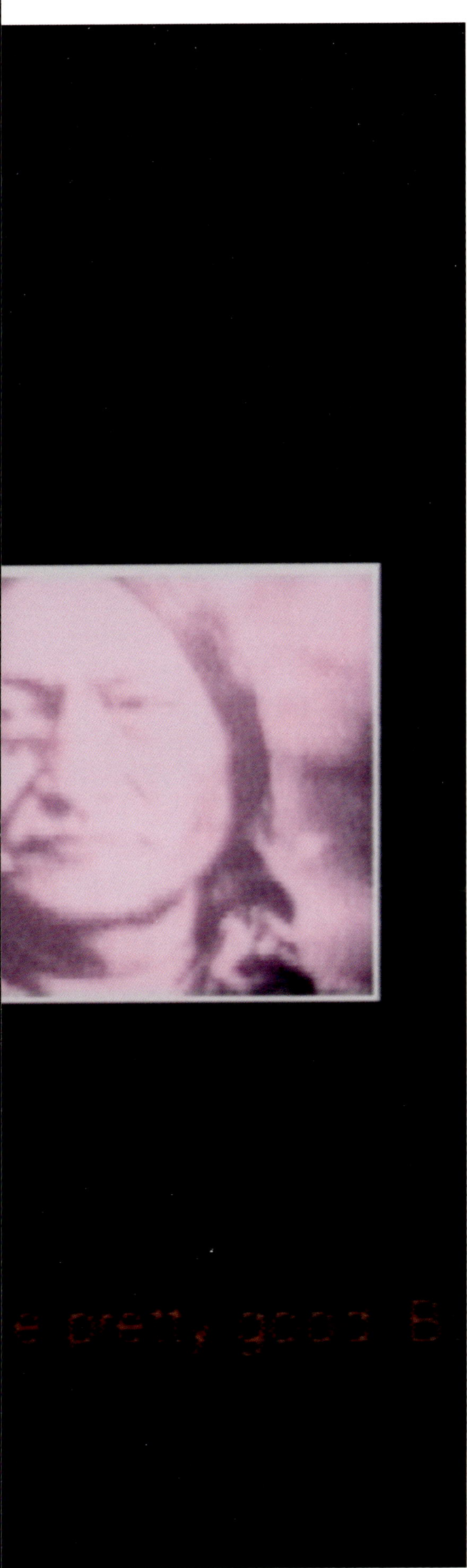

The strategy of intertwining the past and the present and creating new simulations to counter the "indian" stereotype as outlined by Vizenor runs through much of Claxton's work. It can, perhaps, be most clearly seen in *The Mustang Suite* (2008) and her *Indian Candy* (2013) project. Taking impetus from the Lakota *wičháša wakȟáŋ* (medicine man or holy man) Black Elk's (1863–1950) dream of the horse dance, in which the dance becomes a ritual of healing, *The Mustang Suite* is a set of five staged photographs of a contemporary Indigenous "family," with individual images of Momma, Daddy, Baby Boyz, the Baby Girlz twins and a group portrait with the family on a blanket. Like all of Claxton's photographs and "fireboxes," *The Mustang Suite* images are obviously staged and, especially when considered in relation to Claxton's performance works, overtly embrace a level of performativity, both on the part of Claxton as a director and the "actors" she directs and depicts. Tradition is wryly brought into the present through the paint on Daddy's face, an emphasis on red—alluding to Red Power and the sacred status the colour holds for the Lakota—in the family's apparel and the traditional Lakota pattern on their blanket. Each member of the family is shown with an attribute that refers to mobility and the horses of the Great Plains: a Ford Mustang car, a pair of mustang bicycles, a live pony, and a Caucasian woman, who appears as the personification of history and wears red paraphernalia from BDSM pony play. The postures and clothing of the family members were chosen specifically to reflect a particular persona. Baby Boyz is "a young urban warrior who likes hip-hop" and, like his ancestors, "rides his pony bareback." The twin Baby Girlz are hip but also wear mukluks and "help on the trap line when their grandfather calls," while Daddy could work "as a computer programmer and dances pow-wow during the summer." Momma, "influenced by traditional woman's dancing, medicine womn, BDSM and burlesque culture" has "slightly humiliated history"and then lets it trot off, "never to be a burden again." Taken together, this layering of references evokes a set of complex questions regarding history and the performance of identity while proposing a space in which tradition and contemporaneity offer the Indigenous subject the possibility to choose from "the best of both worlds."[14]

Most of the images that make up the *Indian Candy* project—a ledger drawing showing Sitting Bull counting coup as he captures a mule wagon, souvenir cards from Buffalo Bill Cody's Wild West Show, correspondence ordering the arrest of Sitting Bull, a lone white buffalo on the open prairie, the acclaimed Osage prima ballerina Maria Tallchief, Jay Silverheels playing Tonto in *The Lone Ranger*, an unidentified young man wearing a shirt, tie and feather

Sitting Bull and the Moose Jaw Sioux, 2004 (video still)

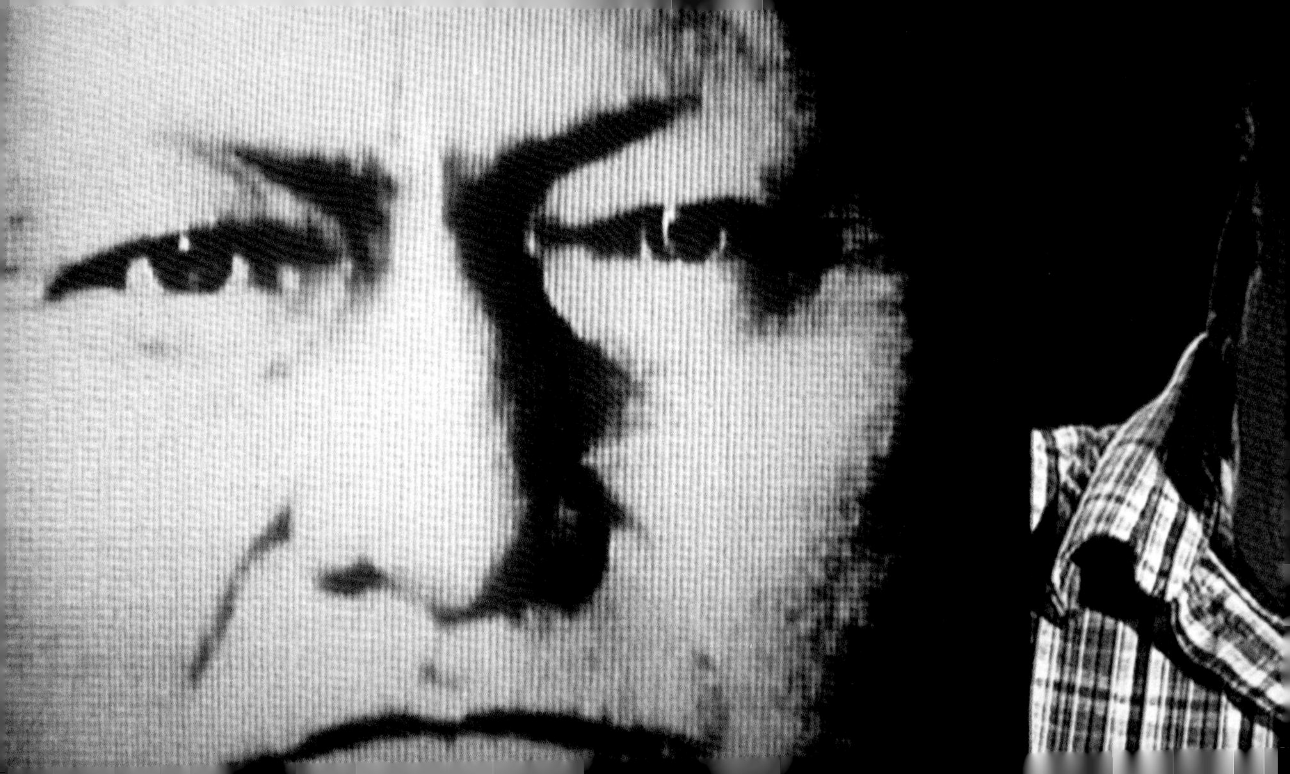

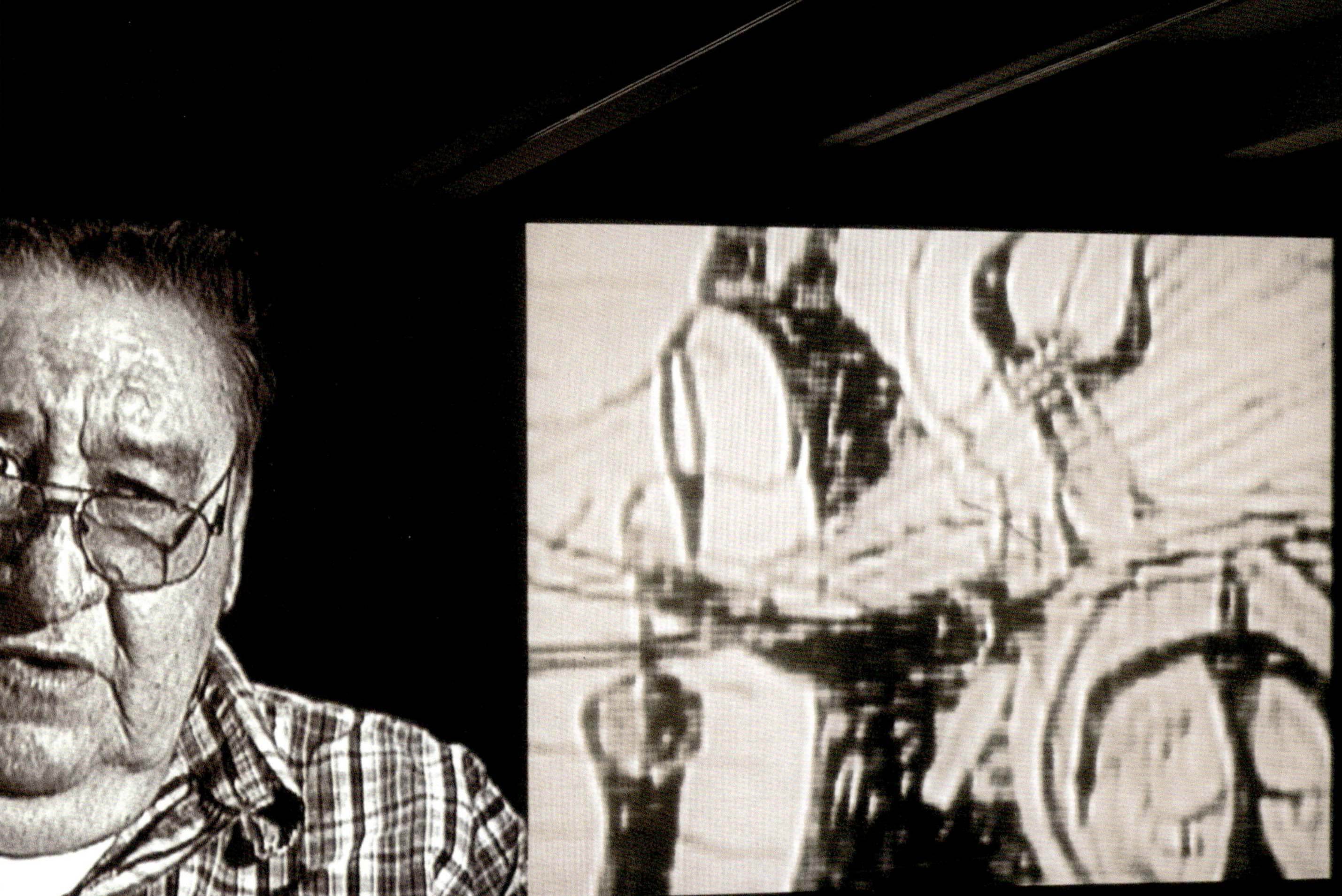

headdress—are what Claxton describes as "archival images" that appeared in Google searches for images of the "Wild West."[15] Mounted on aluminum with no frame, the seductive glossy surfaces, intense saturation and confectionary colour of the prints gives them a fetish-like pop culture slickness. The pixellation in the images highlights the layers and modes of technology that lie between the represented subject and the viewer of Claxton's work and, in some instances, takes on a patterned texture that has "an uncanny resemblance"[16] to the beadwork traditionally produced by Indigenous women of the Great Plains.

The *Indian Candy* project can be seen as the assembly of an archive made up of pictures from other archives, in which acute remediation—as in, the transfer of an image from one media to another—draws attention to and seeks connection with suppressed histories and subjectivities. In *Blue Headdress*, for example, we can—with enough distance from the picture—just make out the image of a young man wearing a feather headdress associated with the Plains tribes, along with a suit or sports jacket, shirt and tie. The era is hard to pin down, but could be the 1960s or 70s. There's a formality to the pose that might recall some of Edward Curtis' photographs from *The North American Indian*, but the young man's clothing has none of the pseudo-authenticity Curtis employed. That's about the extent of detail that can be made out; the heavy pixellation precludes the standard conventions of viewing an archival photograph, implying a wariness toward the history of picturing Indigenous people to a non-Indigenous public and emphasizing that any meaning we might take from the image is incomplete and speculative. Which is not to say speculation is discouraged; following *The Mustang Suite* we might wonder what sort of occasion is implied by the headdress and clothing, what elements of tradition and contemporaneity the young man was able to choose from and what acts of survivance he may have performed. This speculative character and the implied refusal to conform to the convention of Indian-ness, together with the project's punning title and the playful use of colour, imply a potential for new meaning to be found in the remediation of the image and the reordering of the conventional systems in which images are categorized.

The departure from "accurate" colour in the *Indian Candy* works recalls the Shirley Card, a reference card with the image of a young Caucasian woman that was first used by Kodak in the late 1940s to calibrate the manufacture and processing of colour film, a method of standardization that was followed by other producers of photographic materials so that Shirley Cards, or an equivalent, were eventually used in photo labs around the world. As a result, the standard tonal range of the colour film used in still photography and motion pictures tended to reproduce white skin better than dark skin. This was particularly evident in cinema, where white actors would have more of a screen presence than actors with darker skin. The choices made in standardizing these materials, as Navneet Alang has noted, "led to some people being able to revel in seeing themselves, but left others to look into a mirror and see no reflection."[17]

There is both a parallel and a point of divergence between Claxton's manipulation of the *Indian Candy* images and the recent work of cinematographers who have developed specific lighting techniques to overcome the Shirley Card bias in feature films and television dramas.[18] While both seek a heightened presence for subjectivities that have been subordinated within the culture at large, Claxton has sought remediation—as in providing a remedy—metaphorically, in a move away from a "realistic" rendering of colour, while in more mainstream cinema the assertion of subjective presence is achieved through enhanced mimesis.

The central role of metaphor in Claxton's work—as seen in the Statue of Liberty as an emblem of displacement in *I Want to Know Why*, the use of spoken Lakota to signify generational memory in *Sitting Bull and the Moose Jaw Sioux*, the violence implied by the censor's marks in the *AIM* photographs, the

Maria Tallchief in Turquoise (from *Indian Candy*), 2013

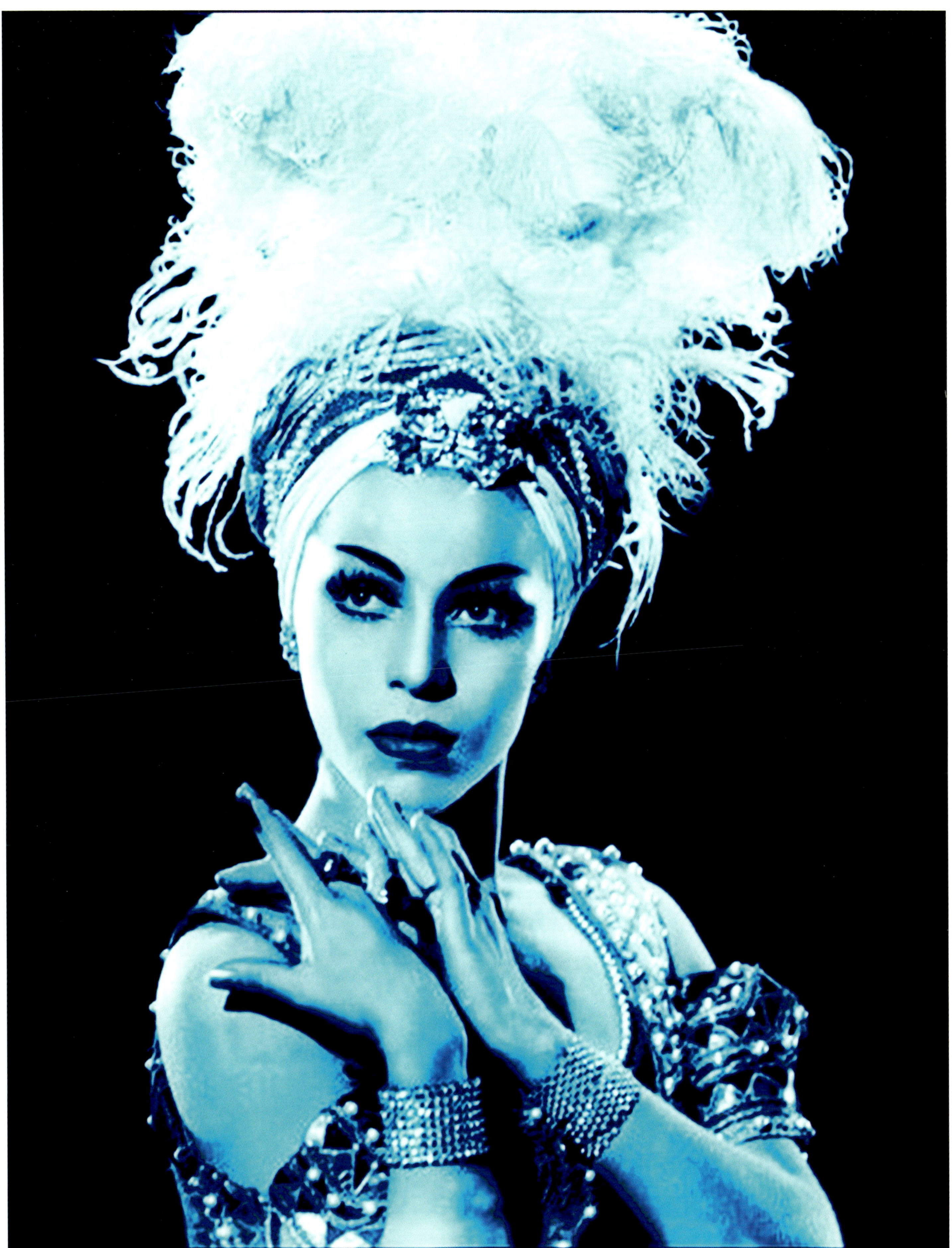

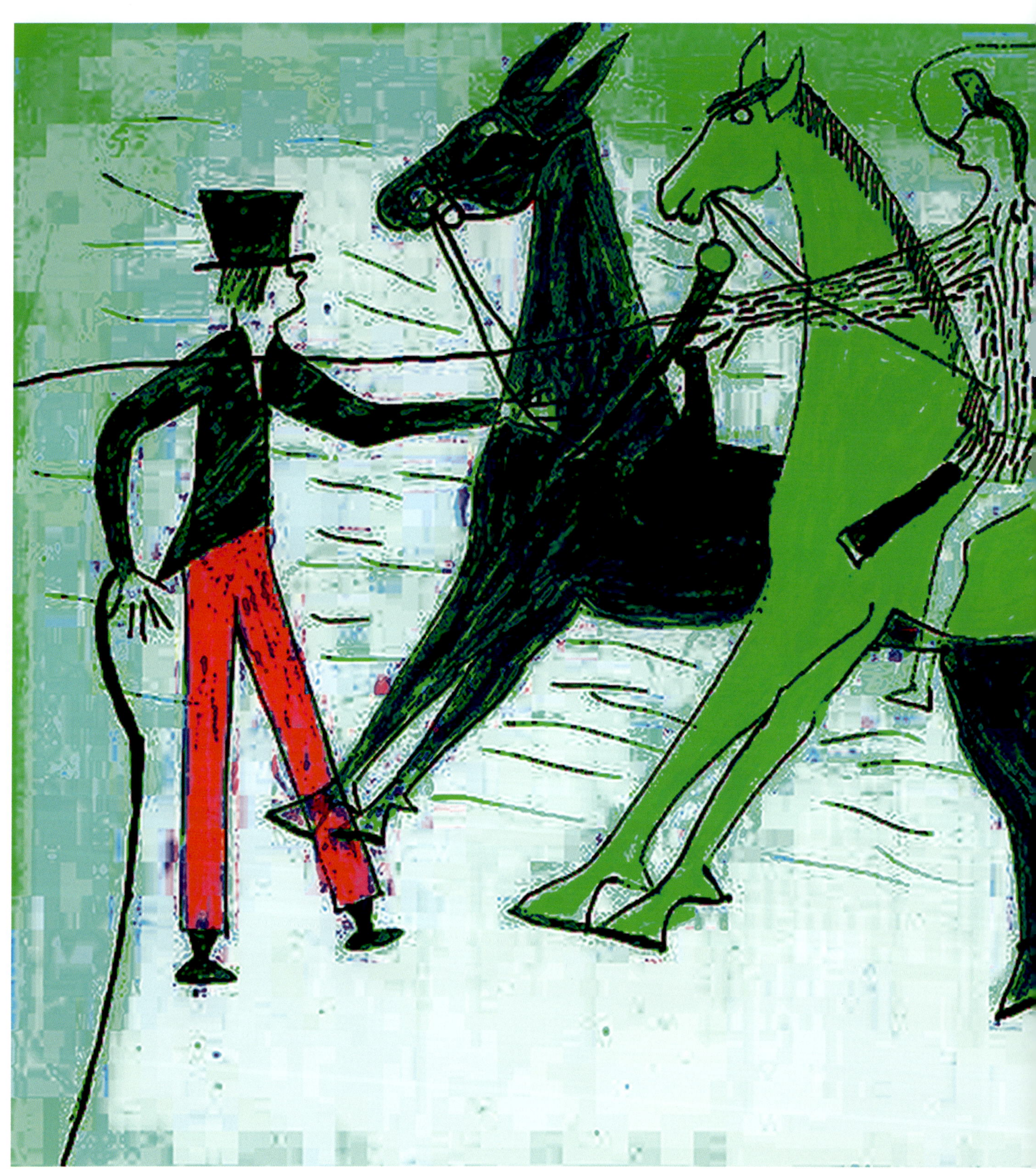

 Sitting Bull Draws the Dandy (from *Indian Candy*), 2013

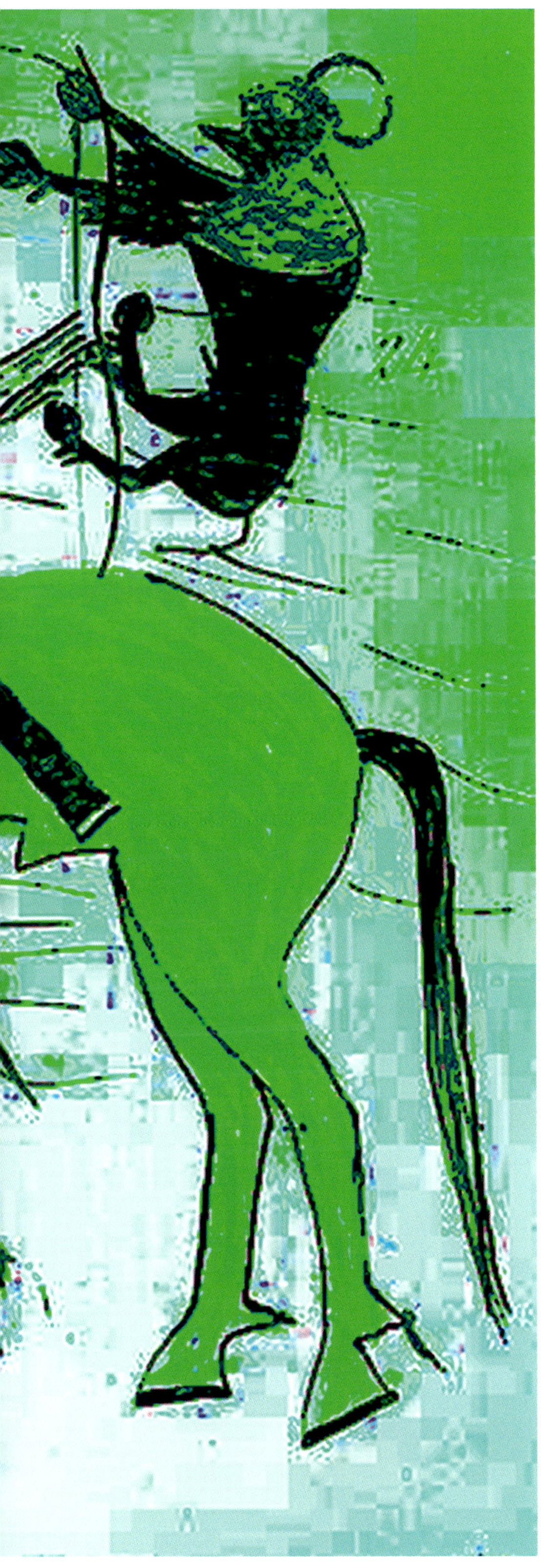

tongue-in-cheek references to horses in *The Mustang Suite*, among many other examples—evokes Vizenor's discussion of metaphor as a mode of articulating Indigenous subjectivity that cannot be contained within established linguistic structures, instrumental logic or conventional Euro-American modes of understanding. Drawing connections between the tradition of oral storytelling and contemporary Indigenous literature, Vizenor, citing philosopher John Searle, argues that metaphor allows for a more expansive mode of signification that moves beyond simple resemblance, and that "the knowledge that enables people to use and understand metaphorical utterances goes beyond their knowledge of the literal meanings of words and sentences."[19]

Considered within this context for articulating identity, Claxton's deployment of metaphor, her dialogical intertwining of Indigenous tradition and contemporaneity, use of punning humour, emphasis on the performative and refusal of stereotypes eloquently and forcefully demand the recognition of Indigenous subjectivities within the museum/gallery and the broader culture. In doing so she simultaneously offers the possibility for Indigenous viewers to see their reflection in the image/mirror and, for the broader culture, proposes a mode of communication in which, in the words of Werner Kogge, "understanding is not simply assumed as given like it is in ordinary linguistic usage but...results from mental movements that mutually induce and open one another up and that are interdependent."[20]

ENDNOTES

1 Gerald Vizenor, "Introduction," in *Fugitive Poses: Native American Indian Scenes of Absence and Presence* (Lincoln: University of Nebraska Press, 1998), 15.

2 Scott Watson, "Whose Nation?" *Canadian Art 11*, no. 1, Spring 1993, 40.

3 Dana Claxton, quoted in Lynne Bell, "Dana Claxton: From a Whisper to a Scream," in *Canadian Art* 27, no. 4, Winter 2010, 104.

4 Dana Claxton, "RE:WIND," in *Transference, Tradition, Technology: Native New Media Exploring Visual and Digital Culture*, eds. Dana Claxton, Melanie A. Townsend, and Steve Loft (Banff: Walter Phillips Gallery, 2005), 16–17.

5 Ibid. 17.

6 Christie's novel was first published in Britain in November 1939. Its original title, *Ten Little N[*****]s*, was taken from a popular children's rhyming song. Concern that the title would be controversial led to it being changed to the, apparently, more acceptable *Ten Little Indians* when it was first published in the United States in 1940. Like the original title, this was taken from a children's nursery song. The novel later appeared under the title *And Then There Were None*. Film versions of the novel appeared under all three titles. *Ten Little Indians* is still a popular children's song; it can be found on numerous internet sites, often with an animated children's video.

7 David Garneau, "Dana Claxton: Sitting Bull and the Moose Jaw Sioux." *Vie des Arts* 197, Winter 2004–05, 93.

8 Gerald Vizenor, *Native Liberty: Natural Reason and Cultural Survivance* (Lincoln: University of Nebraska Press, 2008), 1.

9 Ibid.

10 Karl Kroeber, "Why It's a Good Thing Gerald Vizenor Is Not an Indian," in *Survivance: Narratives of Native Presence*, ed. Gerald Vizenor (Lincoln: University of Nebraska Press, 2008), 25.

11 Gerald Vizenor, *Manifest Manners: Narratives on Postindian Survivance* (Lincoln: University of Nebraska Press, 1994), vii.

12 Ibid. 4.

13 Winfried Siemerling, *The New North American Studies: Culture, Writing and the Politics of Re/Cognition* (London: Routledge, 2005), 93.

14 Claxton, cited in Amber Berson, "Dana Claxton, The Mustang Suite and Hybrid Humour." Amber Berson. 2010. https://www.amberberson.com/academic-writing.

15 The images of the ancient petroglyphs that depict humans and animals that make up the other component of the project were shot by Claxton in Writing-on-Stone Provincial Park / Áísínai'pi National Historic Site in Alberta.

16 Dana Claxton, "Artist Statement," in *Dana Claxton: Indian Candy* (Vancouver: Winsor Gallery, 2013): 6

17 Navneet Alang, "Ways of Seeing," *Globe and Mail*, January 27, 2018.

18 Alang cites the example of Ava Berkofsky, the director of photography on the current HBO drama *Insecure*.

19 John Searle, "Metaphor," in *Metaphor and Thought*, ed. Andrew Ortony (New York: Cambridge University Press, 1979), 93; quoted in Vizenor, "Aesthetics of Survivance: Literary Theory and Practice," in *Survivance*, 13.

20 Werner Kogge, *Die Grenzen des Verstehens: Kultur–Differenz–Diskretion* (Weilerswist, Germany: Velbrück Wissenschaft, 2002), 247; translated by Helmbrecht Breinig and quoted in his "Transdifference in the Work of Gerald Vizenor," in *Native Authenticity: Transnational Perspectives on Native American Literary Studies*, ed. Deborah L. Madsen (Albany: State University of New York Press, 2010), 127.

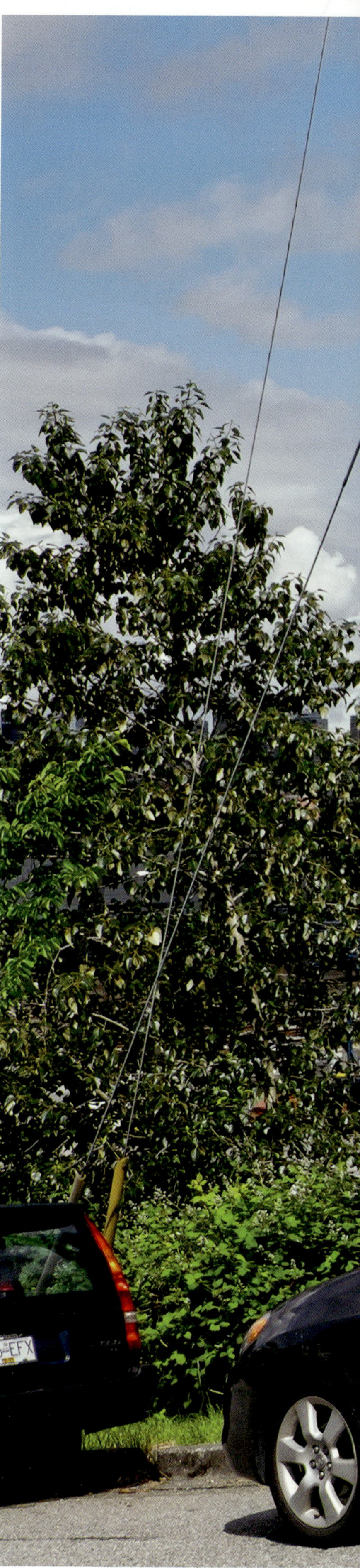

Tonto Prayer (from *Indian Candy*), 2013 (installed in Vancouver in conjunction with the 2014 Scotiabank CONTACT Photography Festival)

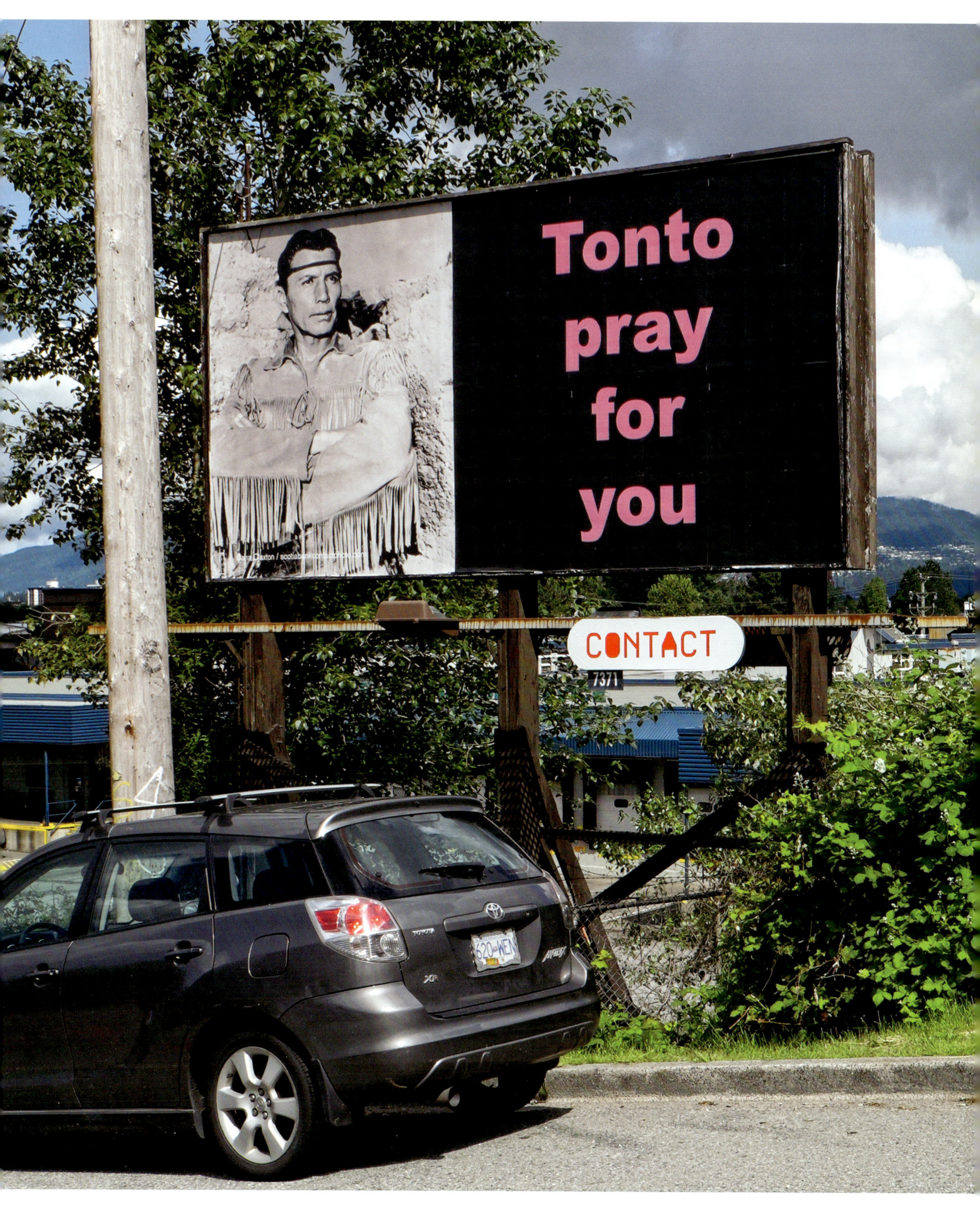
Tonto
pray
for
you
CONTACT
7371

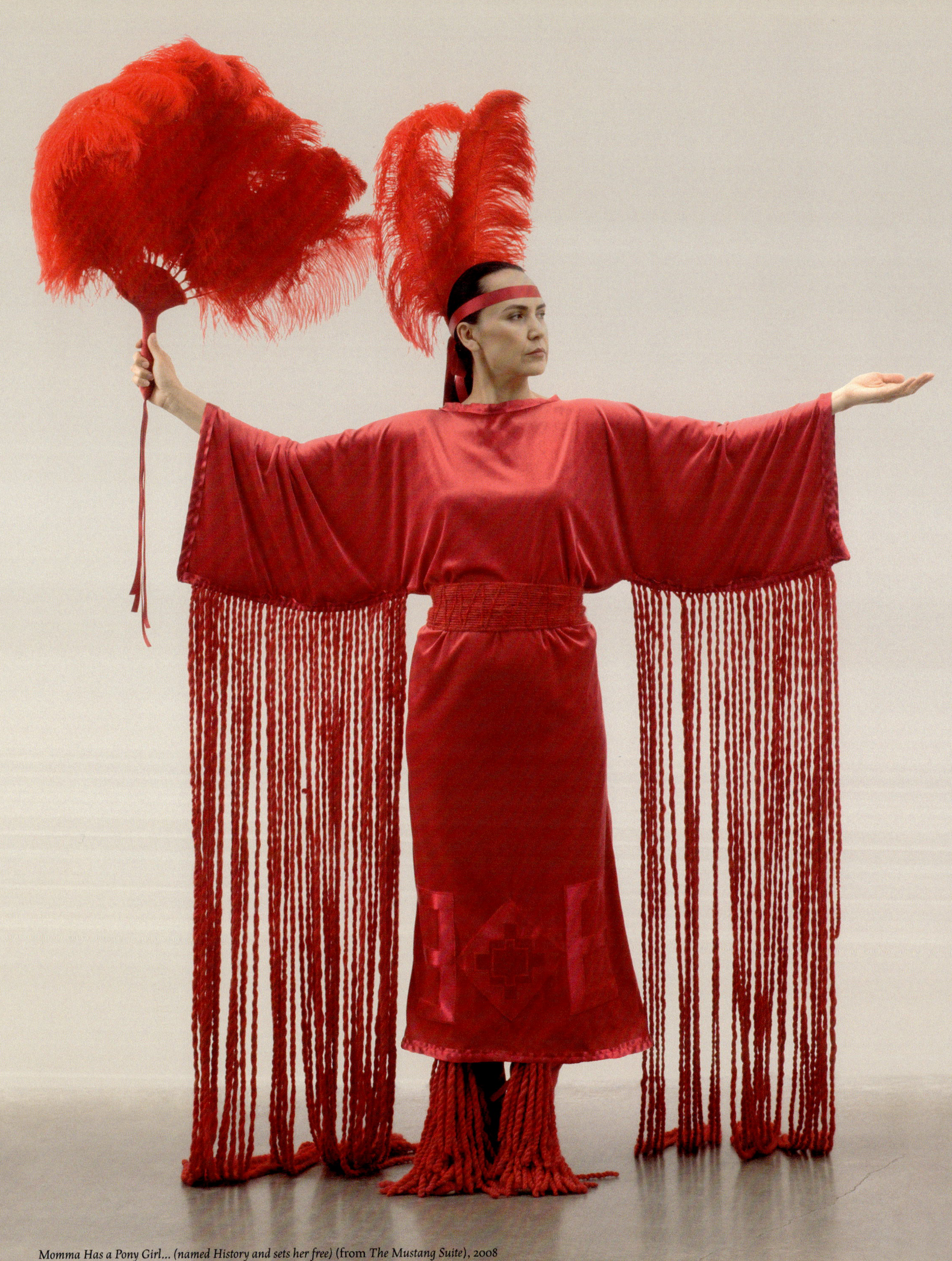

Momma Has a Pony Girl... (named History and sets her free) (from *The Mustang Suite*), 2008

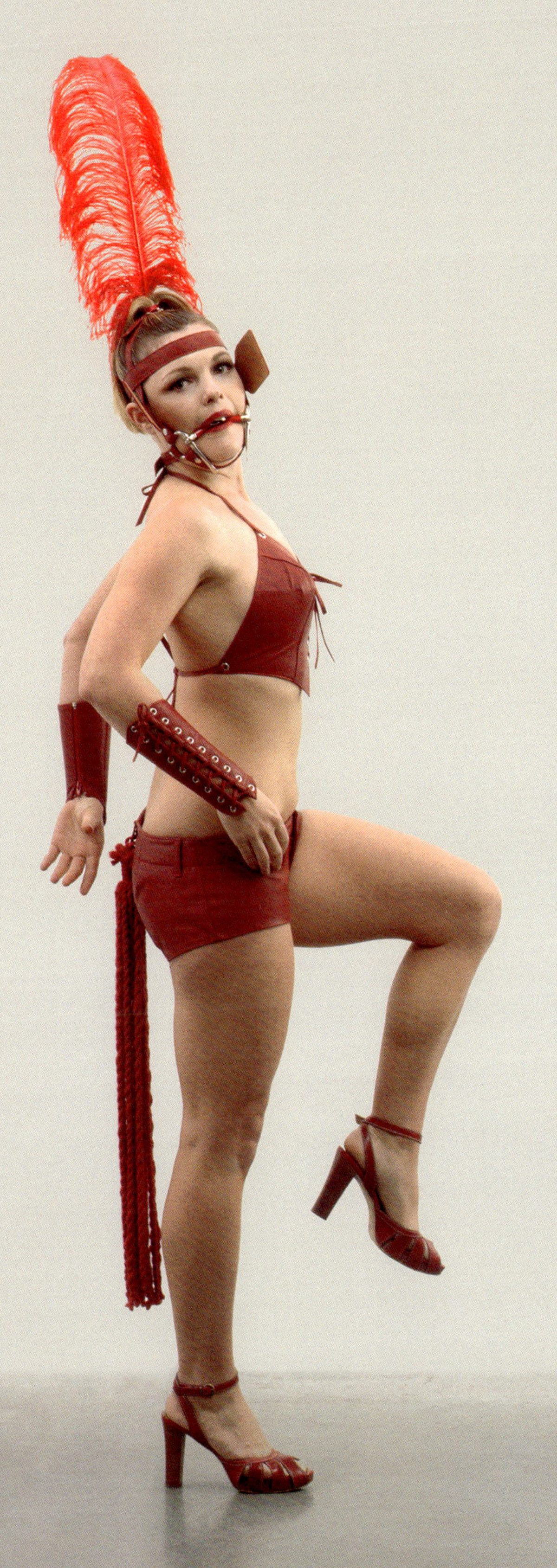

Family Portrait (Indians on a Blanket) (from *The Mustang Suite*), 2008

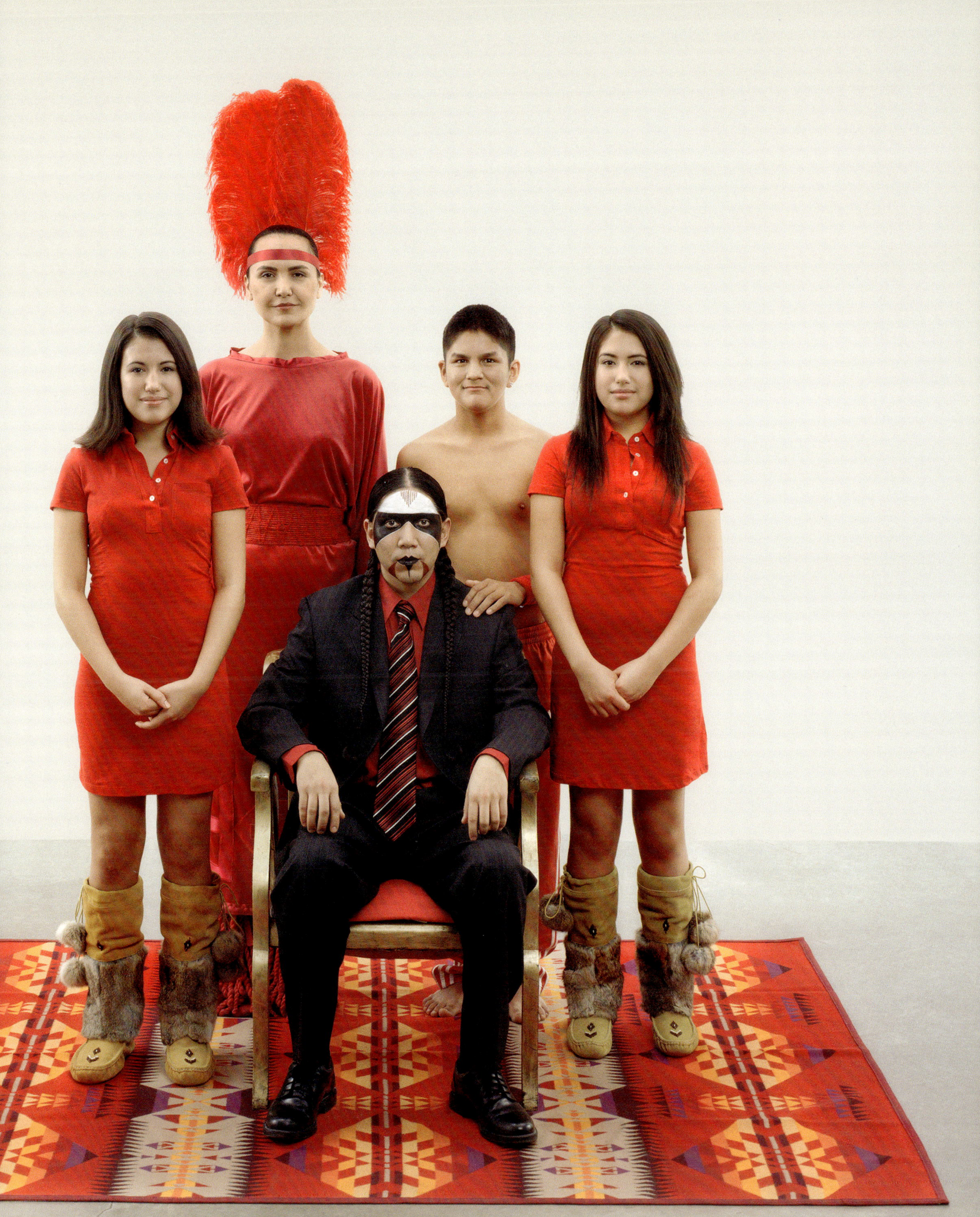

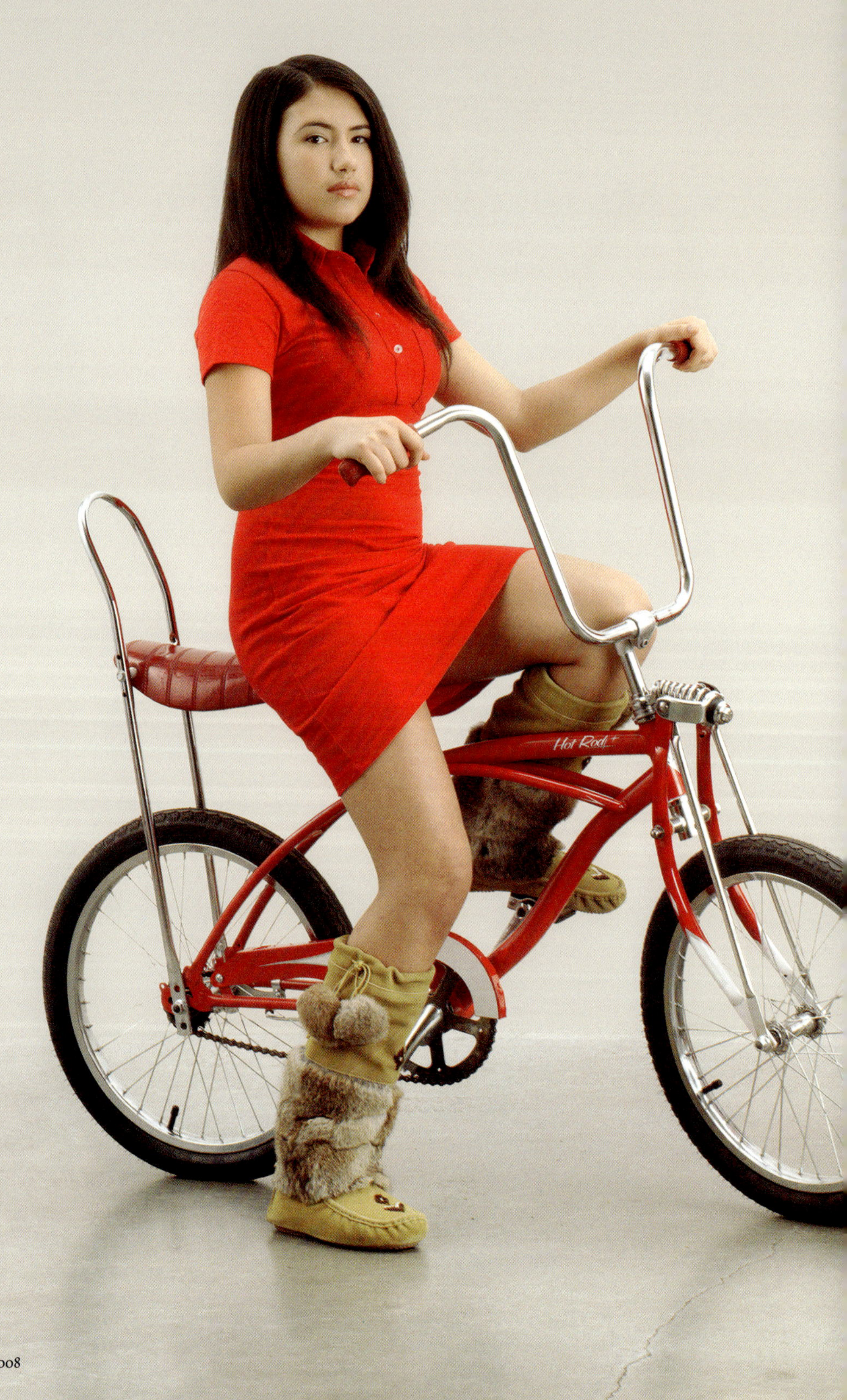

Baby Girlz Gotta Mustang (from *The Mustang Suite*), 2008

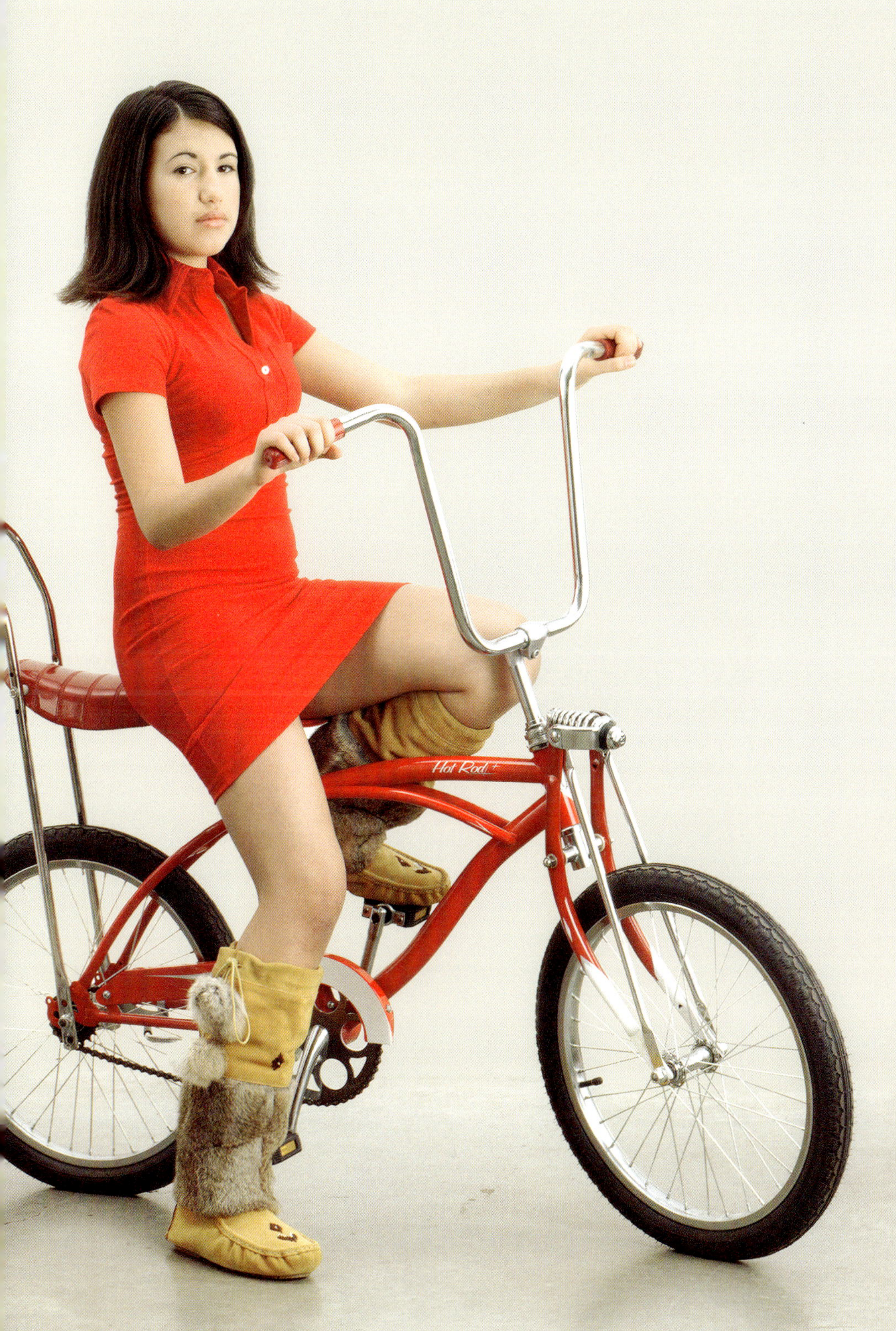
Hot Rod

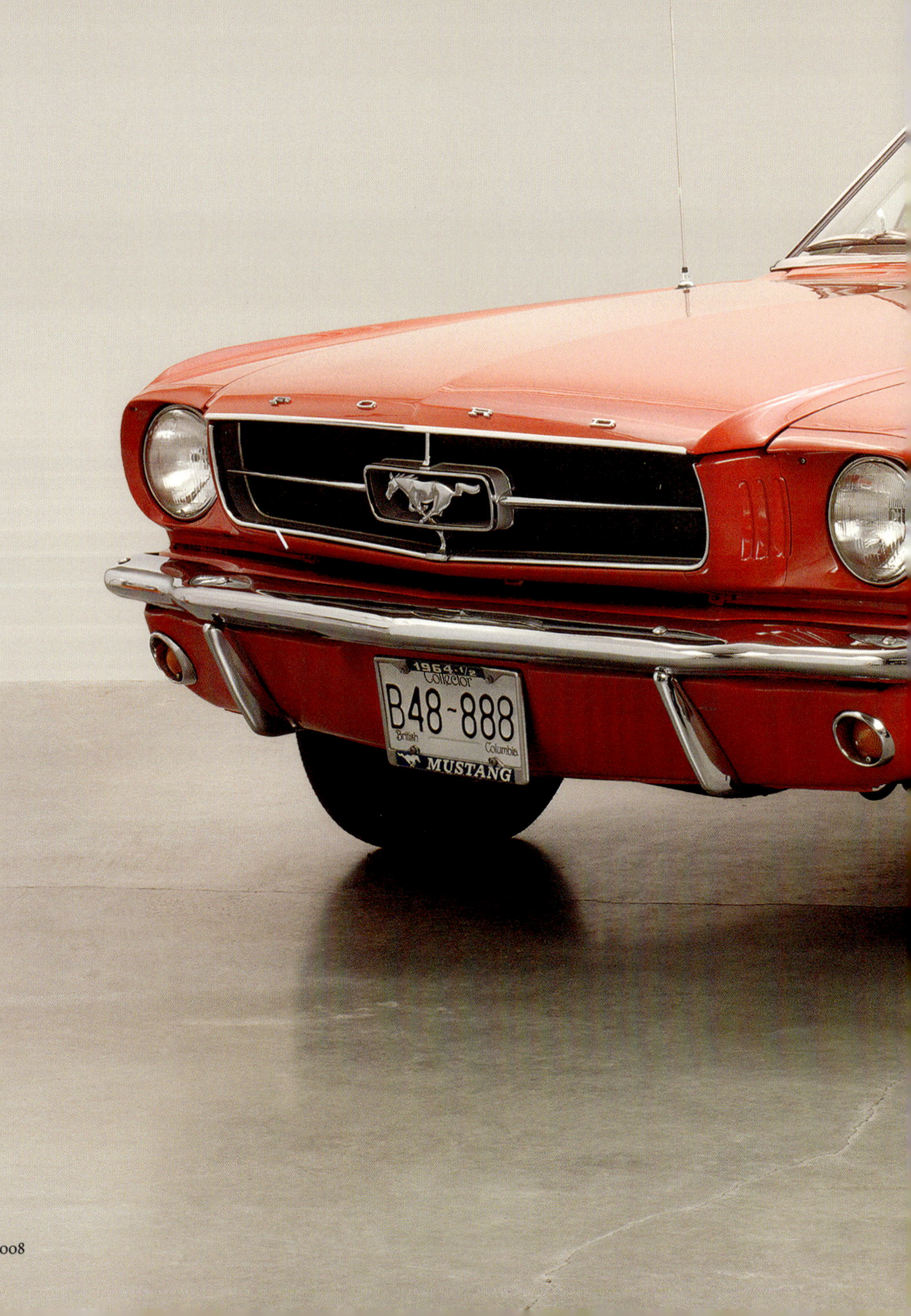

Daddy's Gotta New Ride (from *The Mustang Suite*), 2008

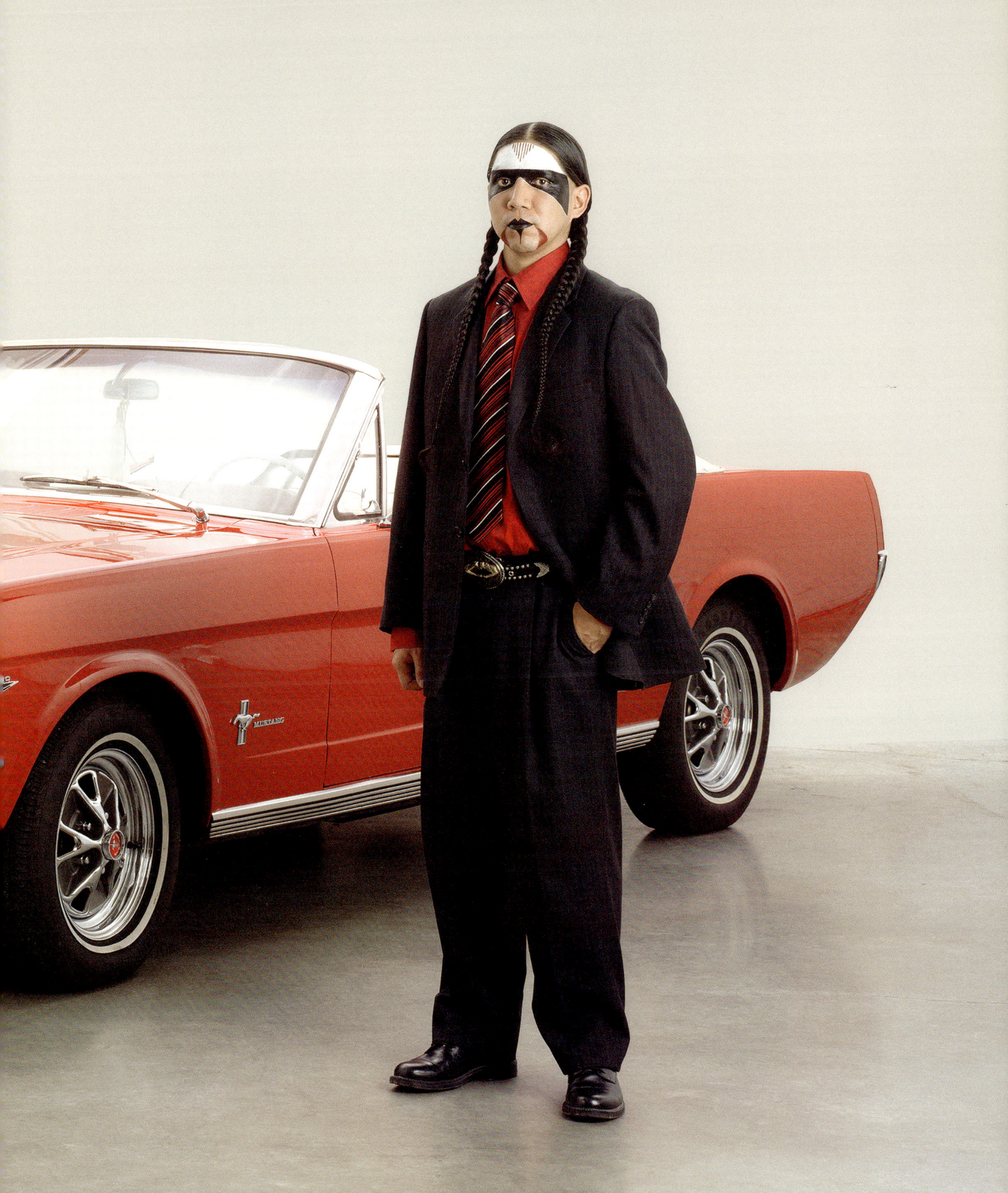
MUSTANG

Baby Boyz Gotta Indian Pony (from *The Mustang Suite*), 2008

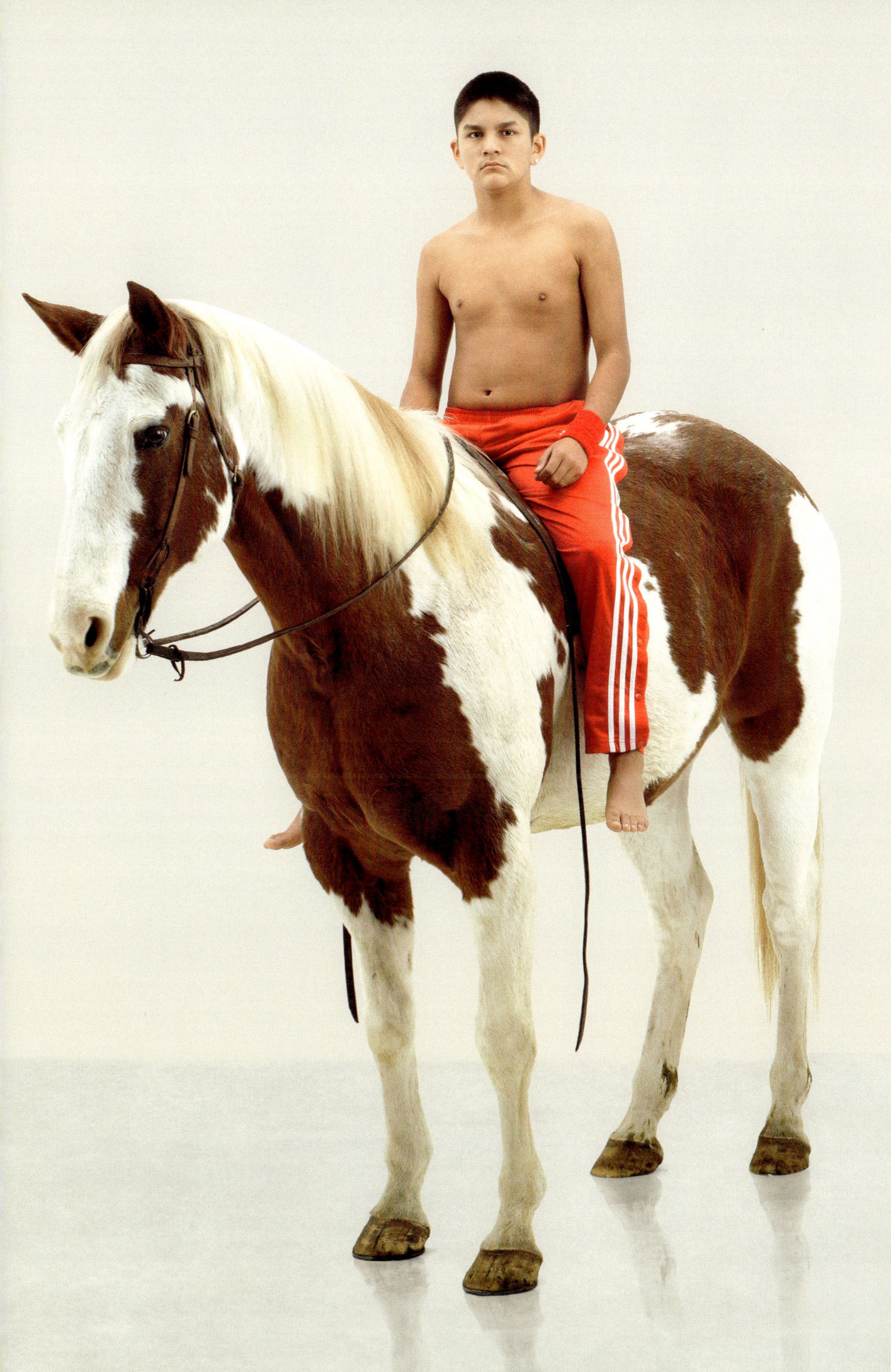

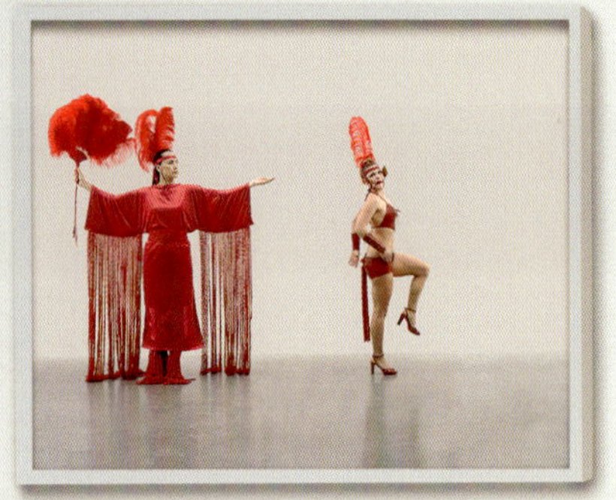

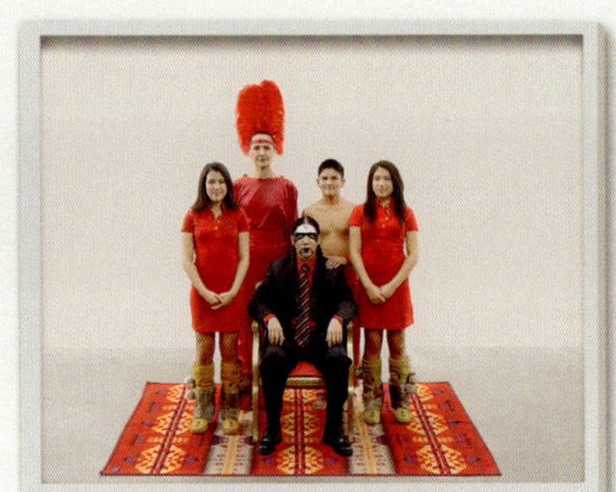

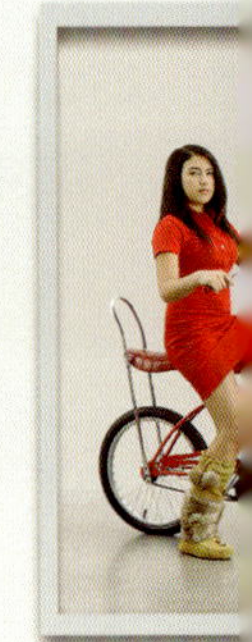

The Mustang Suite, 2008 (installation at the National Gallery of Canada, Ottawa, 2009)

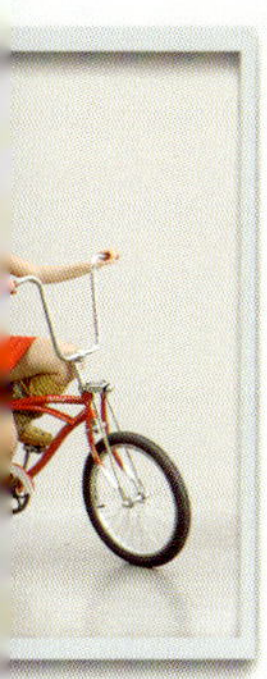

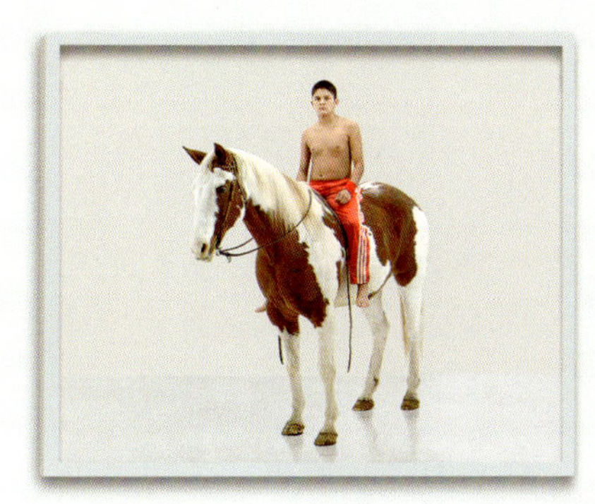

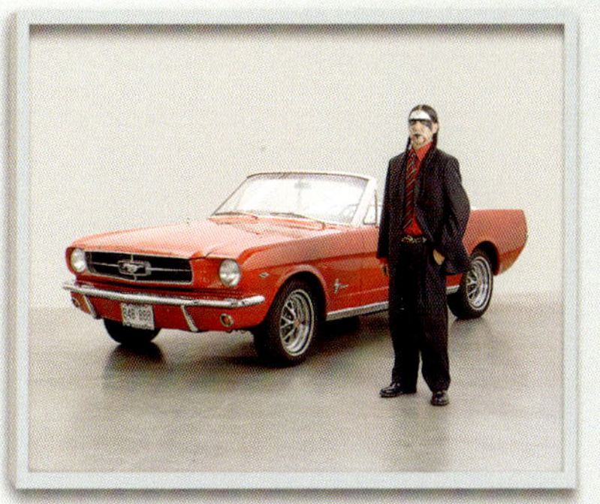

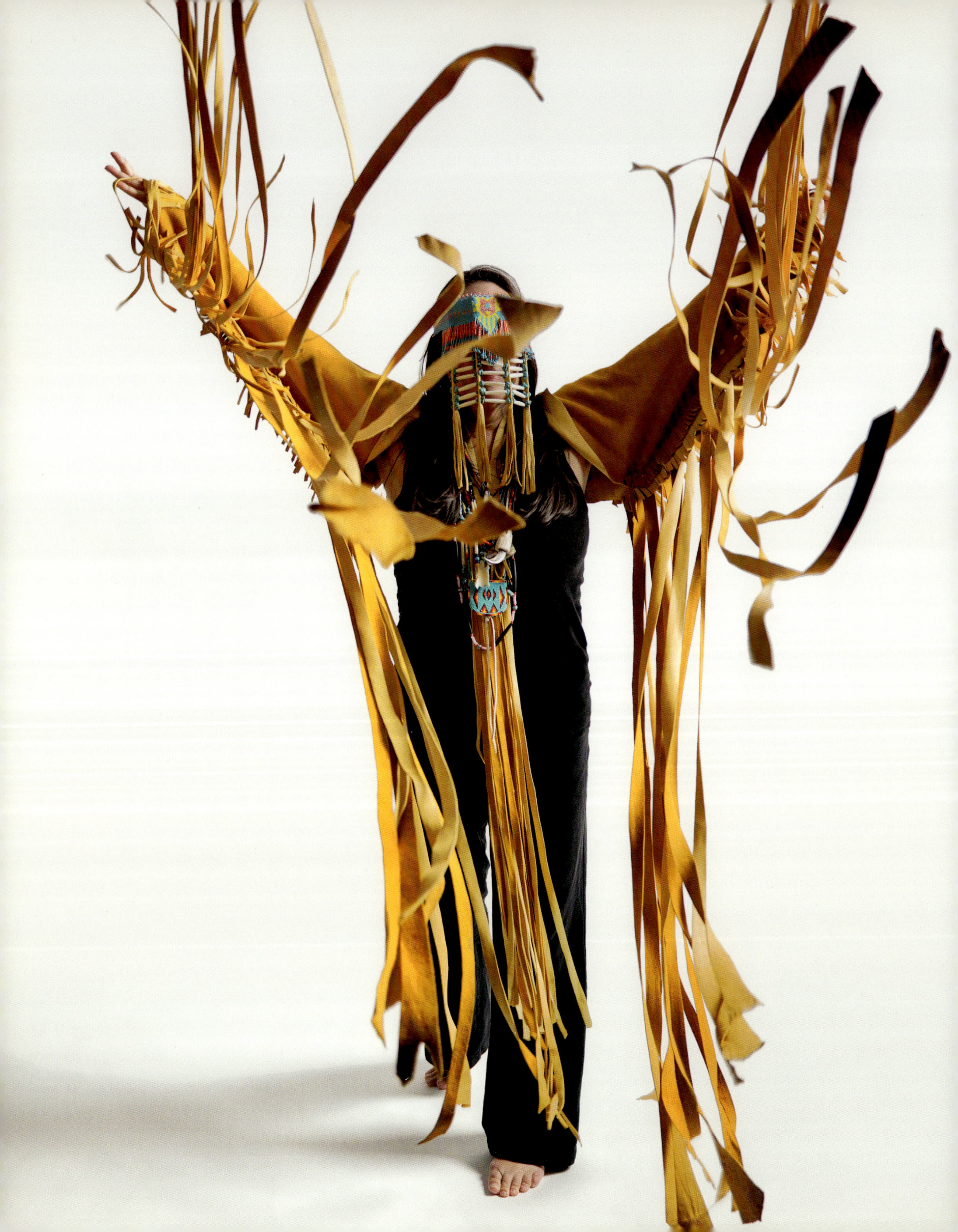

GIFTS OF FRINGE

MONIKA KIN GAGNON & OLIVIA MICHIKO GAGNON

Fringe

The materiality of fringe. The performance of fringe.[1] The gift of fringe.

"Fringe on garments has both practical and spiritual purpose. It sweeps away water, and it moves with the wind, keeping the wearer keenly aware of the connection between his or her body and the elements."[2]

Fringe as connective tissue. Fringe as an Indigenous "made-to-be-ready": an item made for *use*, but one which is also imbued with spiritual and aesthetic energies. An attunement to the "everyday aura of aesthetic forms."[3]

In an email, Dana Claxton tells us that "fringe is an entity of sorts—it sways with the wind, has sound, and makes aliveness—dynamism—as well [as having] a practical side in the rain. It's a Plains aesthetic that has adorned everything from clothing to horse gear, to warfare items, to dolls. An adornment, embellished.

I think fringe is about autonomy."[4]

—

Tradition
Gift-giving
Performance

as transmission.

—

We are sitting in the Grace Rainey Rogers Auditorium at the Metropolitan Museum of Art in New York City on March 15, 2015.

Olivia | Monika

We have made our way through the museum's Great Hall with its majestic, immense domes and arches through thrumming crowds here to see some of the two million objects in the Met's famous collections. It's no secret that many of these objects are imbued with contested stories of acquisition, some violent, surreptitious, even illicit! Others reciprocal. Some objects enthrall. Their juxtapositions teem with complicated energies in our fields of vision, as do most anthropological, ethnological institutions in the twenty-first century. We walk amongst Egyptian sarcophagi and the *Book of the Dead* as we make our way to the theatre. Exhibition vernaculars: display cases, low light and controlled temperatures, didactic panels (year, geographical origin, description, provenance), instructions for movement, stanchions.

We wait.

As Claxton walks from the back of the darkened auditorium toward the stage, she holds a pair of antlers in front of her body. At first, we only hear her; she moves to the front of the room, taking (her) time. Resplendent in fringe made by her sister Kim Soo Goodtrack, she thumps out a rhythmic beat through the clatter of antlers. They seem to propel her forward, like what one teacher once described to me as "objects that get you there"—a colloquial riff on D.W. Winnicott's *transitional object*.[5] Teaching—like collaboration, like the gift of fringe—is also a form of transmission that elaborates (new) webs of sociality. And Claxton has brought two of her graduate students with her: she dances Jamey Braden and Eric Angus—who will be part of the performance—in. (My mother has brought me; I have brought my friend L. We all sit together in the darkened auditorium with several hundred other people.)

> *"What is an Indian Action and why were Indian Actions criminalized in Canada for over 80 years? What is the threat of dancing and singing? [...] What is an Indian Action? Shaking a rattle, shaking a tent? What is an Indian Action? Beading, drumming, singing, dancing, praying?"*
> Tania Willard and Dana Claxton[6]

FRINGED. METROPOLITAN MUSEUM OF ART, NEW YORK CITY. MARCH 15, 2015.

A video projection of the plains—blue sky and green grass—lights up the screen at the front of the darkened auditorium. Claxton dances her way around this room, fringe moving on and with her body, fringe covering her eyes (*covering*, here, a gesture of refusal or withholding). She approaches the stage, trailed now by Jamey, who cradles a red

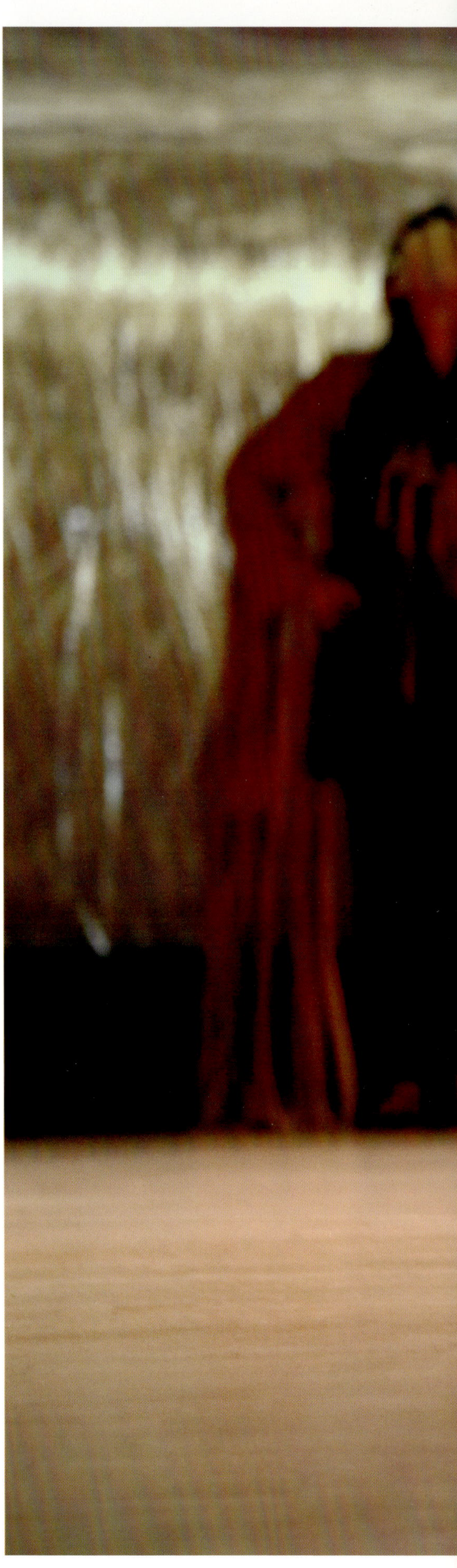

Fringed, March 15, 2015 (documentation of performance at the Metropolitan Museum of Art)

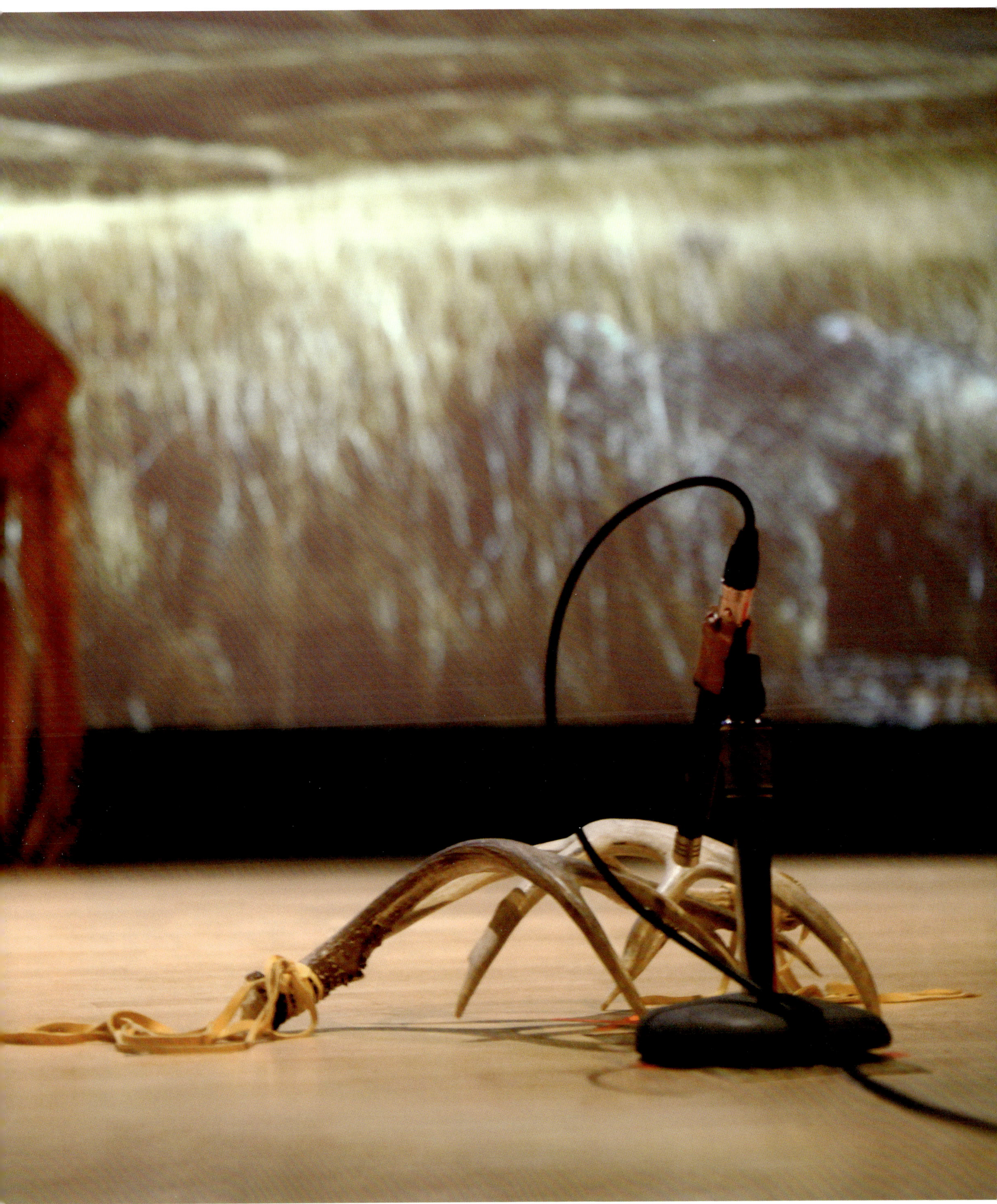

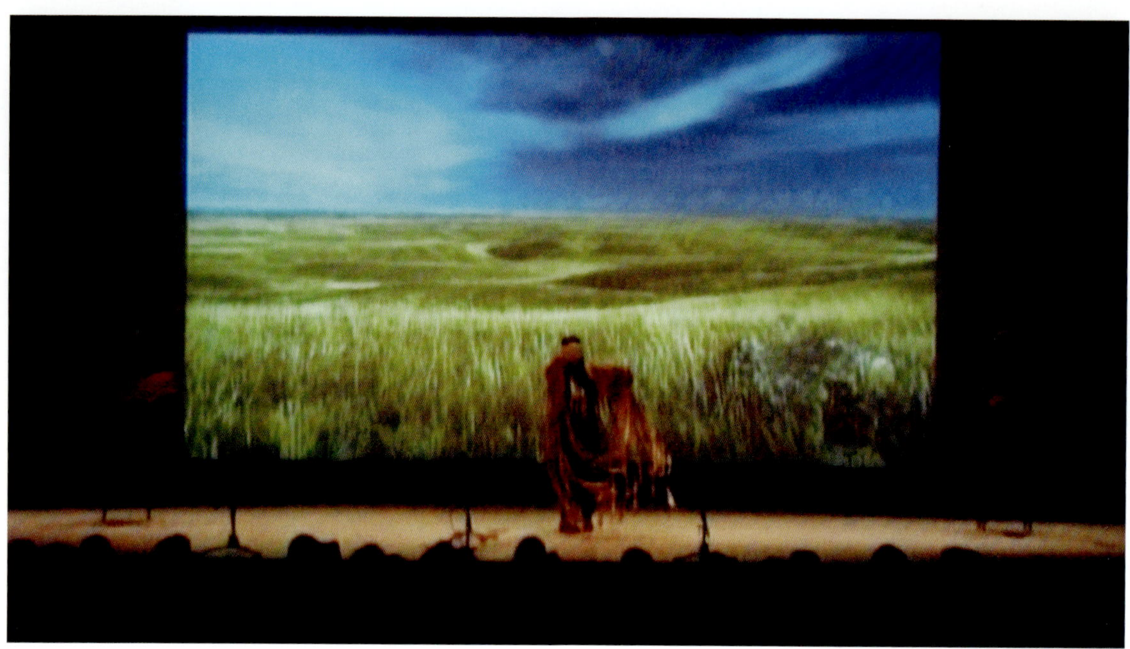

bundle in her arms. Claxton seats her and leaves her up there, returning to the back of the room. And now, she has returned again, trailed this time by Eric, who also holds a small bundle in his hands. He, too, sits. And these two—her students—flank, or frame, her. Taking centre stage, Claxton raises the antlers above her head—dancing or keeping time or holding the beat—projected blades of grass dancing with and across her fringe. Now, the antlers beat low, close to the ground. They settle at her feet. She makes the long fringe hanging from her arms dance and swing and sway and (a)live. Then, she takes the bundle from Jamey's arms, raising it high above her head, moving around the stage's perimeter. This bundle, too, will eventually come to rest with the antlers, and when Claxton unwraps it, we find that its red fabric holds a fringed bustle holder, made of buffalo hide. Claxton handles it, tosses it above her head—as if getting to know it, as if learning to use it. *(A) Made-to-be-Ready.* The bustle holder is placed back in Jamey's arms. And now, Eric's bundle circles the stage, held high. It too is lowered, it too unwrapped. But it holds a pair of headphones, which are plugged into Claxton's iPod. And then, she dances—the fringe moving—to a beat we cannot hear (this, too, a gesture of withholding, a refusal). At some point, we begin to hear her breath of exertion. She keeps dancing until she's done. And then, removing the headphones, she places them on a small boom mic, so that we can hear what she has heard—pow-wow music—though muffled, mediated. She takes the bustle holder, dancing still, and places it on the ground in front of the stage, just by the headphones. The music continues, but the performance is over.

Later that evening, Dana gifts me the antlers from her performance. Today, they perch over my books, keeping watch. After the performance, Dana gifts a small wrapped package to Jodi Archambault Gillette (Hunkpapa and Oglala Lakota), Special Assistant to the President for Native American Affairs under President Barack Obama. Dana has been adorned in fringe, made from hide, gifted to her by her sister.

Fringed, March 15, 2015 (documentation of performance at the Metropolitan Museum of Art)

Gillette has spoken some opening words about Dana's performance and the opening of *The Plains Indians: Artists of Earth and Sky* exhibition located upstairs. This was preceded by an artists' conversation between Edgar Heap of Birds (Cheyenne/Arapaho) and Claxton, both of whom are in the show.[7] Gillette speaks of her work with the Obama administration, a commitment that had originally been planned for one year and at this moment in 2015, has turned into six, or is it eight. She is in her dance regalia, a jingle dress, which is causing her some consternation—what am I doing in my regalia, standing here, she says out loud, I should be at home dancing with my community.[8] We read at *Indian Country Today* that she departs Obama's administration two months later.[9] Hers is the Standing Rock Reservation that will be catapulted into public view on April 1, 2016, when the Dakota Access Pipeline project will be contested and resisted by the Stand with Standing Rock movement (also known as #NoDAPL) which is ongoing.

In 2005, Dana, Kim and I drive the 700 km to Standing Rock from Regina to attend the Sitting Bull Sundance in Little Eagle (South Dakota), where Dana has Sundanced for many years. We visit with Dr. Beatrice Medicine in Mobridge, and stay en route at the nearby Prairie Knights Casino and Resort (where Kim wins at the slot machines). There are several hamlets located at Standing Rock; Dana and Kim's relatives lived in Wakpala and Little Eagle. Ten years later in 2016, we plan again to go to the Sundance, but there is flooding in Estevan (Saskatchewan), complicating our route; but also, extreme thunderstorms on the days we plan to travel, and record-high temperatures of 49 degrees celsius at Standing Rock, finally avert our journey. We visit Kim instead at her/their home reserve of Wood Mountain (Saskatchewan) where Kim lives, the only Lakota Reserve in Canada with direct descendants of Sitting Bull, Black Moon and others who fought at the battle of Little Bighorn in 1876. We eat "prairie oysters" sautéed in butter. We camp for several nights at Grasslands National Park near Wood Mountain, a Dark Sky Preserve where we see a most extraordinary full buck moonrise, so named to mark the seasonal moment when male deer—bucks—begin sprouting antlers.

supernatural

While Gillette is talking at the podium, another spectacular dress that she has made—a fully beaded yoke dress—is displayed upstairs as part of the exhibition, which has just opened. She designed the patterns in Adobe Illustrator and "turned for help to accomplished bead workers within her family and circle of close friends."[10] Like the connective tissue between a bustle holder and an iPod, this dress yokes past and present—traditional cultural aesthetic practices and contemporary technology—in ways that also bind generations together, ensuring that such practices are transmitted, even as they are transformed. History and kinship—a line of Lakota women as artisans—converge in and on this dress, flushed pink "in memory of a Cheyenne great-grandmother."[11]

The Plains Indians: Artists of Earth and Sky brings together approximately 150 artworks by Plains Indigenous artists spanning hundreds of years. It was described by critic Christopher Green as the Met's "greatest and most ambitious exhibition of indigenous art from North America in recent history."[12] And indeed, there are display techniques and didactics at use here that foreground the presence of artists in ways that

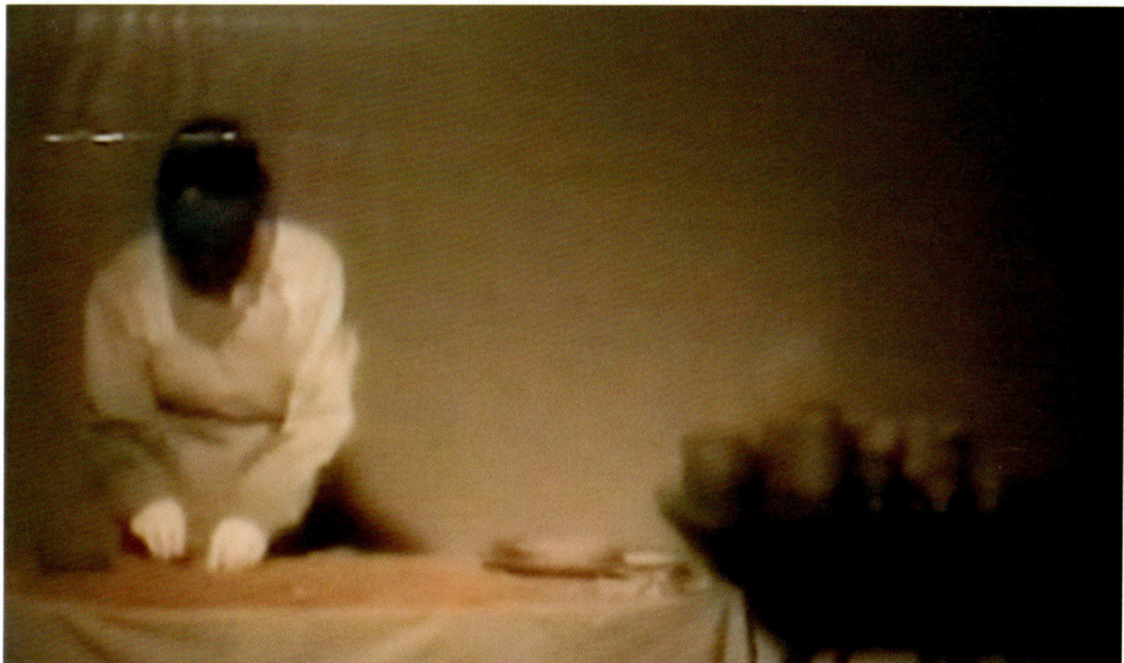

depart from the conventions of ethnographic and ethnological presentation, notably the inclusion of artists' names. On the walls, four curatorial voices intermingle to suffuse the layers of museological-ethnographic-aesthetic-supernatural investments at work in this gathering, which captivate, absorb and sadden.

In his *New York Times* review, critic Holland Cotter writes:

> Some of the earliest surviving art by native North Americans left America long ago. Soldiers, traders and priests, with magpie eyes for brilliance, bundled it up and shipped it across the sea to Europe. Painted robes, embroidered slippers and feathered headdresses tinkling with chimes found their way into cupboards in 18th-century London and Paris, and lay there half-forgotten. Now [...] some of those wondrous things have come home.[13]

Giving an account of the (most recent) provenance of many of the objects featured in the exhibition—various European collections, including the impressive one housed at the Musée du quai Branly in Paris—Cotter misreads the meaning of "coming home." For what kind of home could the museum—*this* museum, *this* site of accumulation—ever be? (And yet, it is undeniable that an exhibition such as this one importantly invites and demands viewers' attention to the contested histories of the United States and its current realities.)

—

In her 2017 collection of poetry *WHEREAS*, Layli Long Soldier's (Oglala Lakota) poem "Hĕ Sápa"[14] contains a page where the following words line, construct and spatialize an empty square—where nothing (or everything fails to) appear(s):

Buffalo Bone China, 1997 (documentation of performance at AKA, Saskatoon)

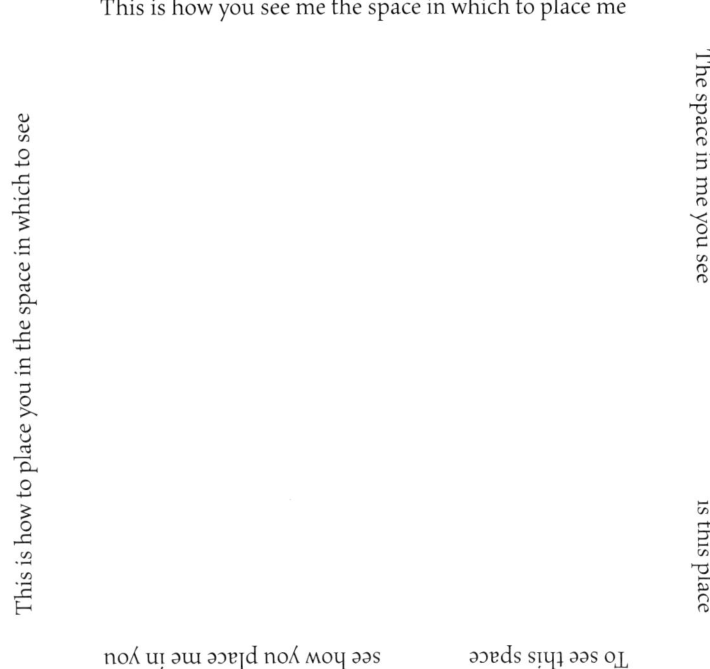

Writing about the imperial museum and echoing Fred Moten's formulation of the resistance of the object, Sarita Echavez See insists that "the imperial project attempts and fails to put in order its vast collection of materials."[15] Objects—and subjects produced as objects of colonial knowledge—are always actively resisting their violent script(ing)s. But performance, too, is one way that See conceives of practices that might upset colonial logics of accumulation.

RATTLE (2003)

Upstairs in the Met's sprawling maze of rooms, we find Claxton's *Rattle* (2003) in the "Artistic Revival in Contemporary Life" section of the *Plains Indians* exhibition. While this part of the show, featuring the work of contemporary artists, is wanting for space (some of the artworks seemingly installed salon-style), the collection of works concludes the visitor's journey through the exhibition—importantly insisting on the continuity of Plains aesthetic practices and their (transformed) contemporary renderings in and as headdresses, painting, sculpture, clothing, collage, drawing, new media and video. This is a powerful testament to cultural transmission and the flexible persistence—which is to say, the (a)liveness—of tradition.

Rattle is a four-channel video installation that combines traditional ceremony and contemporary technology, what Claxton describes as "a visual prayer attempting to create infinity... [m]uch like a palindrome."[16] Rendered in shades of blue, the first sequence shows Claxton shaking horsehair rattles that she has made—two screens in real time, two in slow motion—set to the sound of synthesizers. Then, only the slow motion rattles remain, as the outer two screens become close-up images of beadwork. This second sequence is set to peyote healing songs sung by singers Verdell Primeaux and Johnny Mike.

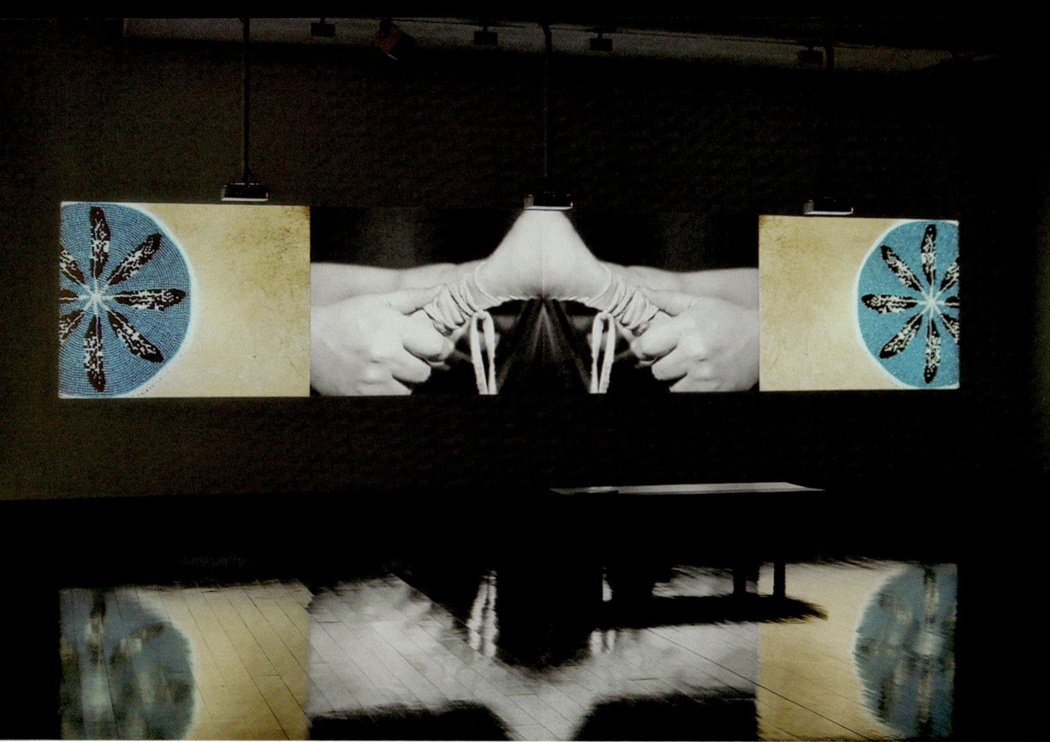
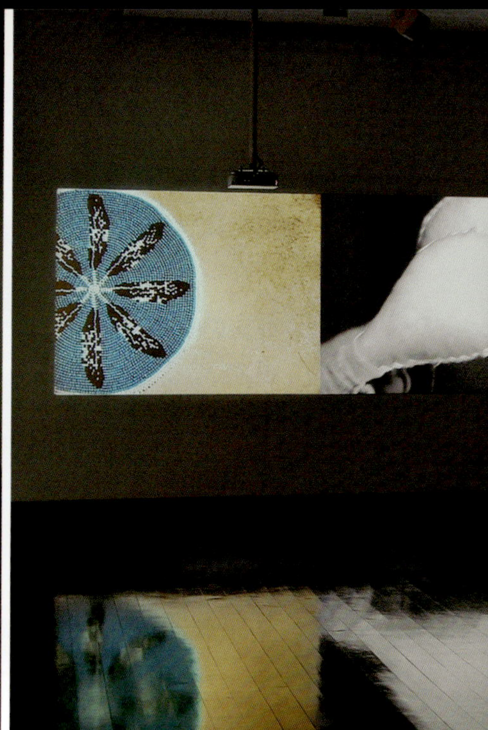

Like a palindrome, these sequences loop without end or start—reflecting "the spiritual Lakota belief that 'The Heart of Everything That Is' and the above skyworld are mirrored directly on the earth below. The doubling of images emphasizes the notion that creation on earth and in the sky, reflect each other to create an existence of timeless continuum—with no ending."[17]

Rattle spatializes with sound, washes us in soothing blue, which is to say that it creates an environment in which one feels not only lulled, but held. But as Green notes, "the sounds [of rattle] haunt the gallery" you almost hear them in every room.[18] A contemporary and endless echo that moves across time, that joints times, that sounds "an existence of timeless continuum—with no ending." This too, is a form of transmission.[19]

Monika writes Dana to ask about her experience of *Fringed*. Dana tells us about "tossing the 'artifact' and [wanting] to place my hands on OBJECTS that the West continues to study and hold with white gloves—I wanted to liberate it and throw it up in the air and catch it—but also with the threat of dropping it."[20]

> Here, Claxton describes a relationship to the Indigenous "artifact" (a man's bustle holder, made of hide)—made possible through performance—that pivots away from the museum's distantiated gaze, which captures the object under glass. Instead, there is use—a *made-to-be-readiness*—and freedom, but also its attendant risk.

These objects (studied and held) have arrived here through theft, trade, gifting, and purchases—the history of America.

Rattle, 2003 (installation at the Samstag Museum of Art, University of South Australia, Adelaide, 2011)

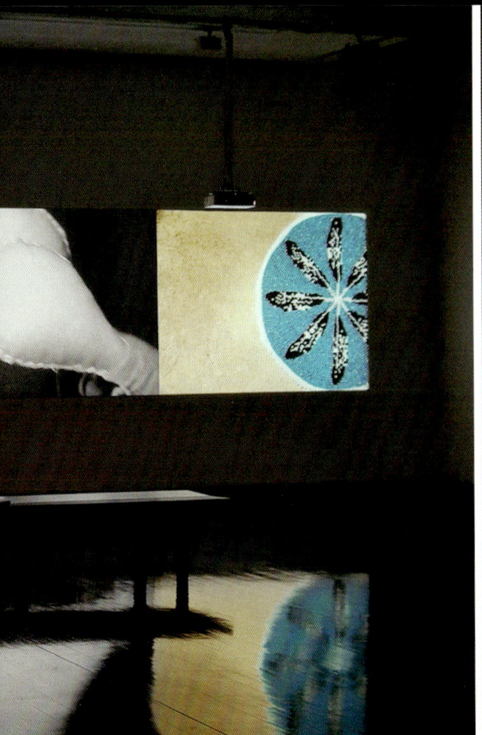
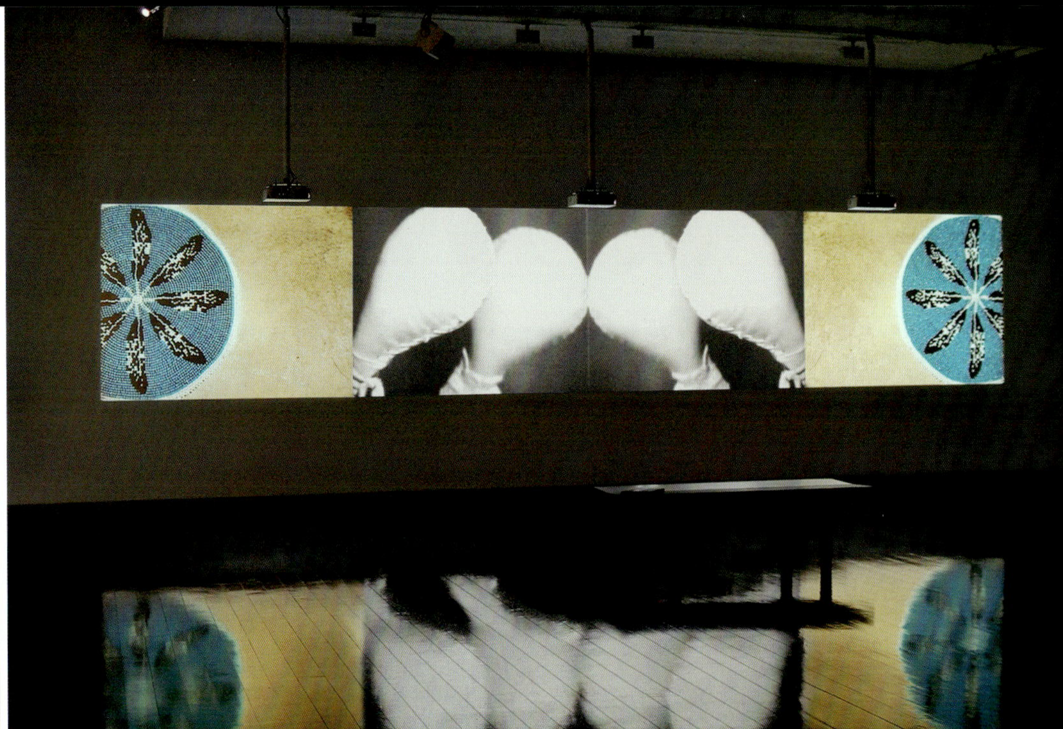

Ask how to "counter the commodification of Indigenous aesthetics and the preservation of 'artifacts.'"[21]

And Claxton might respond: "Performance art is an act of giving and receiving."[22]

Transmission as one possibly anti-accumulative mode.
Women as the keepers and transmitters of *Lakol Wicoh'an.*
Women as gift-givers.

"DR. MEDICINE: I just want to say one thing, that when we talk about these things we have to contextual(ize) them, there are certain things that are sacred and they remain sacred and certain things that are secular. It all depends upon one's commitment to one's community and their ritual as opposed to the commodification of art—we have to look at this—[INAUDIBLE]—I think this is something that we need to discuss more. Because it comes up in every art conference and it's never going to be solved—and it is something that we have to discuss. The contextualization of art—the commodification of art or rituals and where they are rightfully practiced."[23]

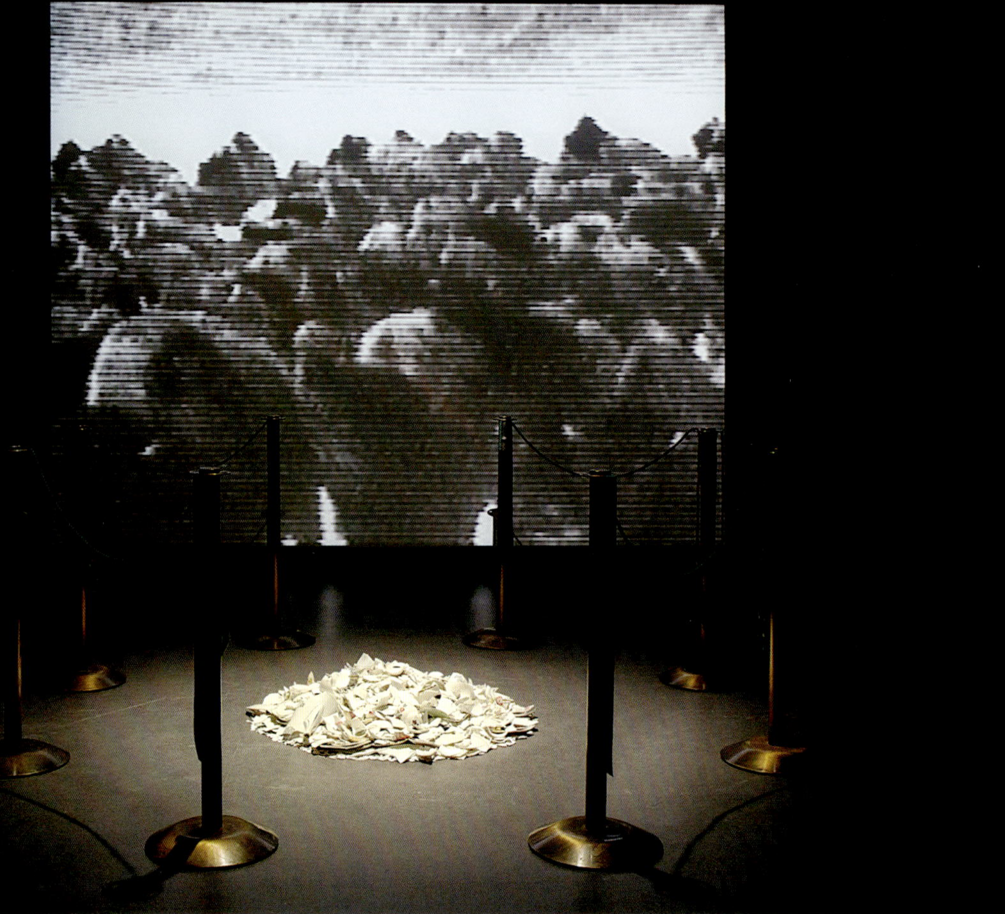

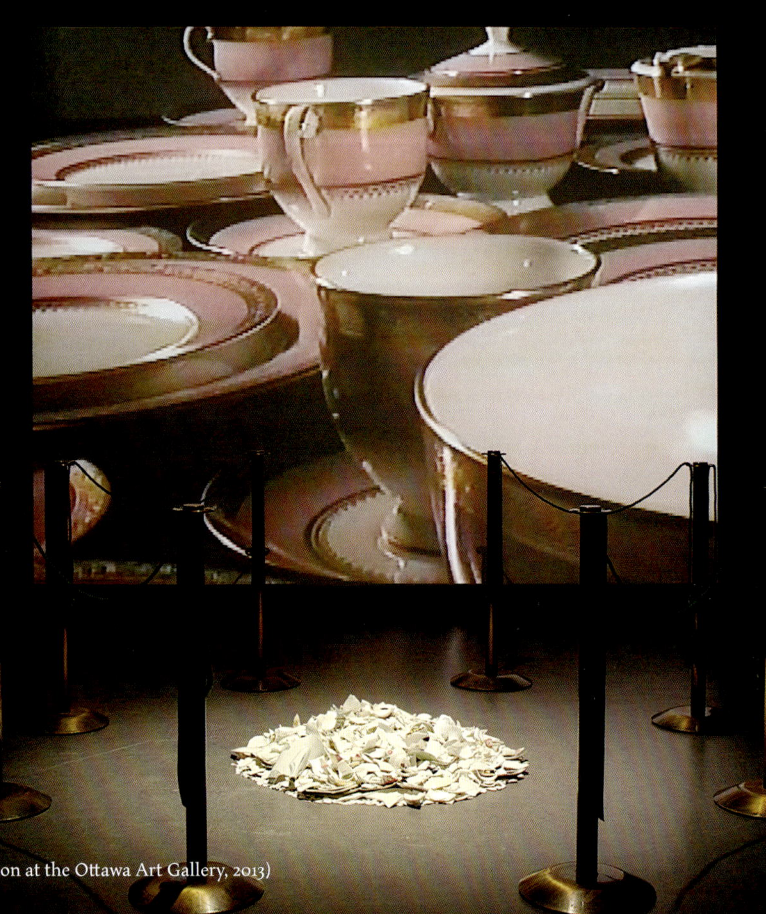

Buffalo Bone China, 1997 (installation at the Ottawa Art Gallery, 2013)

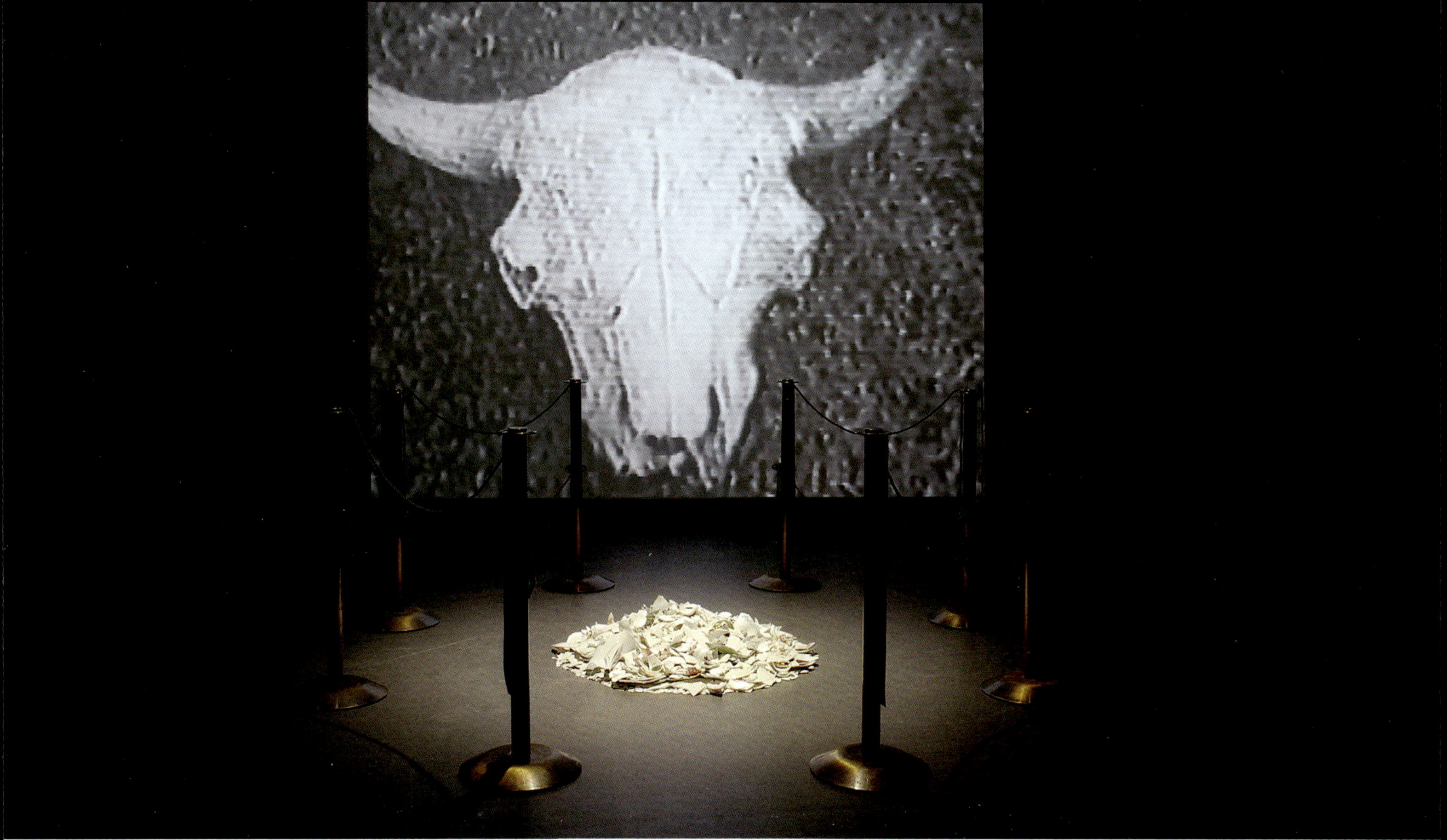

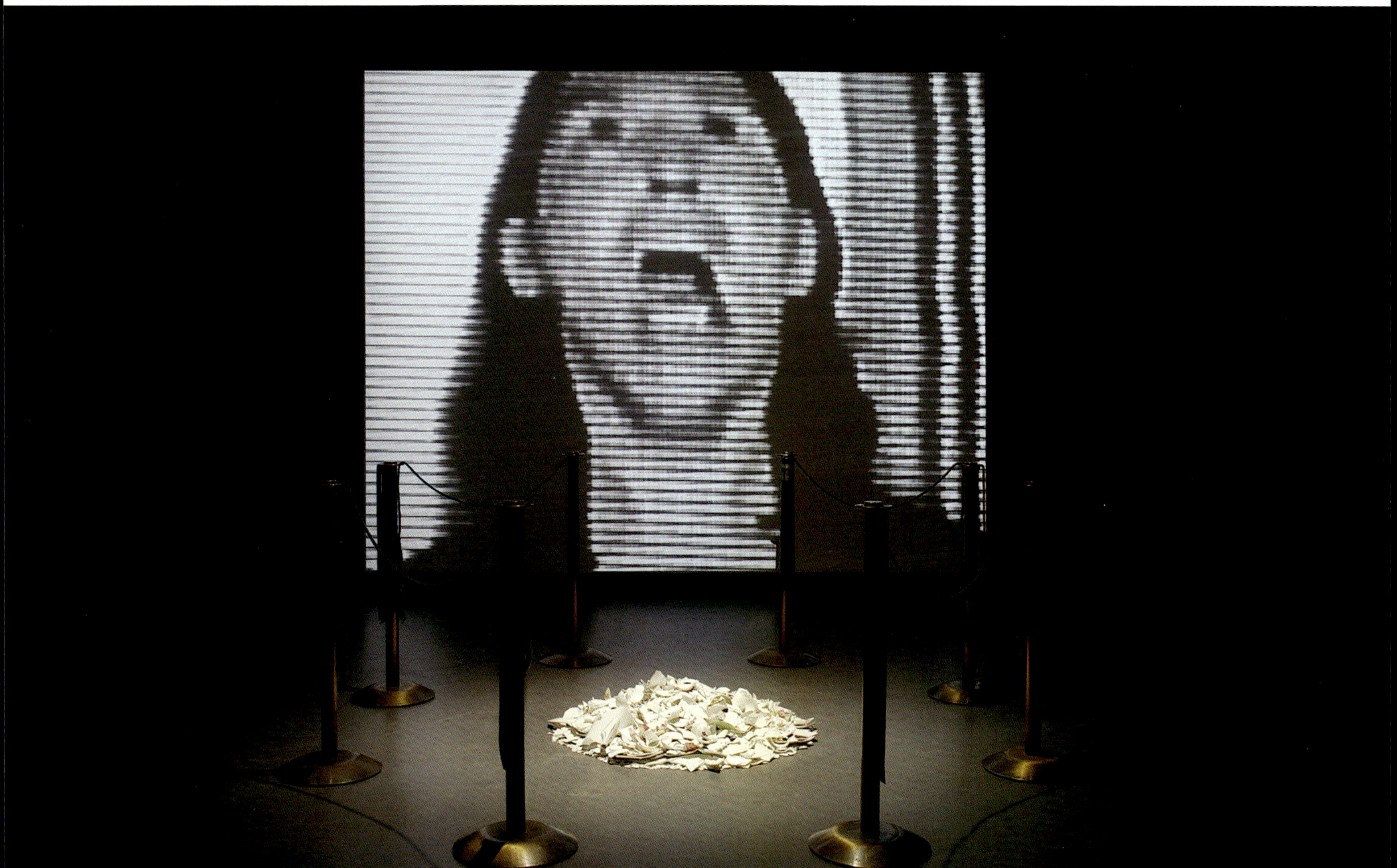

BUFFALO BONE CHINA. A TRIBE PROJECT WITH AKA, SASKATOON, SK. FEBRUARY 14, 1997.

A performance: forty-five minutes of industrial Northwest Coast healing sounds while gently smashing British fine bone china and wrapping these shards into four bundles of purple cloth.

An installation: The four bundles of china pieces are brought into a "sacred" circle on the gallery floor, Claxton makes a prayer, then a ten-minute video begins looping slow motion archival film footage of a buffalo hunt, slow pans across stacks of bone china, a man who screams in (muted) rage. In situ, the thundering buffalo seem life-size as they move onscreen. Several elements in this early performance–video–installation will recur over the next two decades—what she will later call the "Indianizing of space" through ceremonial actions, a measured, rhythmic pacing, the creation of the bundles and the unwrapping of bundles, prayer and ceremony, the thresholds between.

Of this performance, Dana writes:

> "At that time I could not wear my actual moccasins for making what I deemed at that time to be making ART. My moccasins were too cultural, too sacred, and too ceremonial for making art, so I thought at the time. At that time, I was completely unprepared to mix ceremony with making art. So I thought. In retrospect, I was mixing the two."[24]

THE ELSEWHERE. LIVE! BIENNALE, WESTERN FRONT, VANCOUVER, BC. SEPTEMBER 15, 2011.

"For me the elsewhere is going beyond matter into the realm of spirit and I was hoping to take the audience with me, which I am told some did! Also, at the end of the performance I had a "giveaway" and offered the audience to come up and have something from the performance—either stones or shells."[25]

FOLLOW THE RED SINEW. BELKIN ART GALLERY, VANCOUVER, BC. MARCH 4, 2016.

Claxton's performance, *Follow the Red Sinew* (2016), opens *Cutting Copper: Resurgent Indigenous Practice* at the University of British Columbia, the traditional, ancestral and unceded territory of the Musqueam. The event explores Indigenous resurgence and cultural

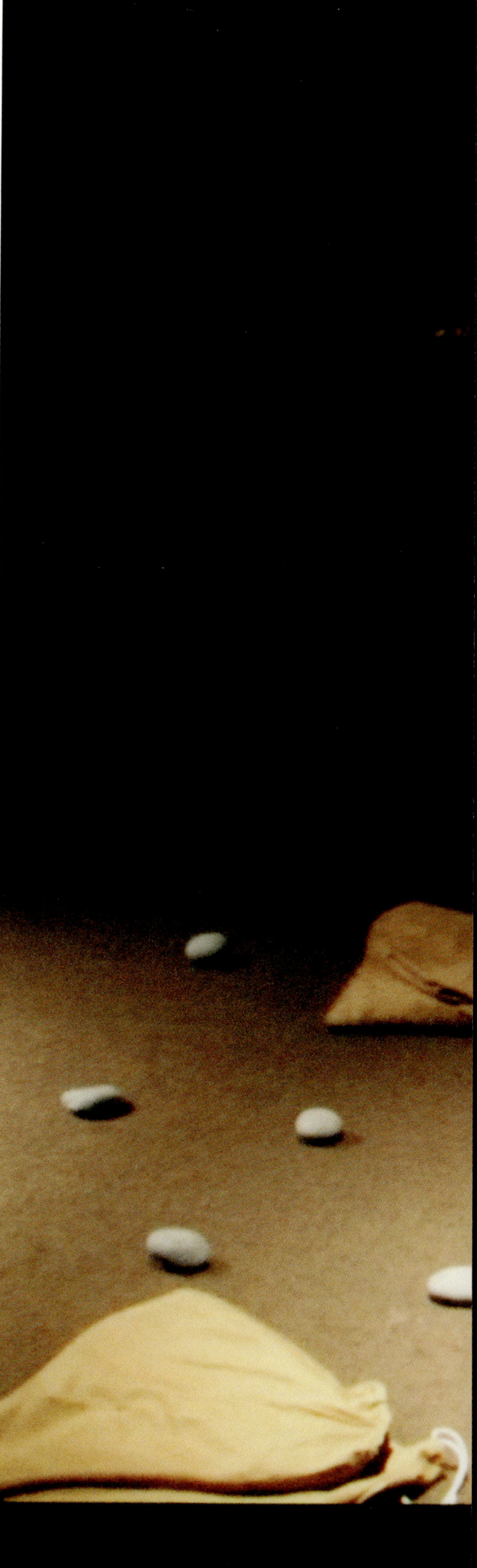

The Elsewhere, 2011 (documentation of performance at Live! Biennale, Western Front, Vancouver)

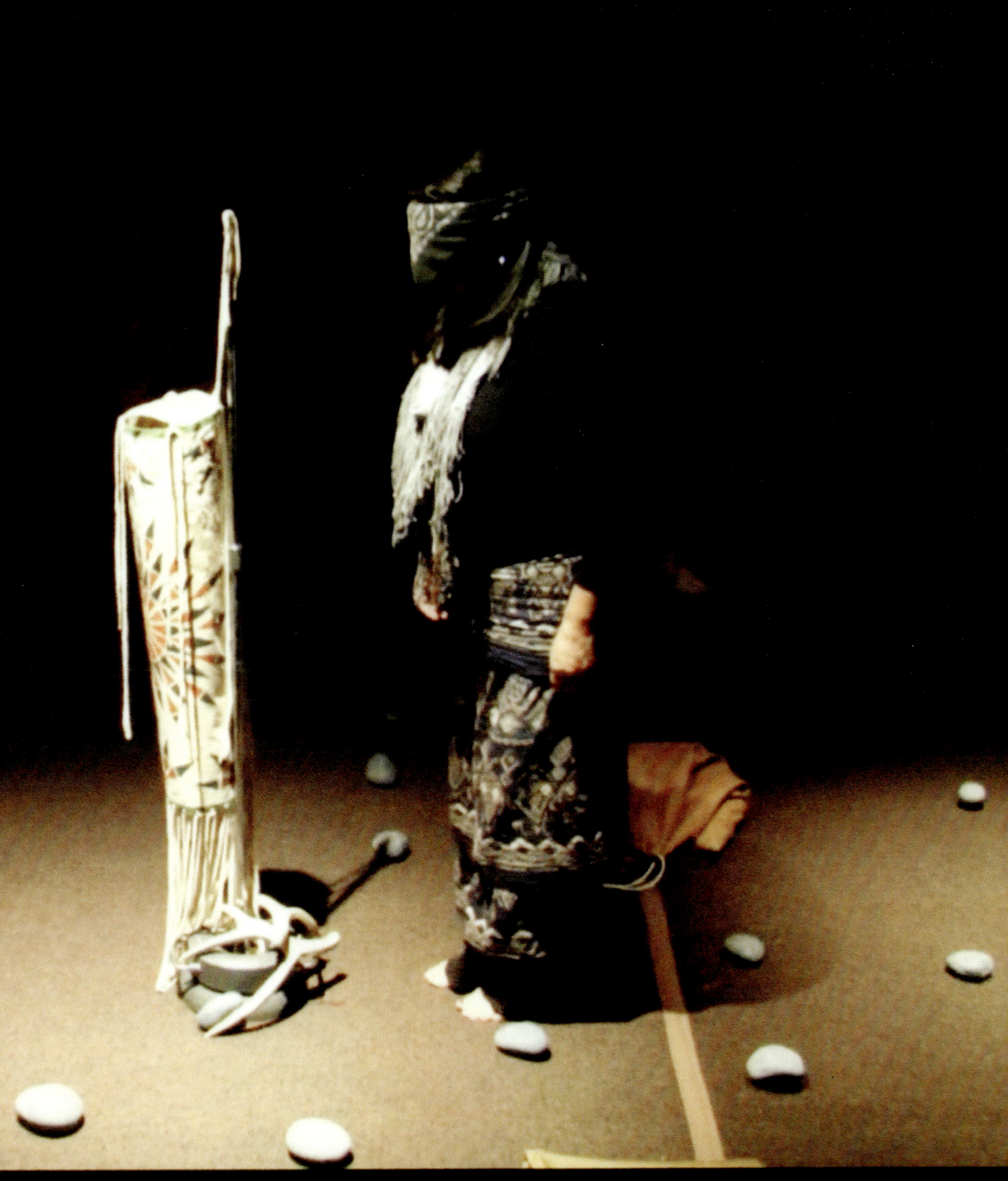

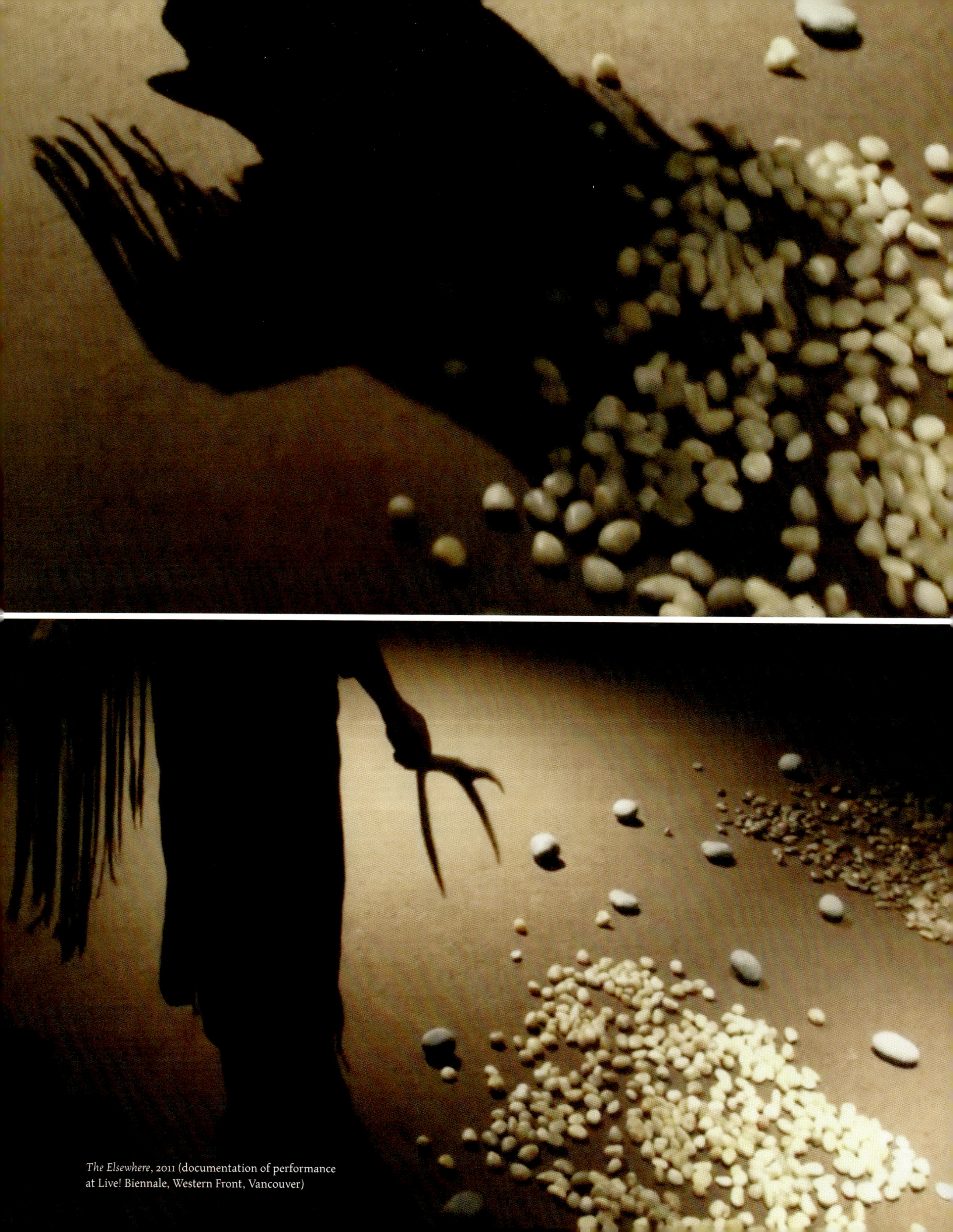

The Elsewhere, 2011 (documentation of performance at Live! Biennale, Western Front, Vancouver)

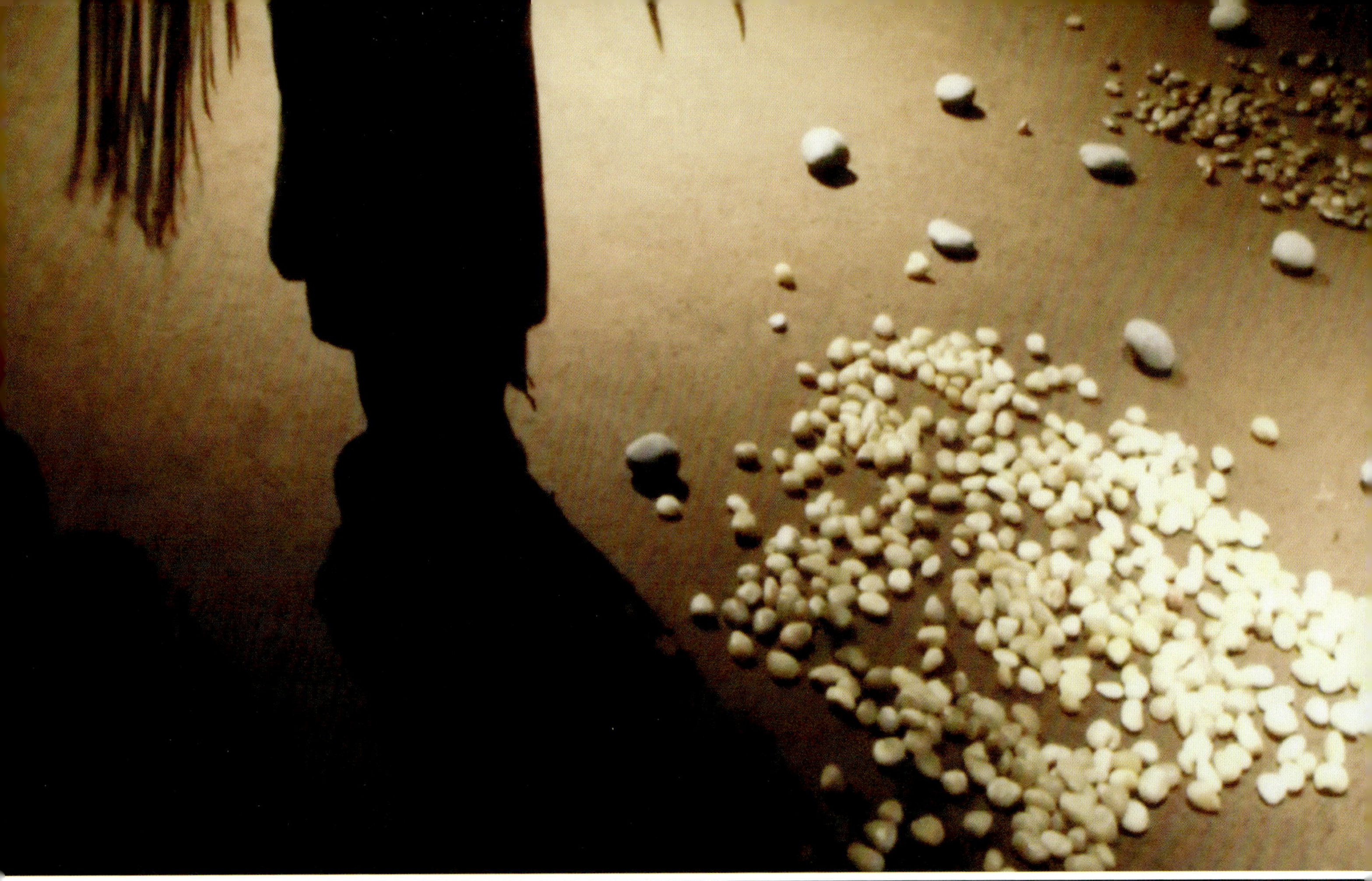

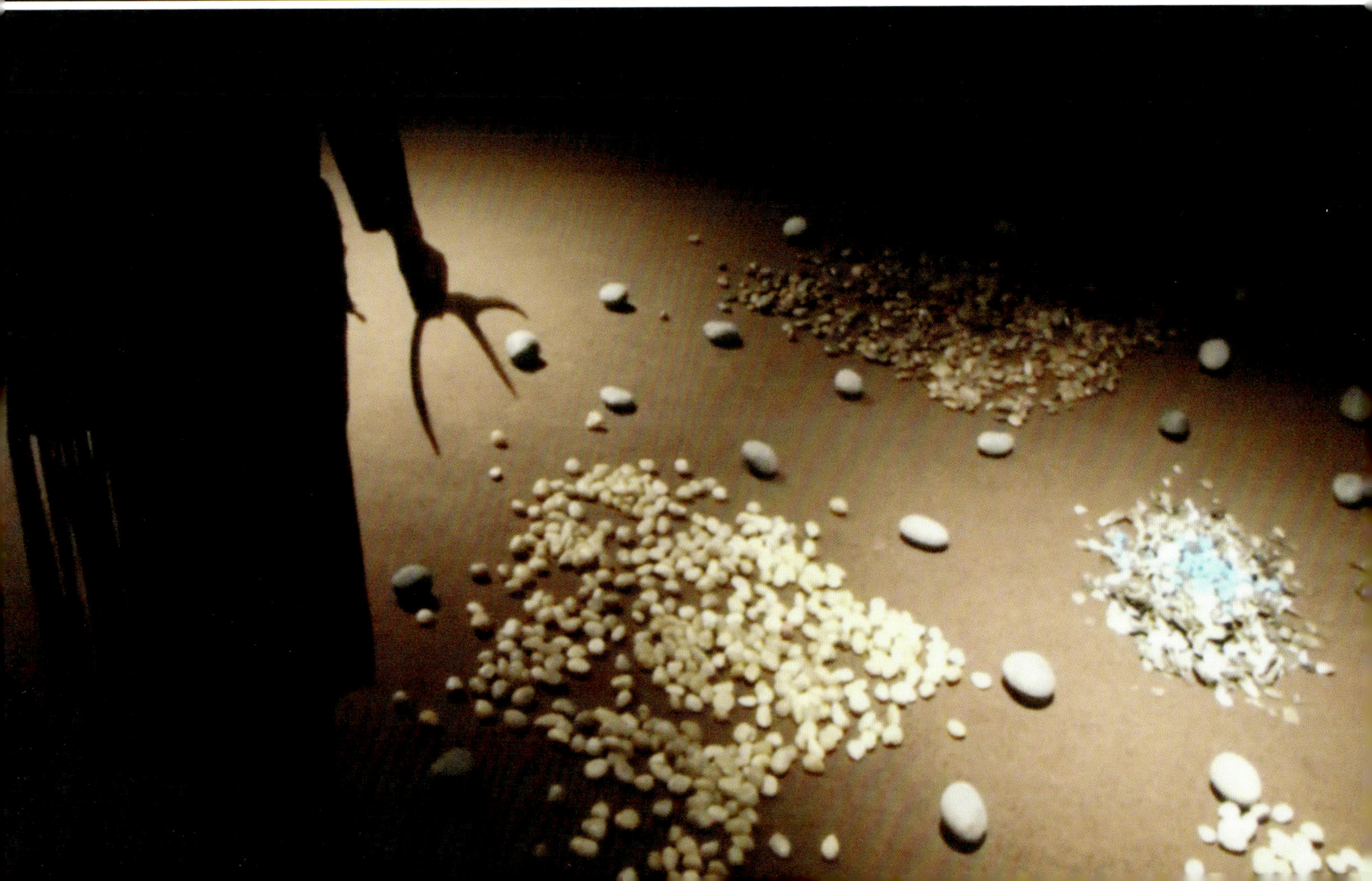

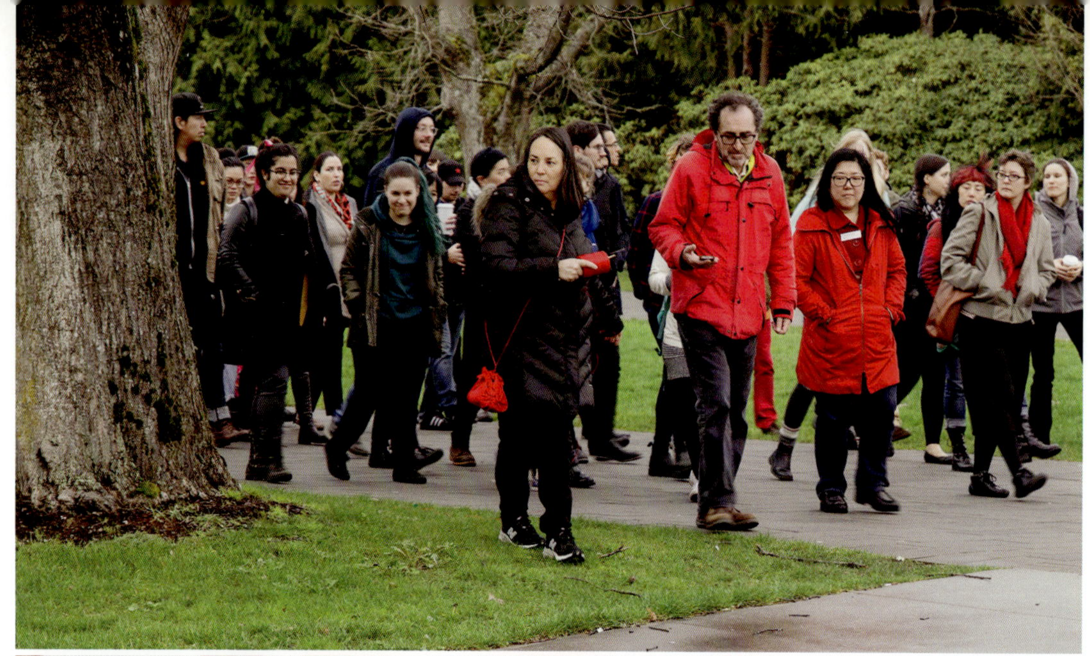

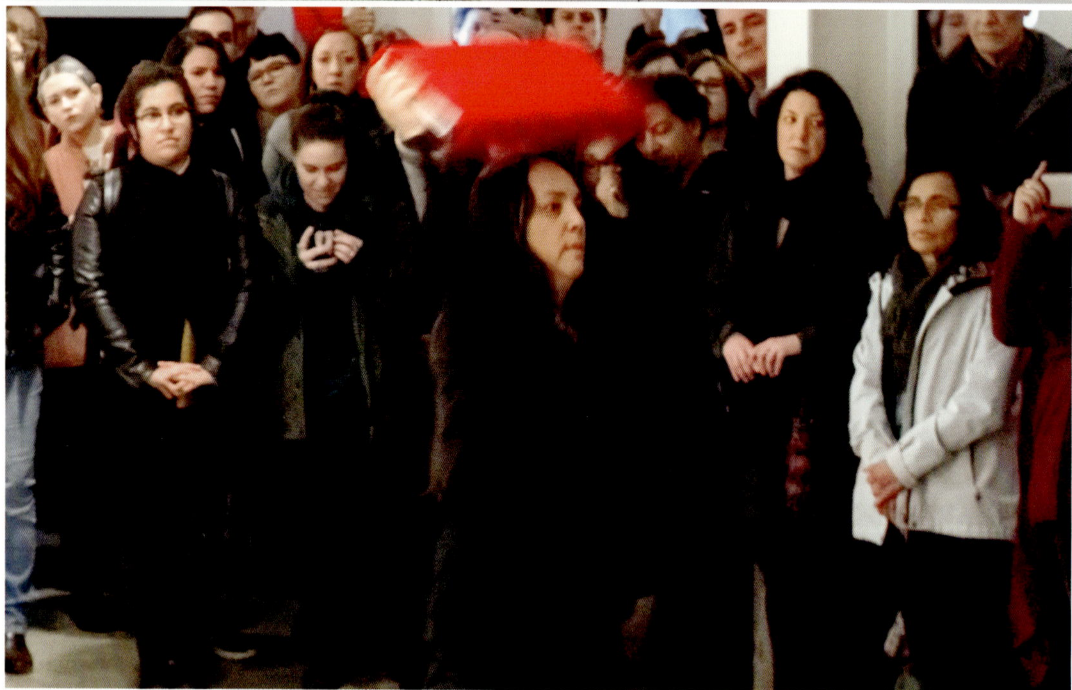

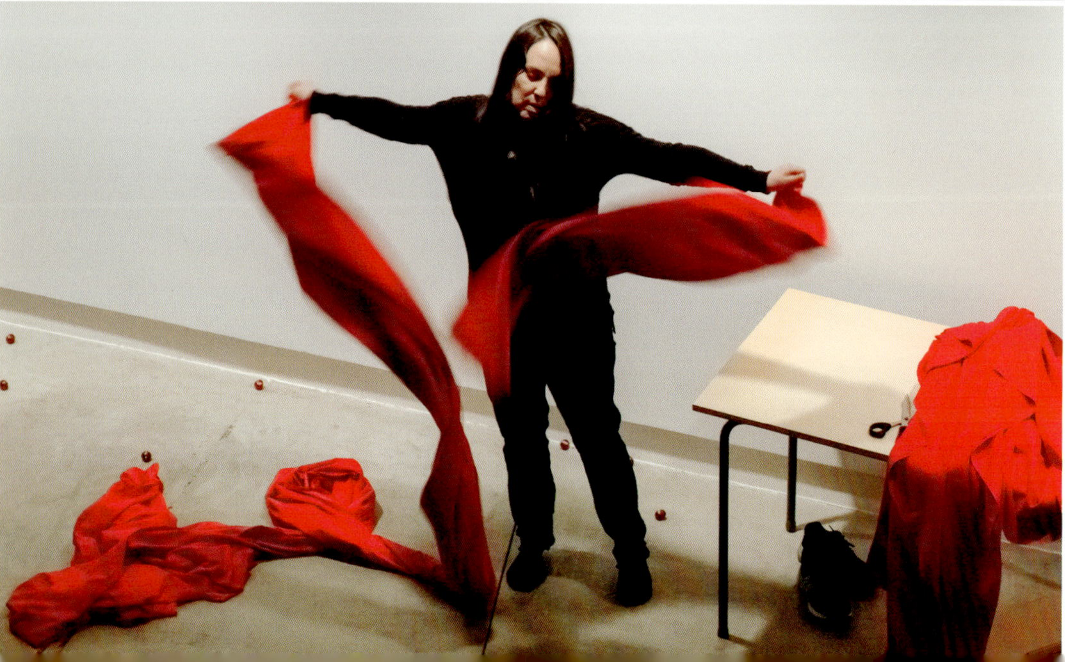

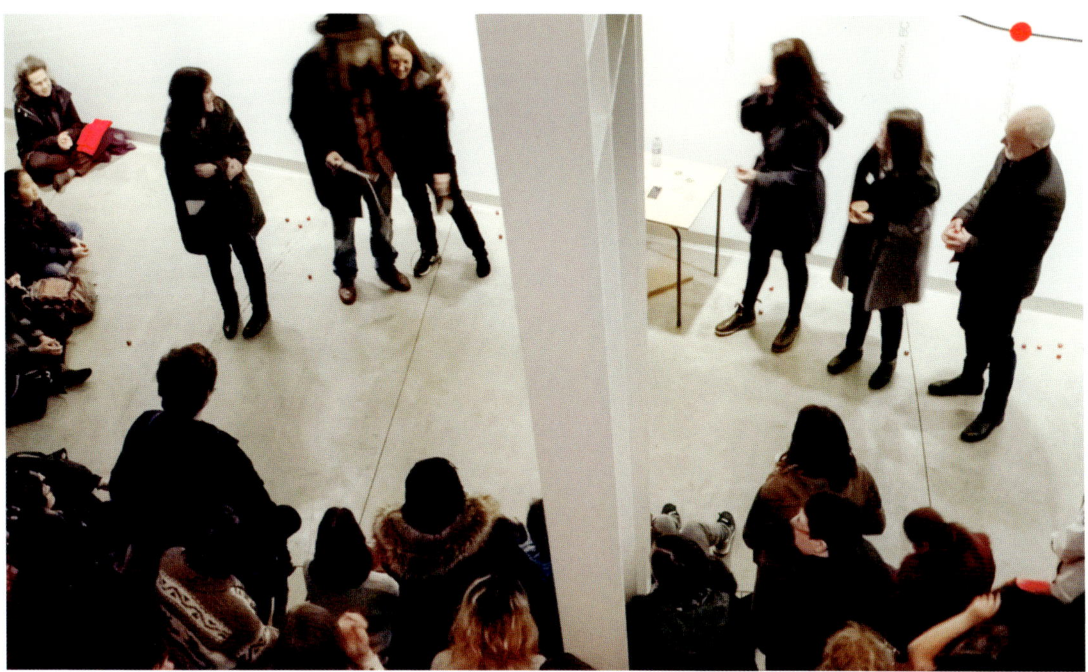

representations, alongside Kwakwaka'wakw artist Chief Beau Dick's exhibition *Lalakenis/All Directions: A Journey of Truth and Unity* (2016).[26] Dick's installation is an assemblage of gifts, artifacts, photos, video and stories gathered along his 2014 journey with twenty-one companions to bring a copper shield known as *Taaw* (a Pacific Northwest symbol of justice that is part of an Indigenous economic system), from UBC to Ottawa: "On July 27, the Taaw copper was broken on Parliament Hill in a traditional copper-breaking ceremony, marking a ruptured relationship in need of repair, and passing the burden of wrongs done to First Nations people from them to the Government of Canada."[27] An earlier journey in 2013 by Geraldine and Linnea Dick, Beau Dick's daughters, brought the Idle No More movement to the British Columbia government. Claxton's performance concludes with a gift-giving.

Follow the Red Sinew begins outside as dozens of participants walk with her as she unravels a spool of red twine along their path. She is flanked by a young girl in big purple rain boots, and Glenn Alteen, a long-time friend and collaborator from grunt gallery who holds a cell phone sending music by Ostwelve, aka Ronnie Harris (Sto:lo/St'át'imc/Nlaka'pamux), to a loudspeaker she is carrying. The motif of a "red thread"—Ariadne's red thread given to Theseus to escape the Minotaur's labyrinth in Greek mythology; the red thread running through Marxist theory which traces genealogies of class struggle; the red thread of Asian legends that connect destined lovers—is Indigenized as *red sinew*, says Claxton, a connector leading participants in Indigenous ways, into the gallery and into the future. She encircles and protects this space of ceremony which assembles cultural belongings and gifts and energies gathered in generosity, hope, love. Inside the gallery, she unwraps a bolt of red fabric, ripping it into sixteen equal segments and folding them, offering them as gifts. *Wopila*—a giving of thanks.[28]

Follow the Red Sinew, 2016 (documentation of performance at the Morris and Helen Belkin Art Gallery, University of British Columbia, Vancouver)

—

In his catalogue essay "Artists of Earth and Sky," Arthur Amiotte (Oglala Lakota) chronicles the forms of trade, violence and dispossession that resulted in the accumulation of non-Native collections of Native objects. But he also writes that *gift-giving*—albeit oftentime a form more closely resembling payment to "school officials, clergy, and doctors"—was one part of "the [beginning] of collections that would find their way into auction houses and museums after several generations of non-Indian owners."[28]

Amiotte describes in great detail the central role that gift-giving—and social events known as *giveaways*—occupied in Plains culture. Early nomadic lifestyles were particularly well-served by such practices. *Saya*: "to ritually paint another person red and to adorn them with precious dress items, household goods, horses, and decorated trappings, and in some case, entire tipis; such gifts exhibited the artistic excellence and industriousness of the female artisans of the giving family."[29] Women—the artisans who transformed "the bounty of the hunt"—were responsible for the preservation of Plains tribal art, and today, they are still charged with "handing gifts to the recipient."[30] The objects they created and gifted were aesthetic *and* utilitarian, works of art that were also embedded in a system of sacred belief.

Women are the keepers and transmitters of *Lakol Wicoh'an*, or, "working, operating, or behaving in ways according to the ideals and beliefs of Lakota Society."[31]

—

After Claxton's performance of *Fringed*, Gillette describes transmission as a deliberate act of love. The transmission of Lakota cultural memory as not only a way of *showing* love, but of *actually loving*—a performative act of generosity and respect. A responsibility and a gift-giving that is also a way to survive.

"Saciya [to paint oneself with pigment] and Lakol Wicoh'an are alive, imparting a clear message: 'we have survived, we are today, well-adorned, in joyous celebration of our heritage as Native Americans.'"[32]

—

Wopila

Of performance and gift-giving, Dana tells us that "the giving of gifts [...] [lets] me be Lakota in my art. The *wopila*—the giving of thanks. They—the audience—are there with me. It's reciprocal really: they give me their attention, I give the performance, and then gifts to acknowledge and honour that the performance has taken place."[33]

ENDNOTES

1 The performance of fringe might also be understood as extending to this writing, whose performativity lies in the sway and (a)liveness of its fragments. In this, it echoes what feminist social scientist and performance studies scholar Della Pollock describes as *performative writing*: evocative (of "worlds of memory, pleasure, sensation, imagination, affect, and in-sight"), metonymic ("a self-consciously partial or incomplete rendering"), nervous ("anxiously [crossing] various stories, theories, texts, intertexts, and spheres of practice"), citational ("[quoting] a world that is always already performative [...] writing as rewriting"); and consequential ("is meant to make a difference"). See: Della Pollock, "Performing Writing," in *The Ends of Performance*, Peggy Phelan and Jill Lane, eds. (New York: New York University Press, 1998), 73–103.

2 Amanda Malcolm,"Dana Claxton to Perform Original Piece, *Fringed*, at the Met," *The Metropolitan Museum of Art*, March 12, 2015, https://www.metmuseum.org/blogs/now-at-the-met/2015/dana-claxton-performs-fringed/.

3 The "made-to-be-ready" is Claxton's Indigenous play on Marcel Duchamp's "readymade" in which ordinary, even dull objects brought into the gallery became imbued as works of art. For Claxton, the made-to-be-ready describes the "life force of Lakota cultural belongings that are to be actively used in domestic work, warfare, social space and ritual." From "Dana Claxton: Made to Be Ready," press release, *SFU Galleries*, Winter 2016 http://www.sfu.ca/galleries/audain-gallery/Upcoming.html/.

4 Dana Claxton, personal email correspondence with the authors, 2018.

5 Thank you to Professor Alexandra T. Vazquez for her generative readings and teachings of Winnicott.

6 Dana Claxton and Tania Willard, "NDN AXE/IONS—a collaborative essay," *INDIANacts: Aboriginal Performance Art*, http://indianacts.gruntarchives.org/essay-ndn-axe-ions-claxton-and-willard.html/. This site is the online continuation of a 2002 conference on Aboriginal performance art, co-curated by Claxton and performance artist Lori Blondeau (Cree/Saulteaux/Métis) with the support of grunt gallery in Vancouver.

7 Edgar Heap of Birds's contribution to the exhibition is *Ma-ka'ta l-na'-zin (One Who Stands on the Earth)*, one of forty aluminum signs from his *Building Minnesota* (1990) series, billboard-like signs placed along Minneapolis's downtown riverfront. The signs recognized by name the forty Dakota men hanged after the 1862 Dakota War, the largest mass execution in American history. The full text read: "Honor / Ma-ka'ta l-na'-zin / (One Who Stands on the Earth) / DEATH / BY / HANGING / DEC. 26, 1862, MANKATO, MN. – EXECUTION ORDER ISSUED BY PRESIDENT OF THE UNITED STATES — ABRAHAM LINCOLN / © HACHIVI EDGAR HEAP OF BIRDS 1990".

8 We are reminded, here, of Brooklyn-based artist Maria Hupfield's (Anishinaabe) work *Jingle Dress* (2002).

9 "Jodi Gillette Steps Down as White House Advisor, Accepts New Role," ***Indian Country Today***, https://indiancountrymedianetwork.com/news/politics/jodi-gillette-steps-down-as-white-house-advisor-accepts-new-role/. During her tenure under the Obama administration, Gillette served as the special assistant to the President for Native American affairs for the White House Domestic Policy Council; deputy assistant secretary to the assistant-secretary, Indian Affairs, at the Department of the Interior; and separately, as the White House associate director of Intergovernmental Affairs.

10 Emil Her Many Horses, "Woman's Dress and Accessories," in *The Plains Indians: Artists of Earth and Sky*, ed. Gaylord Torrence (New York: Skira Rizzoli; Paris: Musée du quai Branly, 2014), 298.

11 Ibid.

12 Christopher Green, "The Plains Indians: Artists of Earth and Sky," *The Brooklyn Rail*, April 2, 2015, https://brooklynrail.org/2015/04/artseen/the-plains-indians-artists-of-earthand-sky/.

13 Holland Cotter, "Review: 'The Plains Indians,' America's Early Artists, at The Met," March 12, 2015, https://www.nytimes.com/2015/03/13/arts/design/review-the-plains-indians-americans-early-artists-at-the-met.html/.

14 Layli Long Soldier, *WHEREAS* (Minneapolis: Graywolf Press, 2017), 8.

15 Fred Moten, ***In the Break: The Aesthetics of the Black Radical Tradition*** (Minneapolis: University of Minnesota Press, 2003), 1; Sarita Echavez See, *The Filipino Primitive: Accumulation and Resistance in the American Museum* (New York: NYU Press, 2017), 3.

16 See: *Stop(the)Gap: International Indigenous art in motion*, John Neylon, ed. (Adelaide: Samstag Museum of Art, University of South Australia, 2011).

17 *Rattle* was originally presented in the travelling group exhibition, *Language of Intercession: Native Media and New Media Artists*, curated by Steven Loft in 2003. See http://dazibao-photo.org/en/past/language-of-intercession-native-media-and-new-media-artists-en

18 Green, "The Plains Indians: Artists of the Earth and Sky."

19 Artist and curator Tania Willard (Secwepemc) says of *Rattle:* "[it] plays with the idea of taking beadwork, which is often seen in a craft context, and blowing it up to this large installation. [Claxton has] talked about wanting to bring this beautiful form and aesthetic into the gallery in a way that contemporary art gallery audiences can perhaps more easily recognize." See Leah Sandals, "Q&A: Tania Willard on Life Beyond Beat Nation," ***Canadian Art***, June 28, 2013, https://canadianart.ca/features/tania-willard-beat-nation/.

20 Dana Claxton, personal email correspondence with the authors, 2018.

21 "Dana Claxton: Made to Be Ready," *SFU Galleries*.

22 Dana Claxton, "Going to the Centre: Performance Works and Other Thoughts," *Canadian Theatre Review* 146 (Spring 2011), https://muse.jhu.edu/article/430911/.

23 Beatrice Medicine, "Mapping the Movement," panel discussion with Aiyanna Maracle, Guy Sioui Durand, James Luna, and Warren Arcan, at INDIANacts: Aboriginal Performance Art conference, grunt gallery, Vancouver (November 29, 2010), transcribed by Warren Arcan, CD 2B, track 8 (00:09). See the video excerpt from Dr. Medicine's commentary on the website: http://indianacts.gruntarchives.org/video-day-1-panel-1-continued.html.

24 Ibid. See also Janice Hladki and Carla Taunton's in-depth discussions of *Buffalo Bone China*: Janice Hladki, "arrives asking, demanding something of us," in *Fierce: Women's Hot Blooded Film/Video*, ed. Janice Hladki (Hamilton: McMaster Museum of Art, 2010); Carla Taunton, "Indigenous (Re)memory and Resistance: Video Works by Dana Claxton," in *Native Americans on Film: Conversations, Teaching, and Theory*, ed. M.E. Marubbio and E.L. Buffalohead (Lexington: University Press of Kentucky, 2013).

25 Dana Claxton, quoted in Elizabeth Neal, "Dana Claxton – Hunkpapa Lakota Sioux," *Contemporary North American Indigenous Artists*, December 19, 2012, http://contemporarynativeartists.tumblr.com/post/39159194194/dana-claxton-hunkpapa-lakota-sioux.

26 See *Cutting Copper* co-organizer Tarah Hogue's description (with Shelly Rosenblum) at http://tarah-hogue.squarespace.com/#/cutting-copper-indigenous-resurgent-practice/.

27 Scott Watson and Lorna Brown, *Lalakenis/All Directions: A Journey of Truth and Unity* (Vancouver: Morris and Helen Belkin Art Gallery, 2016). Gallery guide.

28 Arthur Amiotte, "Artists of Earth and Sky," in ***The Plains Indians: Artists of Earth and Sky***, ed. Gaylord Torrence, 35–48 (New York/Paris: Skira Rizzoli/Musee du quai Branly, 2015), 41.

29 Amiotte, 37.

30 Amiotte, 39.

31 Amiotte, 36.

32 Amiotte, 45.

33 Claxton, personal email correspondence with the authors, 2018.

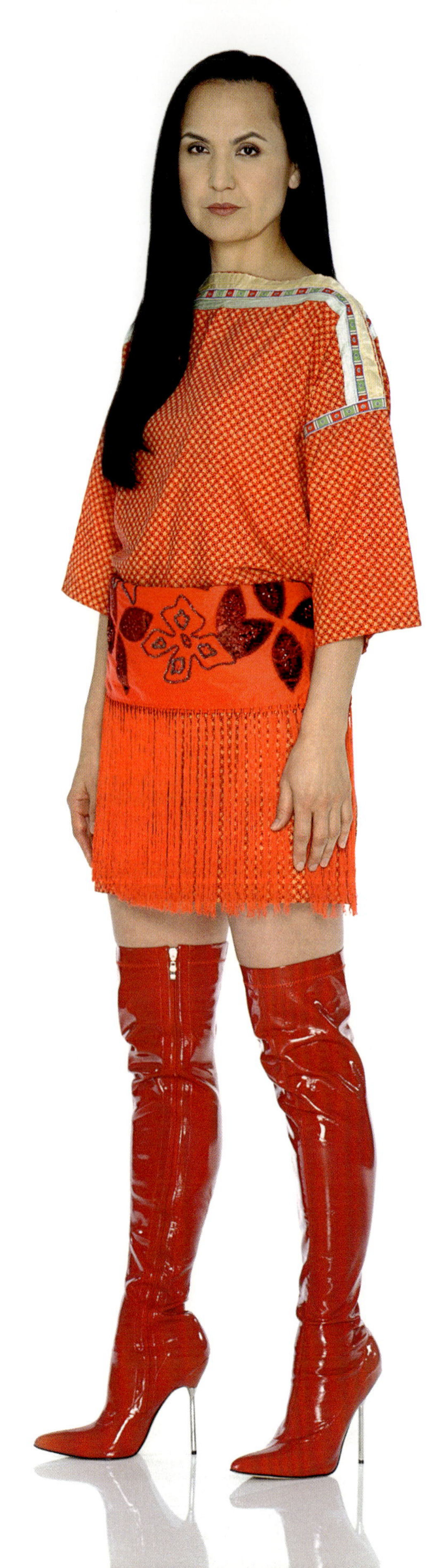

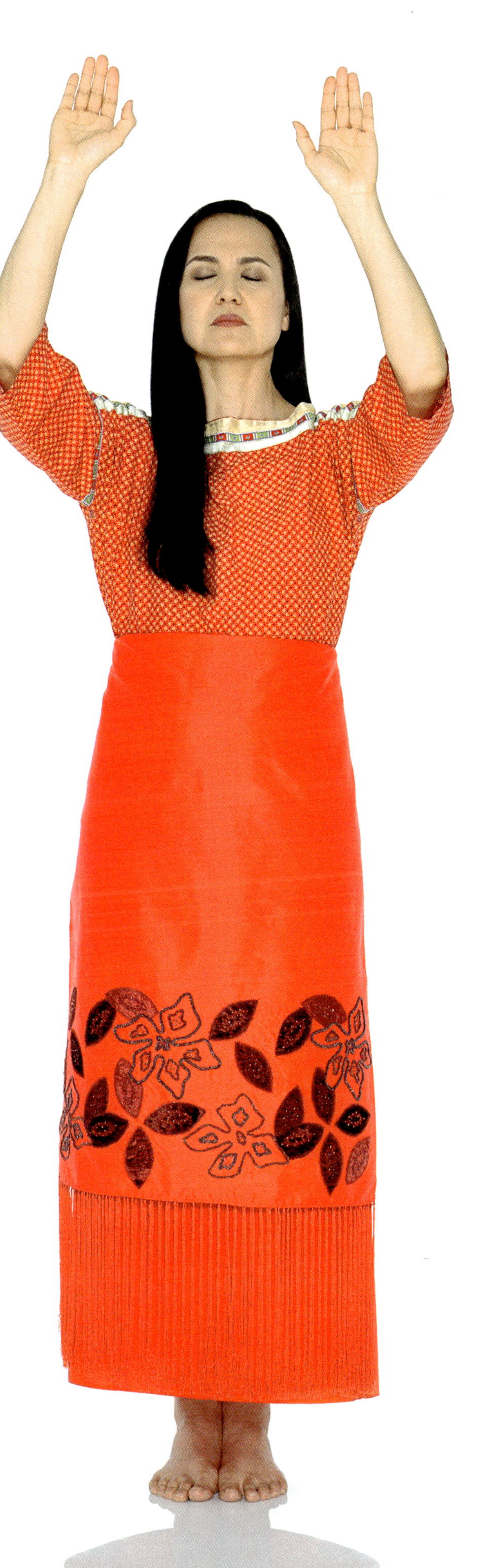

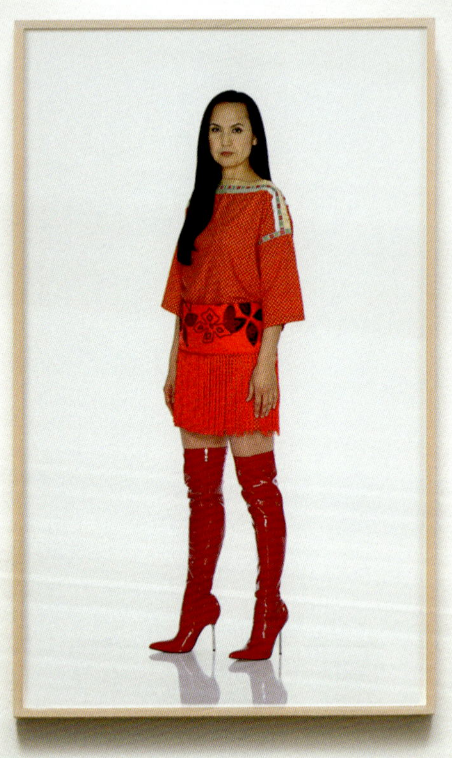

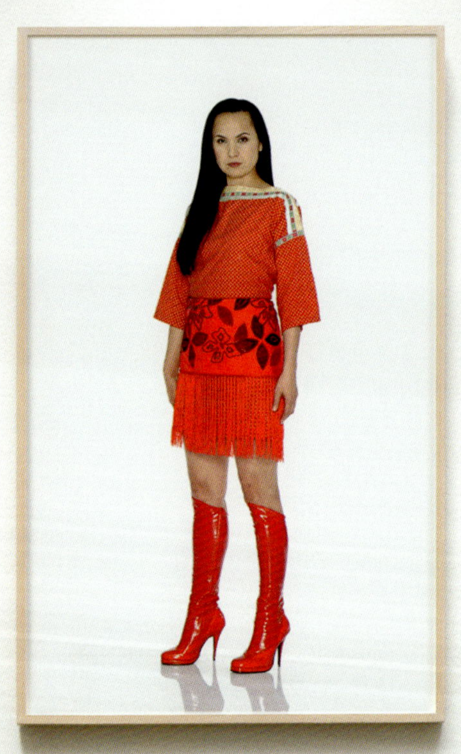

PREVIOUS: *Onto the Red Road*, 2016 (details)
ABOVE: *Onto the Red Road*, 2016 (installation view)

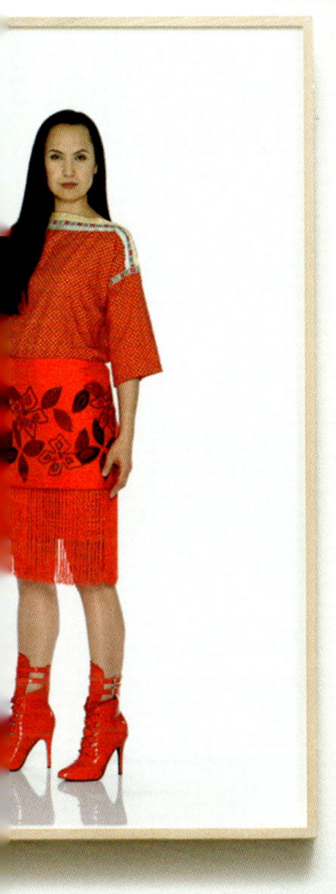
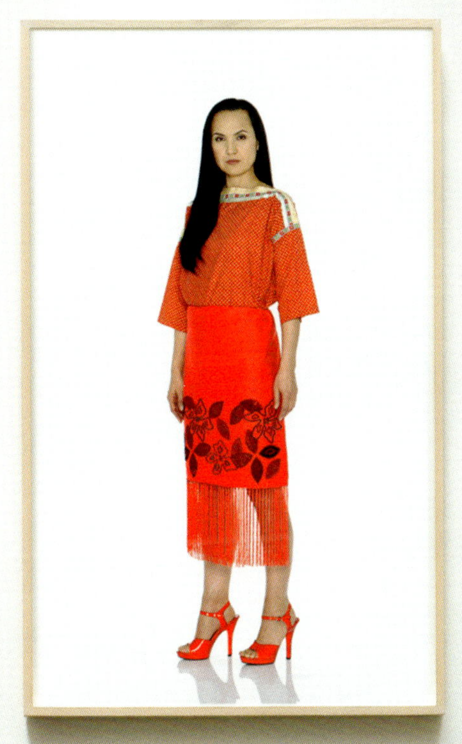
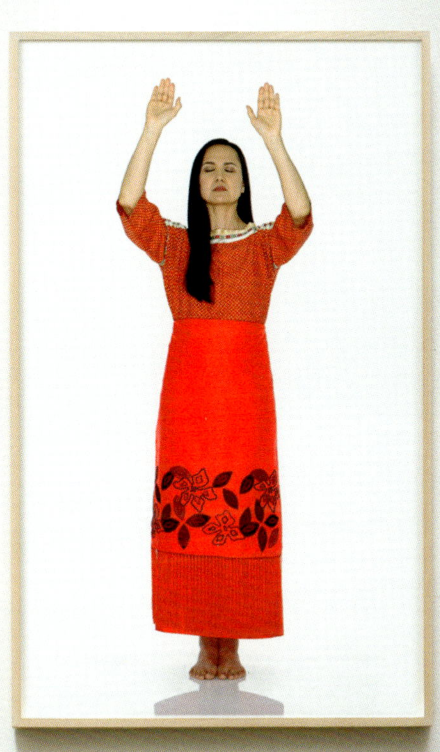

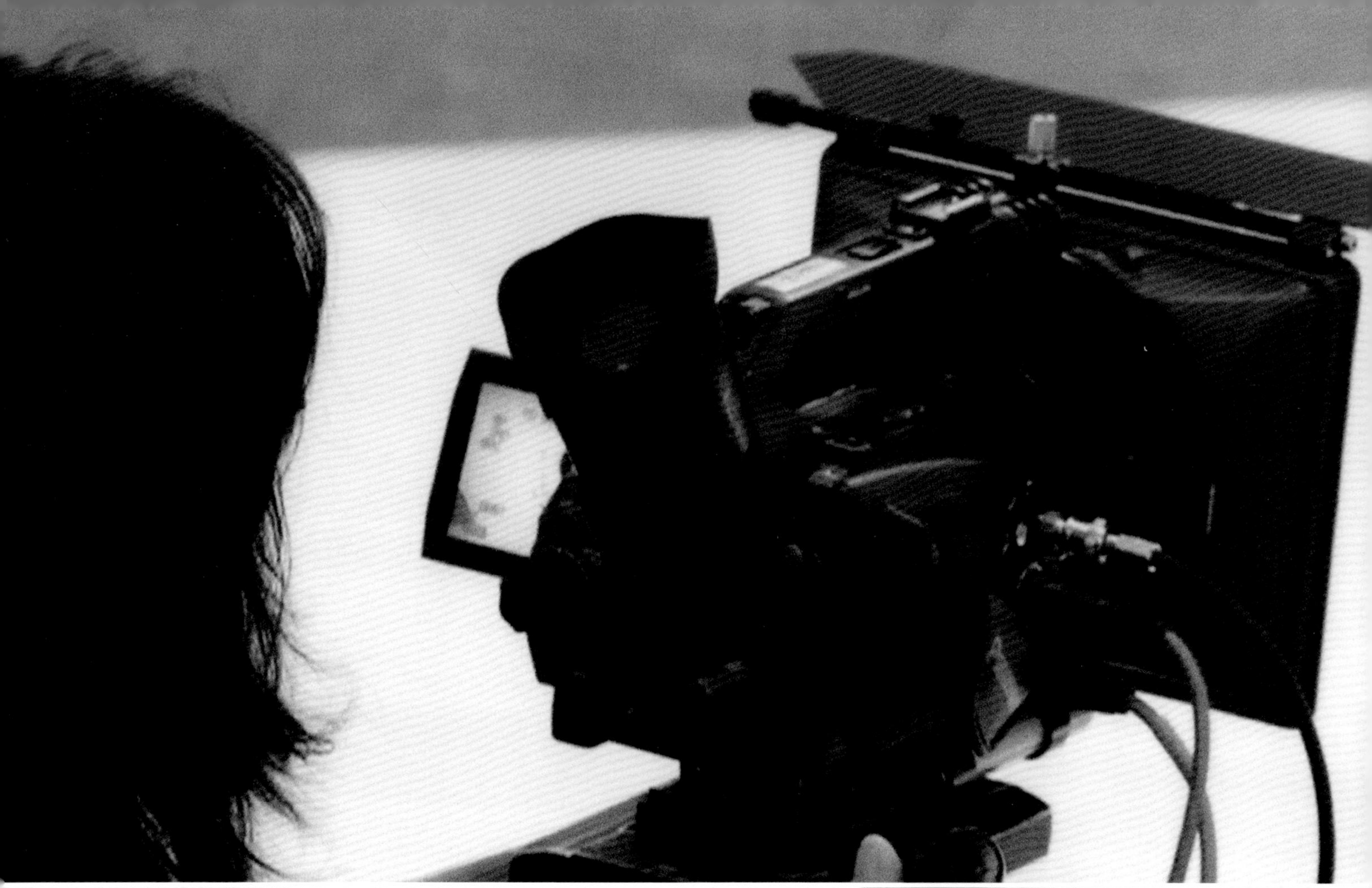

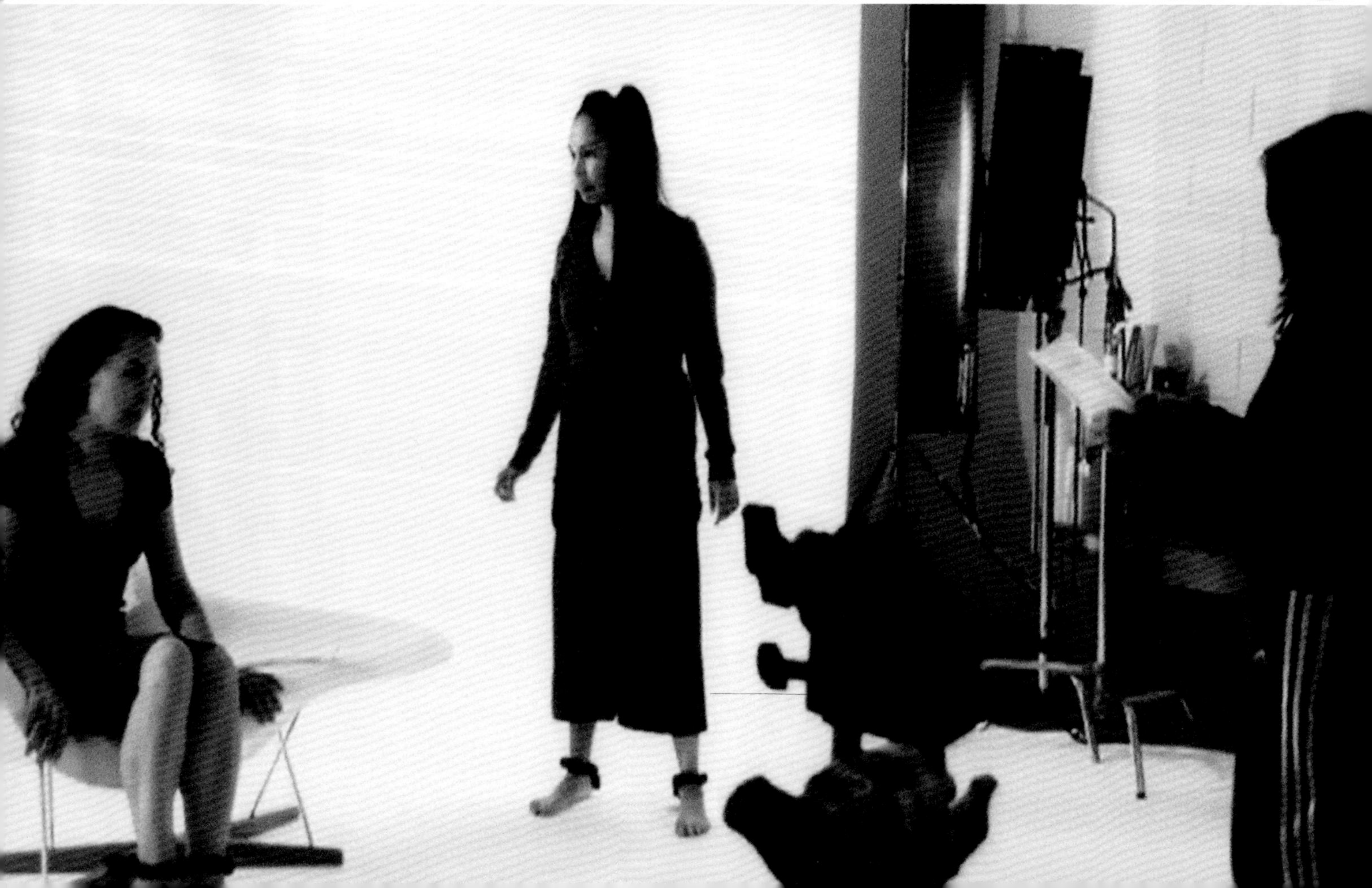

DANA CLAXTON'S PATIENT STORM

DAVID GARNEAU

Indigenous presence in the popular media is usually a cue to stories of crime, abuse, poverty, loss, fluff and feathers pride, or government sponsored success. And Aboriginal self-representations, when they don't mirror mainstream narratives, are often self-reflexive tortured recitations on: "what does it mean to be Native in contemporary times?" and "how will we ever get over the damage?" Meta-discourse is instructive but not very inspiring. So, I took a small pleasure in seeing two beautiful, confident Aboriginal women talking with each other in Dana Claxton's 2006 online video, *The Patient Storm*.[1]

While mainstream representations of Aboriginal people grow with our population, Aboriginal knowledge has not received proportional air time. There is talk in these circles about Aboriginal knowledge—a lot of preteritive gesturing toward and around—but the general public is rarely served more than a glimpse of the content. Resistance to engage may be because this knowledge is not just information; this knowledge is embedded in committed practices and requires more than reading and thinking. Engagement may also be difficult because the traditional Aboriginal world view contradicts the currently dominant one. It is metaphysical, deeply ecological and communitarian.

Elders at pipe ceremonies have told us many times that aboriginally generated knowledge is not just for First Nations people, but should be shared with everyone. Real knowledge transcends the particular, the nation, even history. However, because Aboriginal ways of knowing are experiential, bound up with communities and rituals, only those willing to repeatedly pass the social and conceptual barriers between peoples have access. Art works can serve as this threshold. They can be non-threatening portals between world views.

The initial gentle pleasure I have with Dana Claxton's *The Patient Storm* comes simply from seeing Aboriginal people not ruminating on colonialism or contemporary aboriginality. They just get on with Being (post-colonial, contemporary Aboriginals). This is not as easy as it sounds. We are colonized by an imaginary that has us read Aboriginal bodies into specific landscapes and stories.[2] However, the work of decolonization need not only be about deconstructing power and reminding us who we were, it is about performing who we are. Perhaps we are ready to trade tropes and exchange irony for allegory.

Dana Claxton's *The Patient Storm* is an allegory of the competing impulses in human beings and societies: conservancy and change. Through the figures of Storm and Lightning, Claxton's legend suggests a system—inspired by Lakota teachings and practices (the Sundance)[3]—in which these seeming opposites become complementary. Tradition, on one side, and the desire for action and novelty, on the other, are usually represented as binaries and often as a generational divide. *The Patient Storm* mimics this convention, only to melt the distinctions and show that traditional ways and modern society are not incompatible.

Such lofty ambitions require an elevated site and grand characters. In order to show her women as themselves and not as colonial subjects, and to have us see the knowledge they figure as exceeding specific

The Patient Storm on set, stills from *Storytellers in Motions, Hunkpapa Woman: Dana Claxton*, produced by Urban Rez productions, directed by Jeff Bear, 2006

cultures, Claxton sets them in a space apart. They are demi-goddesses suspended above the world, beyond stereotype and historicity in a timeless continuity. However, they are not detached. Storm and Lightning only achieve their full being when they descend and meet the land and join its people in the Sundance.

The scene couldn't be simpler. The set consists only of a white La Chaise chair.[4] The background is a changing projection of clouds: in post production, Claxton keyed in images of clouds from mid-day to sunset, from accumulation to forming storm. In the middle are images of stars and celestial spirals. The characters are two women who personify natural forces. Claxton describes the older woman, Storm, as "an elegant, knowledgeable patient woman;"[5] and Lightning as "a trickster type, crazysexycool girlish woman." Their brown outfits suggest a timeless, earthy style; but the cuts reflect different generations and temperaments: Storm wears a smart, knee-length business dress; Lightning is dressed in more casual culottes, a T-shirt and hoodie. What links them, besides the brown cloth, are wrist and ankle bands, which Claxton explains, "are worn by Sundancers, along with a crown around the head. They are [traditionally] made from sacred red cloth and sage." The costumes signal the traditional and enduring alongside the contemporary and fashionable. They are different, but not opposites. This theme is echoed in the sound-track, which features a gently throbbing synthesized music accompanied by what sounds like a traditional rattle.

The plot is just as lean. Storm and Lightning prepare to descend to the earth but are held up by late members of their party. The scene opens with Storm (Samaya Jardey), a woman in her late thirties reclining on a large, cloud-like chair. Her head is tilted back; her long dark hair drapes down. The camera jumps back to a mid-shot revealing Lightning (Marie Prince),[6] who is in her early twenties. They talk. Storm mostly stays seated; Lightning twirls an orbit around her. After seven minutes and forty eight seconds, it's over. Not much happens, but a whole cosmos emerges.

While we only see Storm and Lightning, at least five other individuals or groups are mentioned. Storm oscillates between lounging languor and straight-spine alertness. She moves slowly and gracefully with fluid and confident gestures. She is stable, dignified, calm. Lightening describes her as sometimes "blue" and complains that she is slow to get going, but acknowledges that once in motion, "the whirl, the twirl brings life to you."

Lightening is energetic. She sits only once. While her initial movements are relaxed, as the scene progresses she becomes more animated, almost dancing. She describes herself as "a grrrrrrl," and as "Exquisite Lady L, keeper of bolt—the rolling zig, zig, zag." Her rhythmic speech is often poetic and strange. Storm finds her impatient and her hip hopish language hard to follow. Storm often makes faces and ignores Lightning when she is particularly obscure.

"Rattling Wings," "the Lightning People" and "the prince" are the only other beings given proper names. Lightning is one of the Lightning People, though, as "keeper of the bolt," she may have an elevated status. Because Storm is waiting for "the others," and regularly restrains and corrects Lightning, we can infer that she is in charge, perhaps even personifies the whole system. "The prince, the tide," is more of an allusion than a character, and even then, he is a confused reference. When Lightning mentions him, Storm is puzzled, suggesting that either she doesn't know him, or doesn't understand the whole sentence.

Lightning's energy is sensual. Her speech is full of rhythm and rhyme: "Stormy Storm, let's twirl the swirl and swirl the twirl, zig the zag and zag the zig." Her words flow and jump as her body glides in near dance. She often seems silly, but just as often wise. Her reference to the prince might be a silly moment. Storm seems to treat it that way. But Storm is clearly repressive and side-steps Lightning's

The Patient Storm on set, stills from *Storytellers in Motions, Hunkpapa Woman: Dana Claxton*, produced by Urban Rez productions, directed by Jeff Bear, 2006

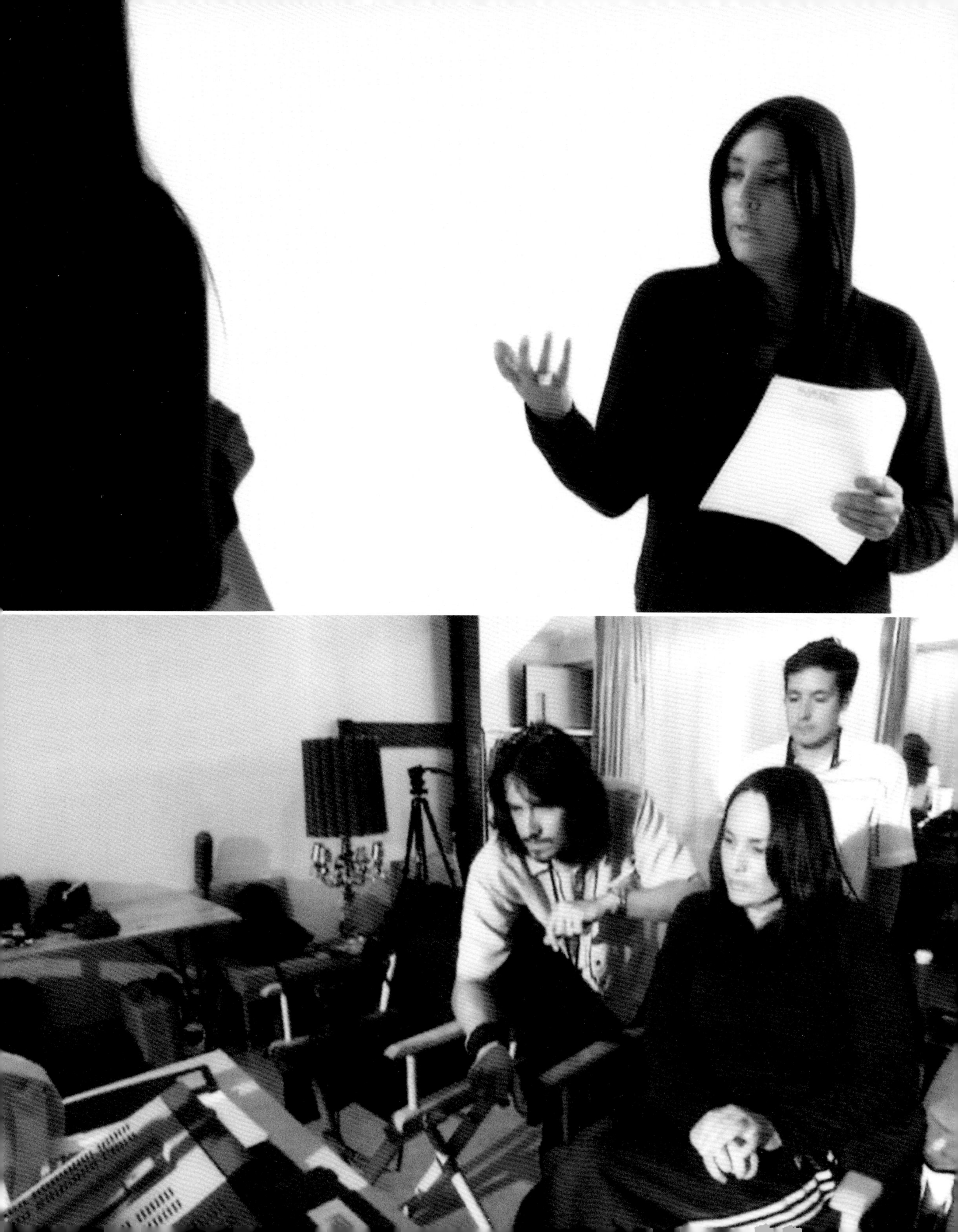

The Patient Storm

many sexual innuendos. "Follow the fellow, the prince—the tide. Become wet, become untied." The building rhythm and force of the tide (here figured as masculine), wetness, and the play on tide and untied seems an obvious string of sexual metaphors. But Storm isn't biting. The building energy, the anticipation, frustration, and concluding off-screen release is the elemental force that drives the story's action.

Lightning speculates that "everyone else," or "the others," meaning Rattling Wings and the Lightning People, may be late because they are "caught up in the valley, the valley of lovvvvvvvvvvvvve." Some sort of polymorphous sexuality seems to be roiling in this snug metaphor: "he and me, or him and you, her and he, or she and she, or him and he, or they and they, which ever way..." Storm looks disturbed and changes the subject. Is she puzzled that these possibilities exist, or that the Lightning knows about them? Whatever the case, she has other things on her mind and wants other things on Lightning's mind. At the moment, the Lightning People are running hot while Storm blows cool.

The Patient Storm is not the retelling of a traditional story; it is a creative, contemporary allegory. Apart from the weather, what do these figures represent? Storm is a slow-moving but dynamic force; not an individual storm but the force behind individual phenomena. Similarly, Lightning is not an instance of lightning, she is "keeper of the bolts," an inexhaustible archetypal energy behind every specific occurrence of lightning. Storm has two aspects: Storm, the storm potential, the burgeoning energy that she tries to conserve, knowing full well that it must eventually erupt; and Stormy, her complementary, violent and generative aspect. We only see Storm in the video. Stormy only manifests when Storm leaves the scene at the end of the video. She explains that Stormy is her "fundamental nature," and that she is impelled by energies beyond herself to reveal her irrepressible force: "I have an obligation to appear and present my...my fundamental nature. Everybody must." This is not an embarrassment, but an acknowledgement of the fundamental rhythm of the universe.

The Patient Storm, 2006 (video stills)

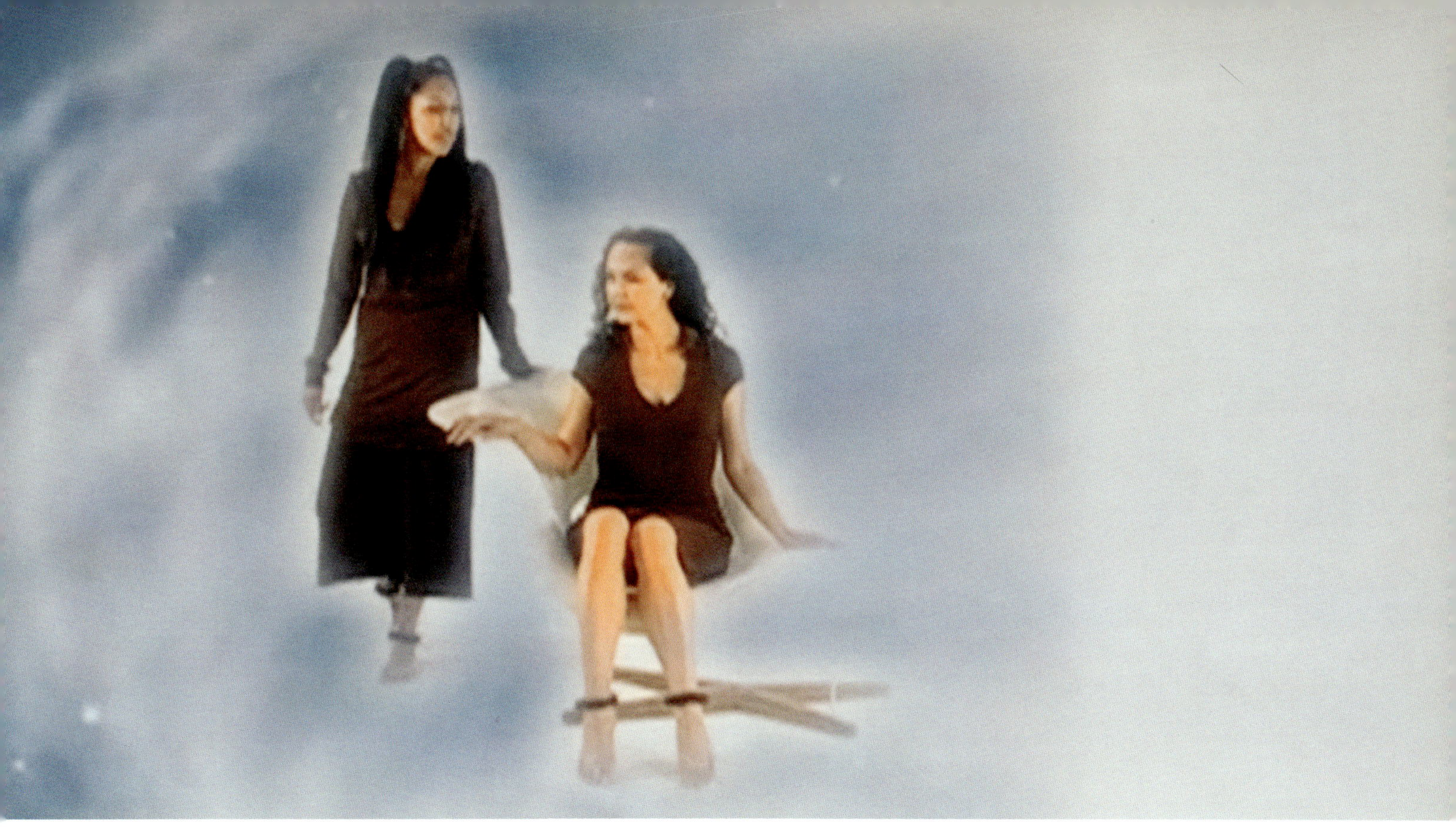

Storm is driven by several forces. As Storm, she is conservative, a leader and regulator, keeper of protocol. She follows the rules and obligations that precede her. These "civil" principles are complemented by an equal force, the Stormy aspect, characterized by whirling and twirling, by dance and pleasure. They conceivably have the same energy—but the static state requires less of it so endures longer; the active state dispels its energy more quickly and subsides sooner. When Lightning describes their transformed character once they present their other aspect, she uses the word "turbulence," which Storm violently rejects in her only burst of anger: "Turbulence! Is that what you call us? No darling, not turbulence...we are the glamorous clamour overhead." The storm/dance is not a disruption, but a beautiful and joyous aspect of a continuum.

Storm is calm and patient before the dance. She is conservative—literally, holding back, cautious, waiting for the right moment. However, when that moment comes, she lets loose, literally loses herself, becomes Stormy. Storm is the figure of tradition. Traditional peoples have a conservative aspect, the teachings and rituals that hold them together. At the same time, traditional societies also set aside a time and place for ecstasy, for rituals, dances, visions, fasts and feasts that attract and release spiritual and physical energy.

Lightning is an apprentice to this duality. While she is drawn to impulsive youthful action, she allows herself to be checked by the older being. She is positioned between the revellers in the valley—a group and activities she seems to know all about and may even have just come from—and the more adult Storm. She signals her willingness to pass from youth to adulthood by being the first of her group to take her place alongside Storm. Symbolically, she even slips into Storm's chair/throne for a moment, as if to try it out. As the elder, Storm is often irritated with Lightning's impatience and imperfect understanding, but does appreciate her timely arrival and playful, revitalizing energy.

Against her foil, Lightning, Storm is less energetic and more of a grown up. And yet, in her shifting from proper sitting posture to draping herself over the chair, she displays sensual possibilities. Her

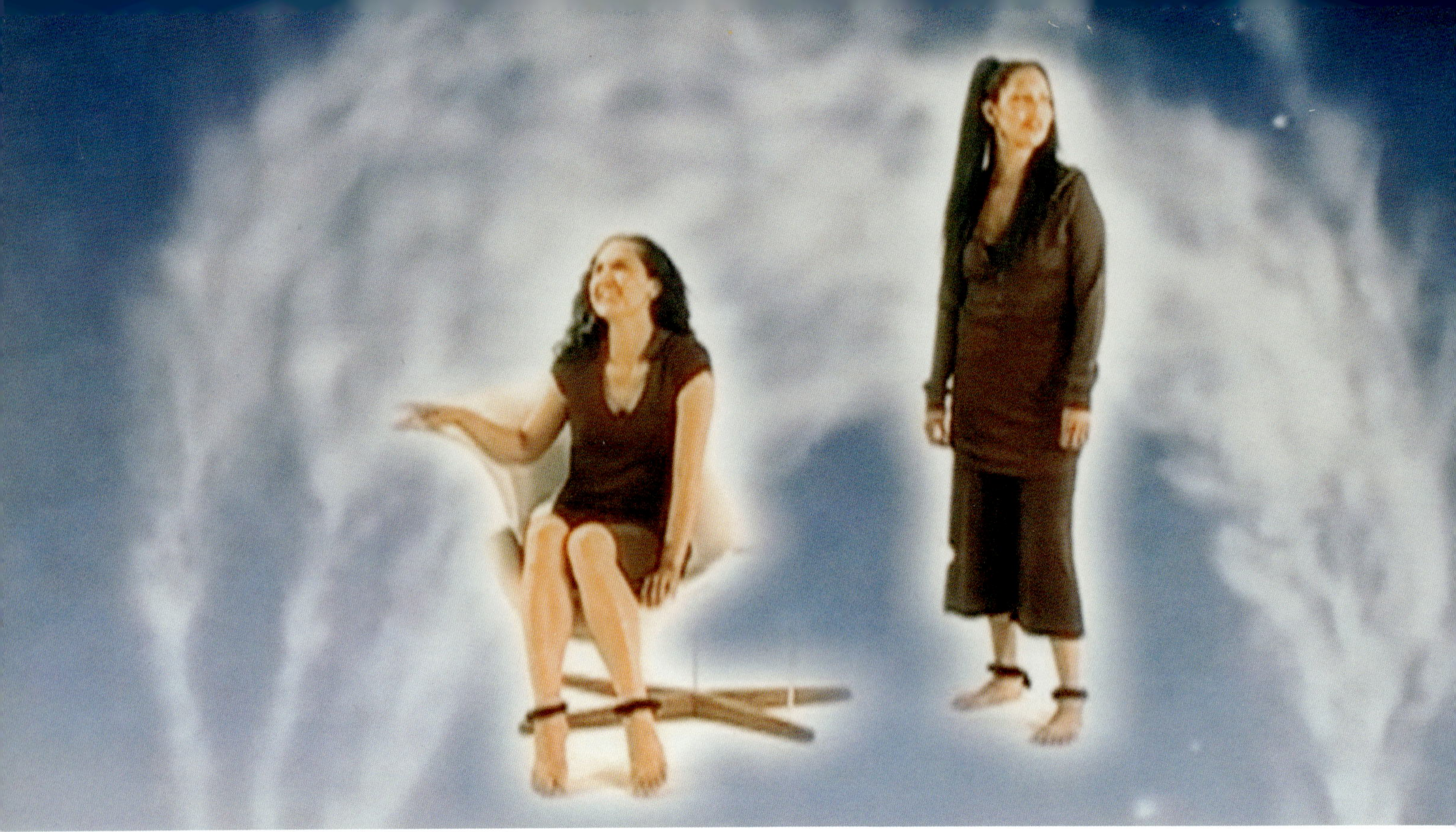

movements hint that she loves to dance, but that there is a proper time for everything. Lightning's body is less regulated. She tries to contain her energy, but it is constantly spilling into dance. She tries to control her language, but it is continuously falling into poetry.

The last figures are "the people," the humans upon which the storm will be visited. In her first speech, Storm says: "If we don't appear—something is wrong. The Cosmos gone crazy—the people will say." She is not a free agent; she is regulated by the force of tradition and unconscious necessity of her nature. The Cosmos is both how things are but also what things mean. Without these recurring events, both natural and social (the storm and the dance) "something is wrong."

The most ambiguous term in the video is "the others." Sometimes it means the late (possibly) orgiastic Lightning and Wind folks; other times it means "the people." The "others," in the sense of "the people," is subdivided into two groups: those mortals who participate in the dance/storm and those who resist. Also, according to Claxton, "the others" are "those who don't believe and those who are anti-Indian in general." But "the others have been opposed to us for so long" also include "those Indians who are so Christianized that they fear their own traditional spiritual practices." Lightning explains: "sacred little scaredy cats. Their knowledge did not fare well to wisdom just. Imagine that. Their opposite stance makes them tall ...even for little little scared fur balls. BUT. ah!!!—not tall enough to see... certainty. Perhaps they are blind...—eyes gone missing, eyes shut, shut!" In this cosmology, ideally, everyone, human and nature and divine will be swept up in the dance, "this moment of connectivity," where all "fundamental natures" are expressed and are one without division. This is the ecstatic experience; "the glamorous clamour"!

Storm and Lightning are given full, complementary natures: physical and metaphysical; responsible, yet sensual; traditional and ecstatic. The oppositional others have knowledge but not wisdom. Lightning further proposes that their status derives from negation. It seems what is rejected may be ecstatic

The Patient Storm, 2006 (video stills)

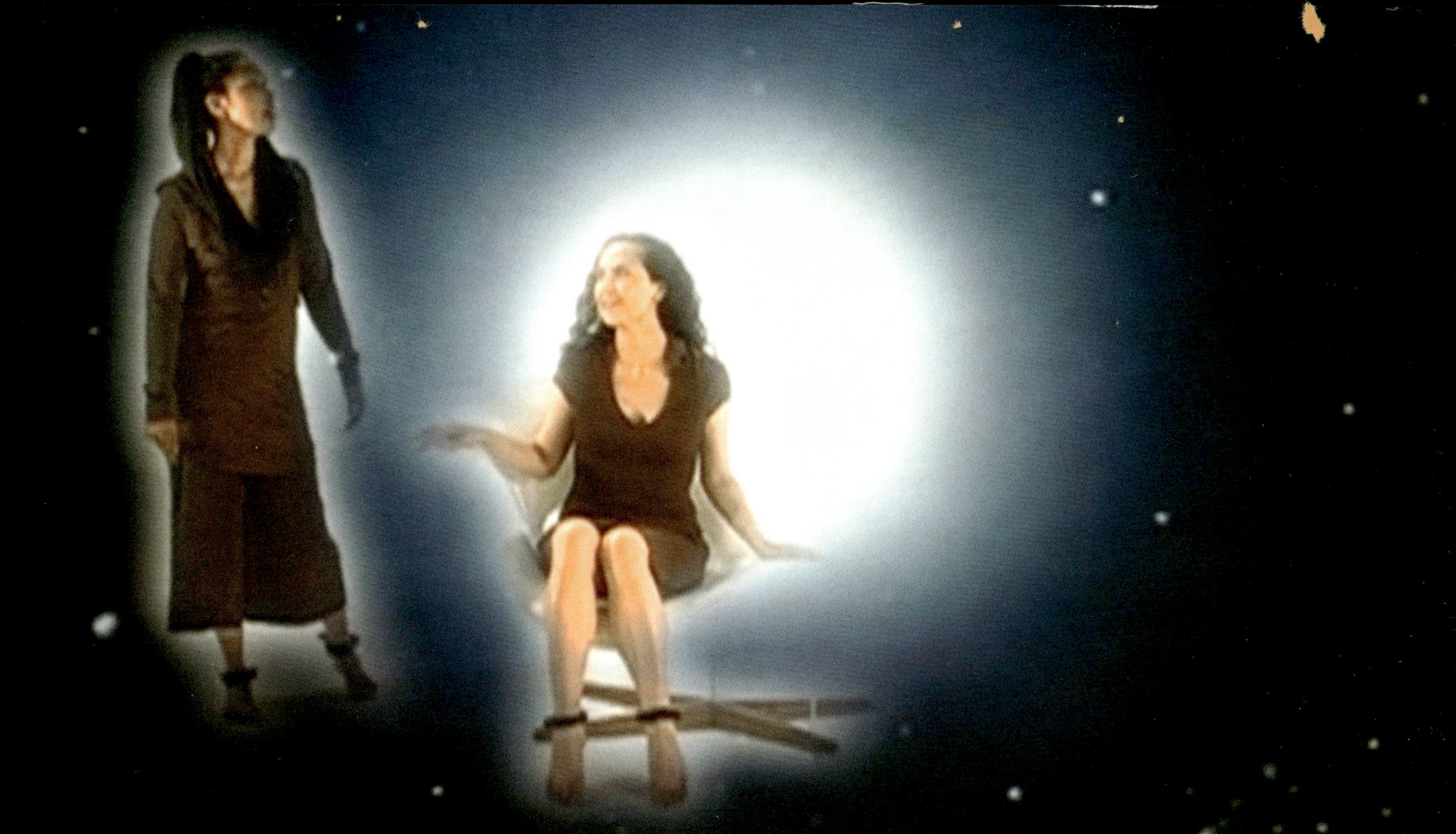

pleasure, losing oneself in a group ritual, in metaphysical belief. While the others' materialism might raise them in one aspect, it makes them not quite tall enough to see into this richer realm. Lightning sees the denial of spirituality as either a tragic or a willful blindness.

Storm and Lightning participate in another sort of knowledge (Aboriginal ways of knowing) that permits you to join the ecstatic moment, dissolve into the dance. Storm says, "Those who know will join us and the others are going to have to wait until they are ready." Lightning repeats, "Join us, those who know, start getting ready....until the others are ready, they will have to wait." This knowledge may be as simple as accepting metaphysical possibilities and being open to community. The lack of this knowledge of how things are is figured as ignorance. Storm and Lightning face the camera and invite us to the dance, but they do not coerce. This is not an evangelical faith looking to win converts. Infidels are not killed; they are recognized as afraid, pitied and left to themselves. The others must simply "wait until they are ready" (to end their otherness).

The video concludes with Lightning saying, "...we dance across the sky—without defeat." Despite the opposition and disbelieving others, they and all who believe and participate, and live with their dualities and in the connectedness of all things, will persist.

This construction of identity through the denial of the metaphysical and its social expressions, Lightning suggests, is based in fear. It could be that Claxton is characterizing this opposition as male ("fur balls!"), or at least as masculine. But that is not necessarily the case. When I asked her about it, she didn't think so. She explained that the scaredy cats refer to people who are afraid of Aboriginal cosmologies and rituals.[7]

Toward the end, the coming storm, which Storm leads but is also subject to and overwhelmed by, is characterized by Lightning as "the moment of hope, this moment of promise, this moment of love, this moment of connectivity." This, according to Claxton, is the Sundance where all the elements come together:

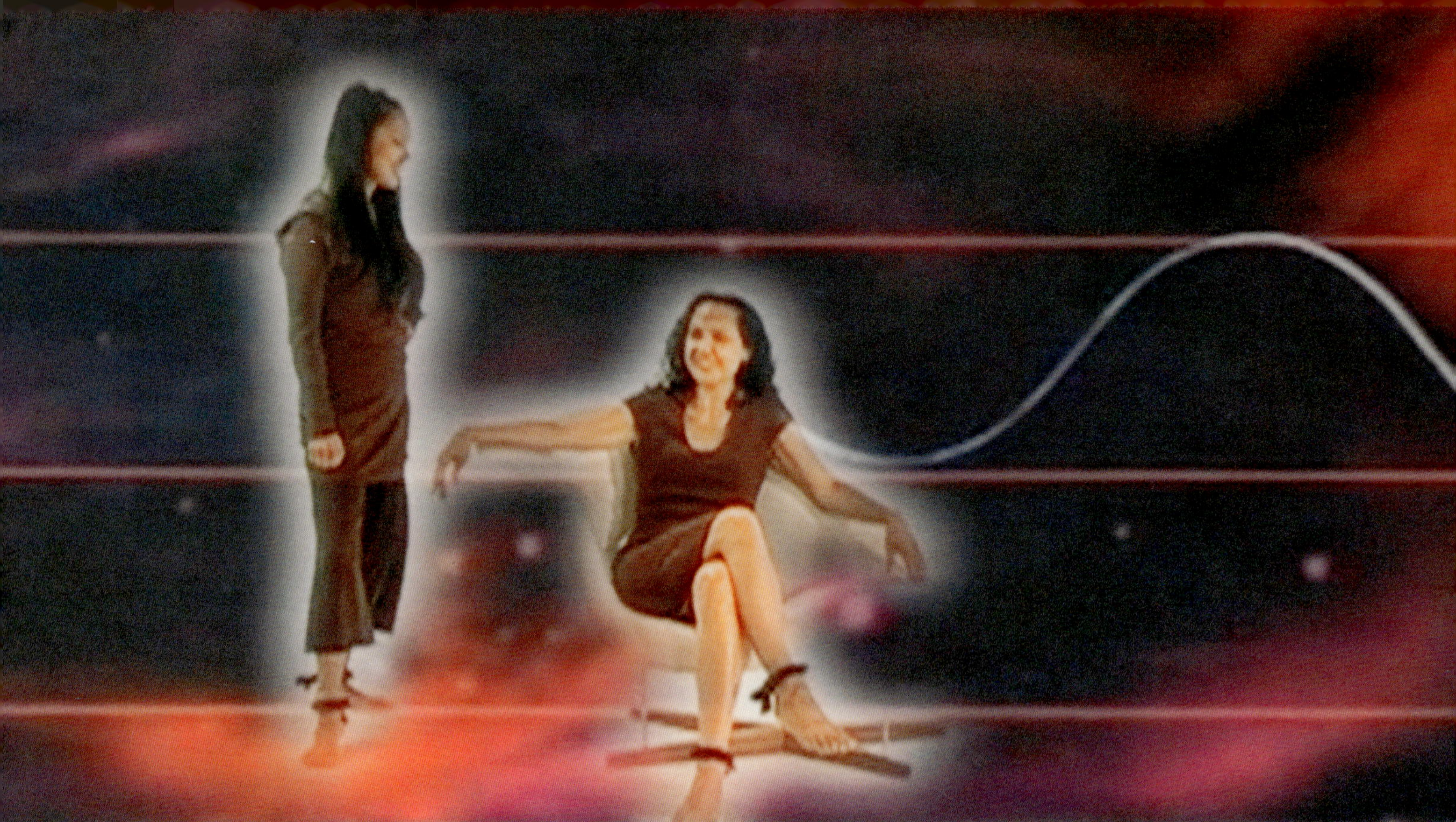

I have been a Sundancer for a while now and the thunder and lightning beings must attend the dance, a storm must make an appearance. Lightning and thunder confirms and rain cleanses. So they make their appearance, the cosmos, as they did the night before our shoot—which doesn't happen very often in Vancouver—a huge lightning/thunder and rain storm that woke Marie Prince. Lightning came into her room. Storm had an experience as well. Me, I slept thru the entire storm...as I had come home 2 days before from Sundancing and needed a good long rest.

With the Sundance, I maintain and enhance my own relationship with the cosmos and the divine. It gives me strength, spiritual strength and connectivity to that realm, as well as strengthens my family ties both in Saskatchewan and South Dakota.

The Patient Storm is designed to cross boundaries, and encourages boundary crossing: between people, peoples, and from metaphysics to spirituality.[8] It is a modern legend that echoes the past to reveal the common dance behind all appearances.

When I watch *The Patient Storm*, I sense something in the wind: a warm, faint, sweet scent that prefigures a glamorous clamour. I feel in the calm; an after-battle exhaustion, longing for home. But nothing is as it was. Is it time to turn from the surging red energy of righteousness; from the tools of struggle to those of rebuilding? Dana Claxton offers hope and possibility.

Dana Claxton's The Patient Storm originally published in ConunDrumOnline, Issue 4, July 2007.

The Patient Storm, 2006 (video stills)

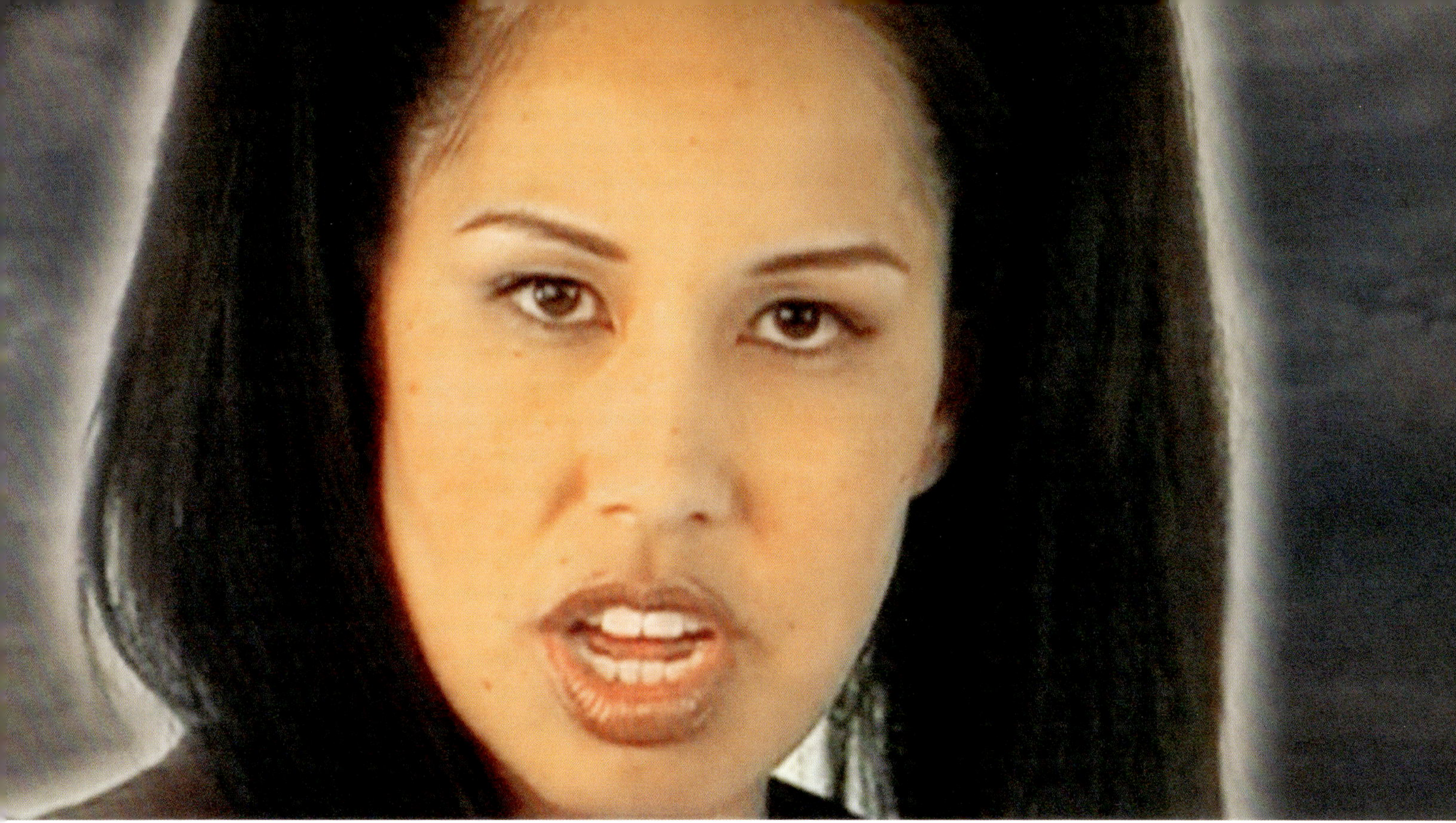

ENDNOTES

1 *The Patient Storm* is an online video project created by Dana Claxton, and commissioned by Urban Shaman for the Storm Spirits – Aboriginal New Media Art project/gallery, http://www.stormspirits.ca/English/Storm/essay.html.

2 Many sources could be cited. But a good recent one is: Greg Younging, "The Indigenous Tradition/New Technology Interface," *Transference, Tradition, Technology: Native New Media Exploring Visual and Digital Culture*, eds. Melanie Townsend, Dana Claxton, and Steve Loft (Banff: AB, Walter Phillips Gallery Editions, 2005), 179–87.

3 "The work does specifically address the Sundance, when Ahawsis invited me to participate, and I read the curatorial intent, the first image I had was of the Sundance and the storm and cloud formations that I have seen. The Lakota teaching, 'everything you need to know is in the sky,' also came to mind" (from a correspondence with Dana Claxton).

4 The La Chaise is an organically shaped chair that invites sitting or reclining equally. Designed by Charles and Ray Eames (1948) for a Museum of Modern Art competition, it is inspired by *Floating Figure* (1927), a sculpture by Gaston Lachaise.

5 All the quotations from Dana Claxton are retrieved from an email conversation I had with her in preparing this essay.

6 "Storm is Salish from Capilano Reserve and Marie Prince is from up north Carrier country" (Dana Claxton).

7 "Certainly...the 'others' are those who are anti-Indian and the furballs are scardee cats...both male and female... perhaps on a subtextual level more male..." (Dana Claxton).

8 "Claxton has described her two new works as an attempt to construct a 'religious art approach,' one that 'hybridizes a cultural process of contemporary art-making and traditional knowledge by creating a site where two seemingly different ways of knowing or being interface." Dana Claxton's "Artist statement," ArtSpeak Gallery, May 2000; cited in Monika Kin Gagnon, "Worldviews in Collision: Dana Claxton's Video Installations," in *Transference, Tradition, Technology*, eds. Townsend, Claxton, and Loft, 70.

Commissioner Indian Affairs,
Department of the Interior,
Washington D.C.

Sir,

I am in receipt of a communication from Sitting Bull dated Fort Yates, Dakota, in which he expresses a strong desire to travel through the East with me during the summer.

As I am not acquainted with the routine of procedure in such affairs, I address you in the hope that you will further his desire in the matter. I have had a long experience in the management and care of Indians, and will guarantee that he shall receive the kindest treatment and safe return to Fort Yates. Major McLaughlin, Agent at Standing Rock knows me well, and will cheerfully endorse your permission to allow Sitting Bull to leave the Agency in my care.

I take pride in referring you further to Genl. Sherman or any officer of Frontier experience as to my character and ability to fulfill all the conditions or restrictions you may impose upon me.

Hoping that you will grant the petition thus set forth, I remain,

W. F. Cody

38

LAYLI LONG SOLDIER

Here, the sentence will be respected.

I will compose each sentence with care, by minding what the rules of writing dictate.

For example, all sentences will begin with capital letters.

Likewise, the history of the sentence will be honored by ending each one with appropriate punctuation such as a period or question mark, thus bringing the idea to (momentary) completion.

You may like to know, I do not consider this a "creative piece."

I do not regard this as a poem of great imagination or a work of fiction.

Also, historical events will not be dramatized for an "interesting" read.

Therefore, I feel most responsible to the orderly sentence; conveyor of thought.

That said, I will begin.

You may or may not have heard about the Dakota 38.

If this is the first time you've heard of it, you might wonder, "What is the Dakota 38?"

The Dakota 38 refers to thirty-eight Dakota men who were executed by hanging, under orders from President Abraham Lincoln.

To date, this is the largest "legal" mass execution in US history.

The hanging took place on December 26, 1862—the day after Christmas.

This was the *same week* that President Lincoln signed the Emancipation Proclamation.

In the preceding sentence, I italicize "same week" for emphasis.

There was a movie titled *Lincoln* about the presidency of Abraham Lincoln.

The signing of the Emancipation Proclamation was included in the film *Lincoln*; the hanging of the Dakota 38 was not.

In any case, you might be asking, "Why were thirty-eight Dakota men hung?"

As a side note, the past tense of hang is *hung*, but when referring to the capital punishment of hanging, the correct past tense is *hanged*.

So it's possible that you're asking, "Why were thirty-eight Dakota men hanged?"

They were hanged for the Sioux Uprising.

I want to tell you about the Sioux Uprising, but I don't know where to begin.

I may jump around and details will not unfold in chronological order.

Keep in mind, I am not a historian.

So I will recount facts as best as I can, given limited resources and understanding.

Before Minnesota was a state, the Minnesota region, generally speaking, was the traditional homeland for Dakota, Anishinaabeg, and Ho-Chunk people.

During the 1800s, when the US expanded territory, they "purchased" land from the Dakota people as well as the other tribes.

But another way to understand that sort of "purchase" is: Dakota leaders ceded land to the US government in exchange for money or goods, but most importantly, the safety of their people.

Some say that Dakota leaders did not understand the terms they were entering, or they never would have agreed.

Even others call the entire negotiation "trickery."

But to make whatever-it-was official and binding, the US government drew up an initial treaty.

This treaty was later replaced by another (more convenient) treaty, and then another.

I've had difficulty unraveling the terms of these treaties, given the legal speak and congressional language.

As treaties were abrogated (broken) and new treaties were drafted, one after another, the new treaties often referenced old defunct treaties, and it is a muddy, switchback trail to follow.

Although I often feel lost on this trail, I know I am not alone.

However, as best as I can put the facts together, in 1851, Dakota territory was contained to a twelve-mile by one-hundred-fifty-mile long strip along the Minnesota River.

But just seven years later, in 1858, the northern portion was ceded (taken) and the southern portion was (conveniently) allotted, which reduced Dakota land to a stark ten-mile tract.

These amended and broken treaties are often referred to as the Minnesota Treaties.

The word *Minnesota* comes from *mni*, which means water; and *sota*, which means turbid.

Synonyms for turbid include muddy, unclear, cloudy, confused, and smoky.

Everything is in the language we use.

For example, a treaty is, essentially, a contract between two sovereign nations.

The US treaties with the Dakota Nation were legal contracts that promised money.

It could be said, this money was payment for the land the Dakota ceded; for living within assigned boundaries (a reservation); and for relinquishing rights to their vast hunting territory which, in turn, made Dakota people dependent on other means to survive: money.

The previous sentence is circular, akin to so many aspects of history.

As you may have guessed by now, the money promised in the turbid treaties did not make it into the hands of the Dakota people.

In addition, local government traders would not offer credit to "Indians" to purchase food or goods.

Without money, store credit, or rights to hunt beyond their ten-mile tract of land, Dakota people began to starve.

The Dakota people were starving.

The Dakota people starved.

In the preceding sentence, the word "starved" does not need italics for emphasis.

One should read "The Dakota people starved" as a straightforward and plainly stated fact.

As a result—and without other options but to continue to starve—Dakota people retaliated.

Dakota warriors organized, struck out, and killed settlers and traders.

This revolt is called the Sioux Uprising.

Eventually, the US Cavalry came to Mnisota to confront the Uprising.

More than one thousand Dakota people were sent to prison.

As already mentioned, thirty-eight Dakota men were subsequently hanged.

After the hanging, those one thousand Dakota prisoners were released.

However, as further consequence, what remained of Dakota territory in Mnisota was dissolved (stolen).

The Dakota people had no land to return to.

This means they were exiled.

Homeless, the Dakota people of Mnisota were relocated (forced) onto reservations in South Dakota and Nebraska.

Now, every year, a group called the Dakota 38 + 2 Riders conduct a memorial horse ride from Lower Brule, South Dakota, to Mankato, Mnisota.

The Memorial Riders travel 325 miles on horseback for eighteen days, sometimes through sub-zero blizzards.

They conclude their journey on December 26, the day of the hanging.

Memorials help focus our memory on particular people or events.

Often, memorials come in the forms of plaques, statues or gravestones.

The memorial for the Dakota 38 is not an object inscribed with words, but an *act*.

Yet, I started this piece because I was interested in writing about grasses.

So, there is one other event to include, although it's not in chronological order and we must backtrack a little.

When the Dakota people were starving, as you may remember, government traders would not extend store credit to "Indians."

One trader named Andrew Myrick is famous for his refusal to provide credit to Dakota people by saying, "If they are hungry, let them eat grass."

There are variations of Myrick's words, but they are all something to that effect.

When settlers and traders were killed during the Sioux Uprising, one of the first to be executed by the Dakota was Andrew Myrick.

When Myrick's body was found,

                                        his mouth was stuffed with grass.

I am inclined to call this act by the Dakota warriors a poem.

There's irony in their poem.

There was no text.

"Real" poems do not "really" require words.

I have italicized the previous sentence to indicate inner dialogue, a revealing moment.

But, on second thought, the words "Let them eat grass" click the gears of the poem into place.

So, we could also say, language and word choice are crucial to the poem's work.

Things are circling back again.

Sometimes, when in a circle, if I wish to exit, I must leap.

And let the body   swing.

From the platform.

                                        Out

                                                                        to the grasses.

Layli Long Soldier, "38" from *Whereas*. Copyright © 2017 by Layli Long Soldier. Reprinted with the permission of The Permissions Company, Inc. on behalf of Graywolf Press, Minneapolis, Minnesota, www.graywolfpress.org.

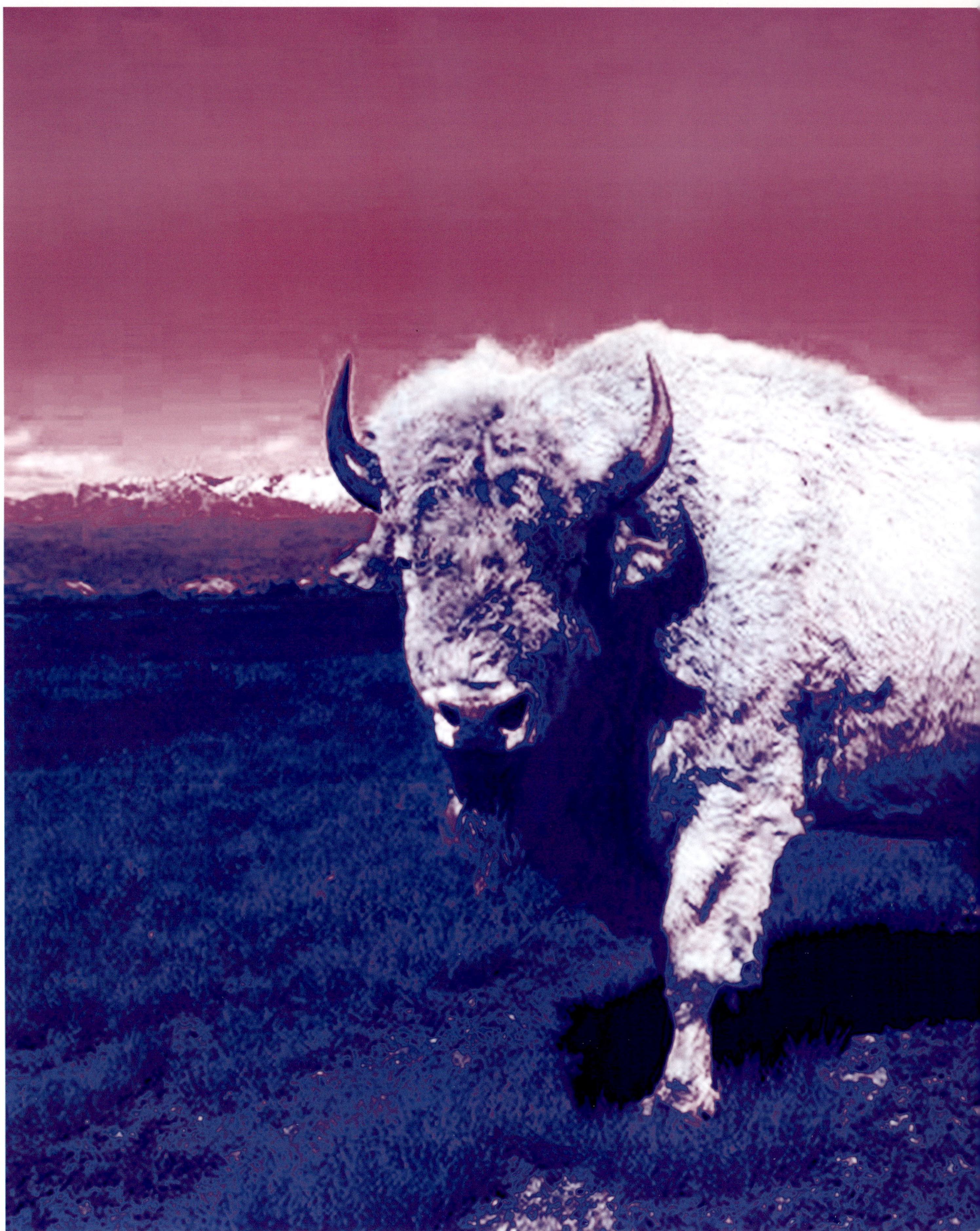

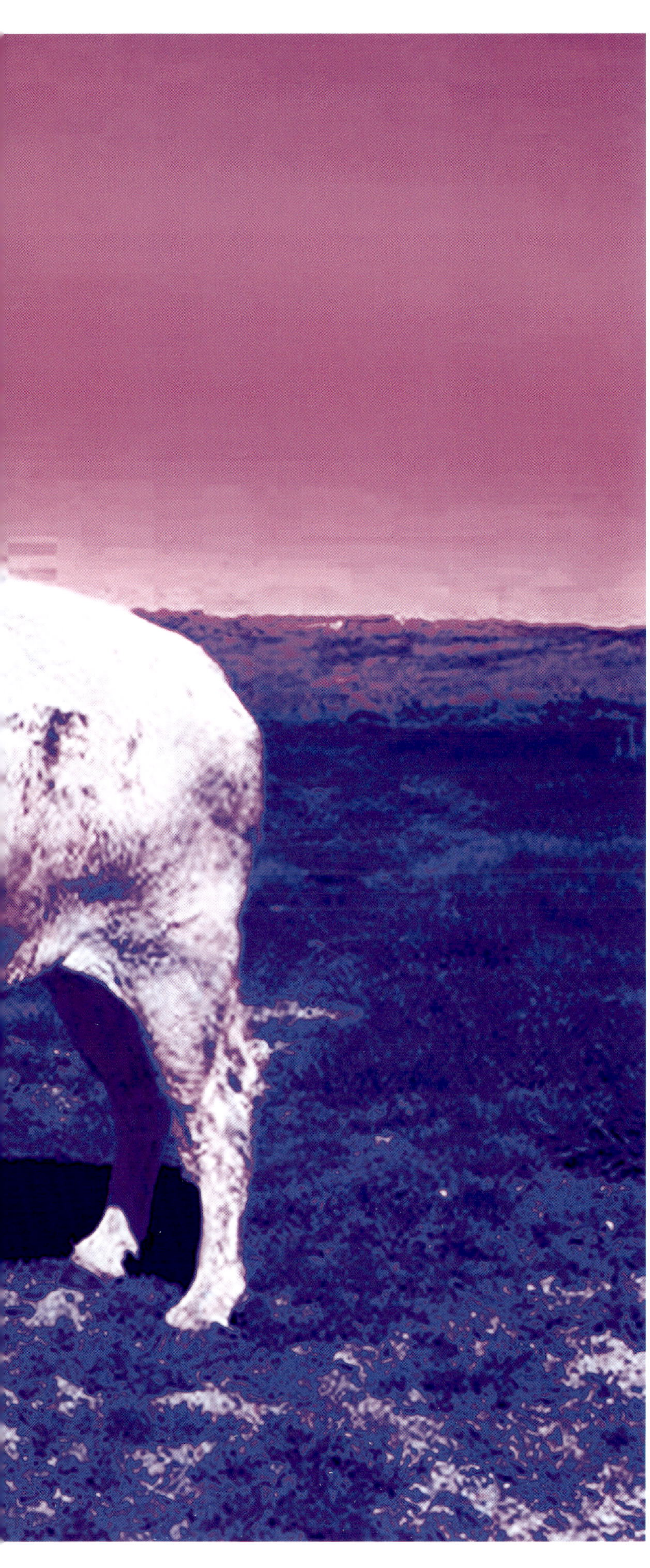

Tatanka (Buffalo) (from *Indian Candy*), 2013

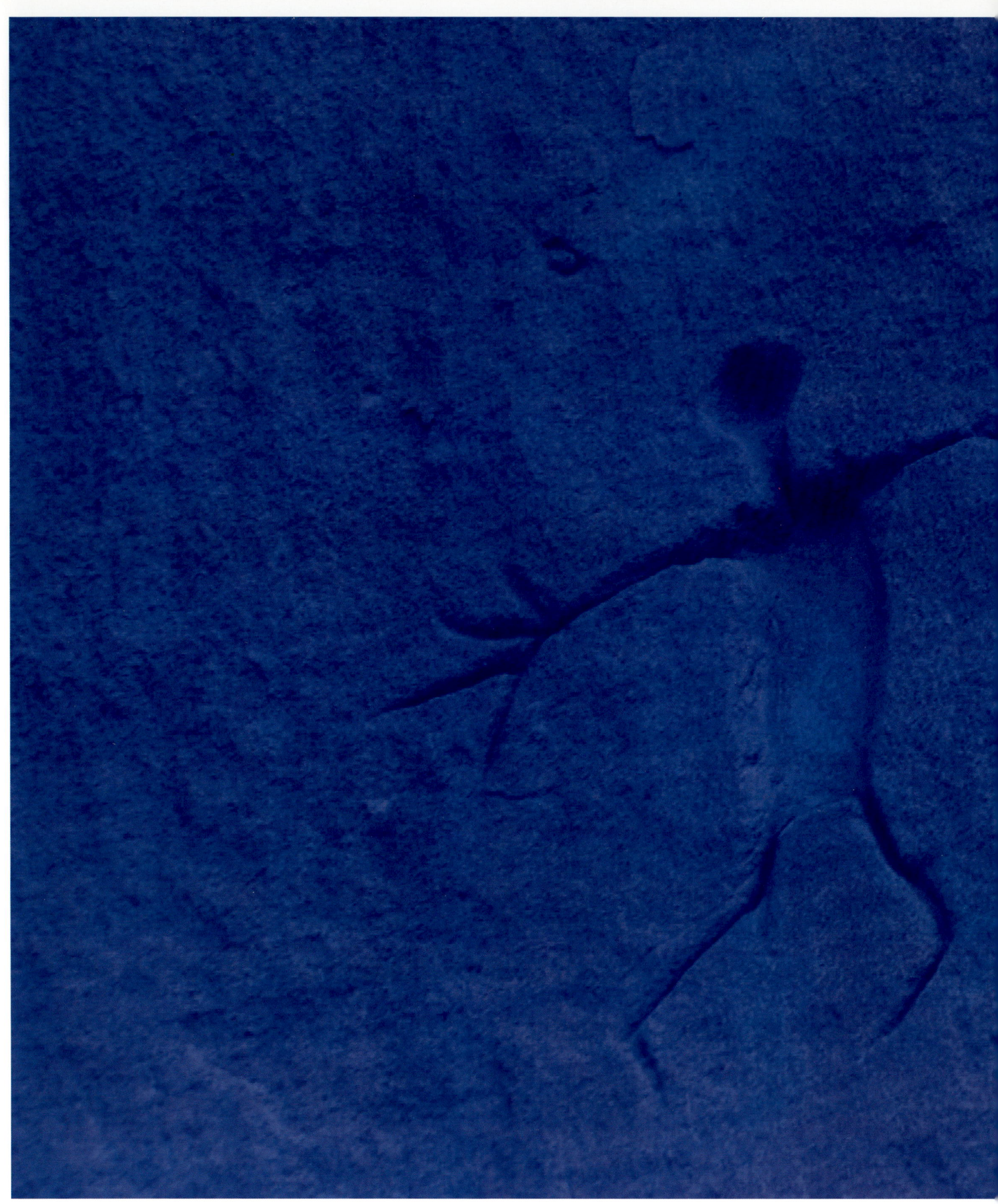

Blue Horse Man (from *Indian Candy*), 2013

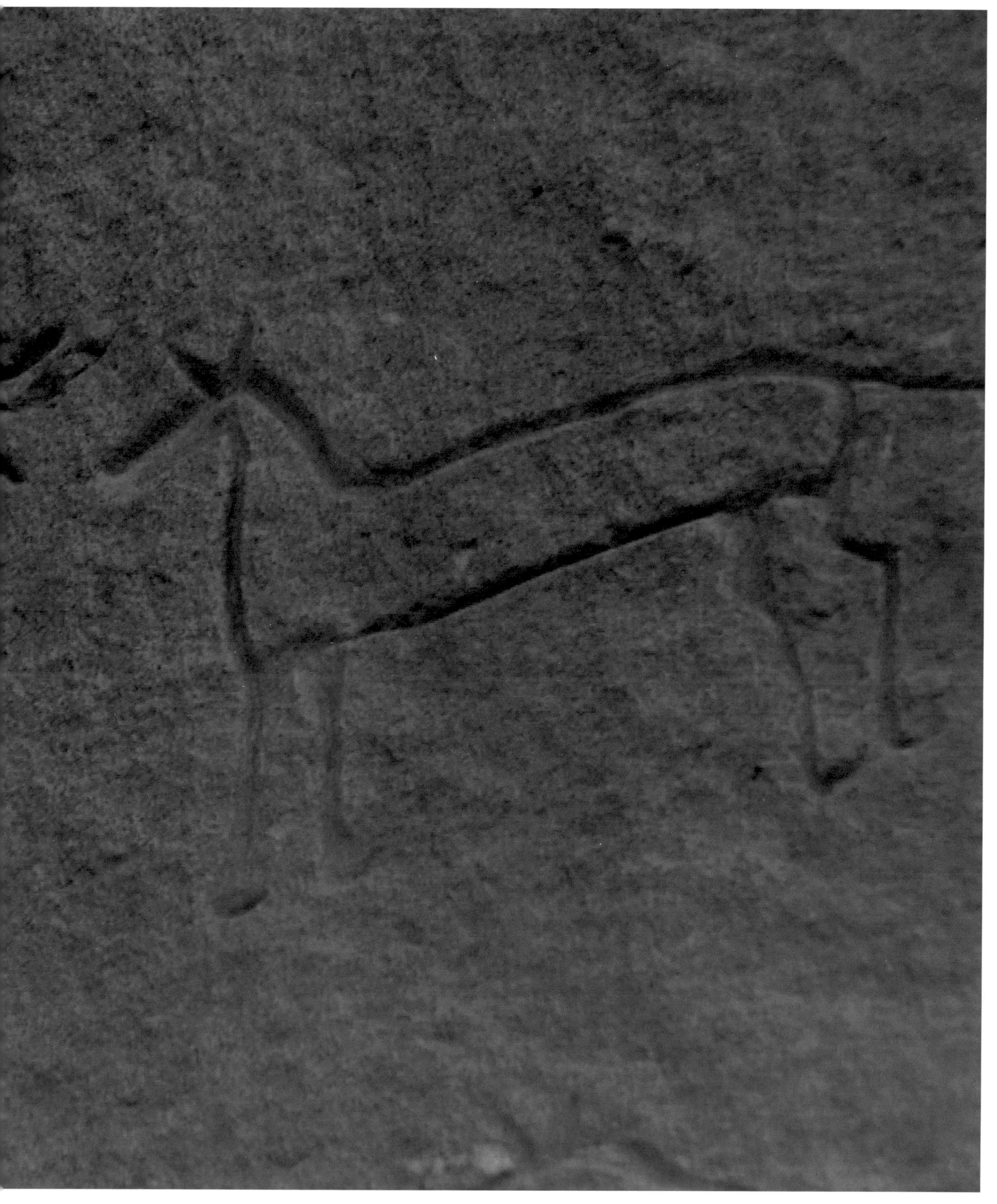

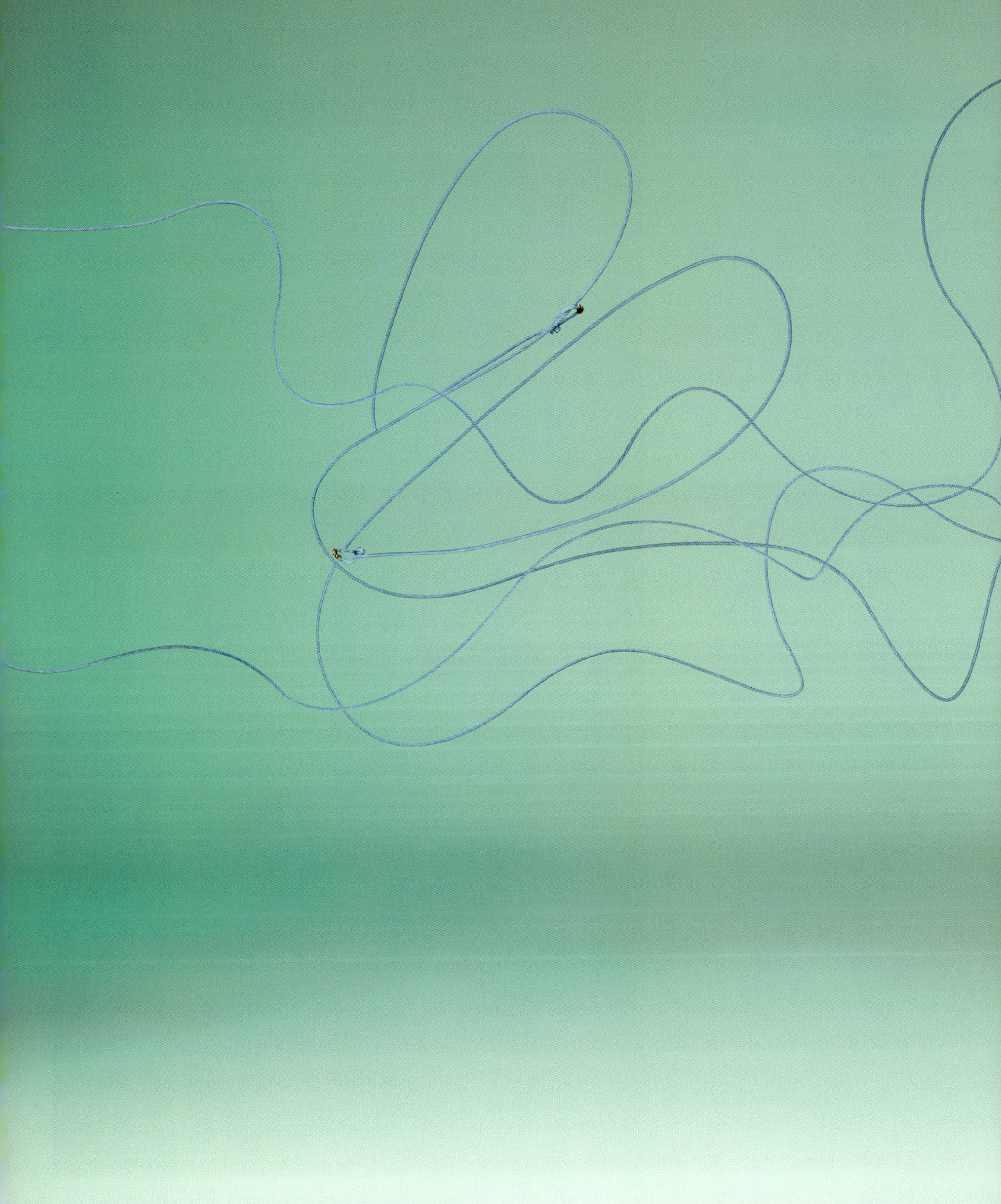

Lasso (study), 2018

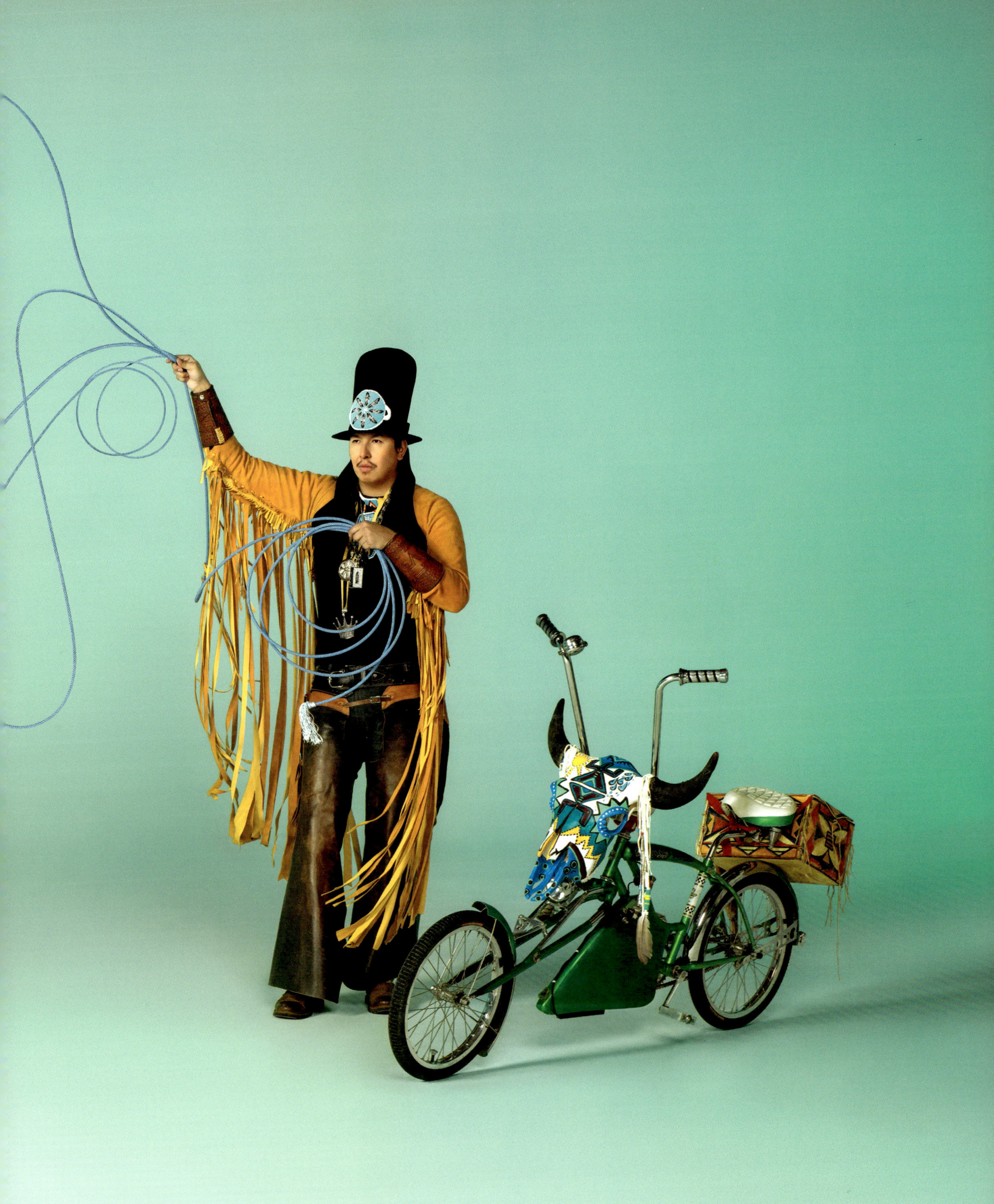

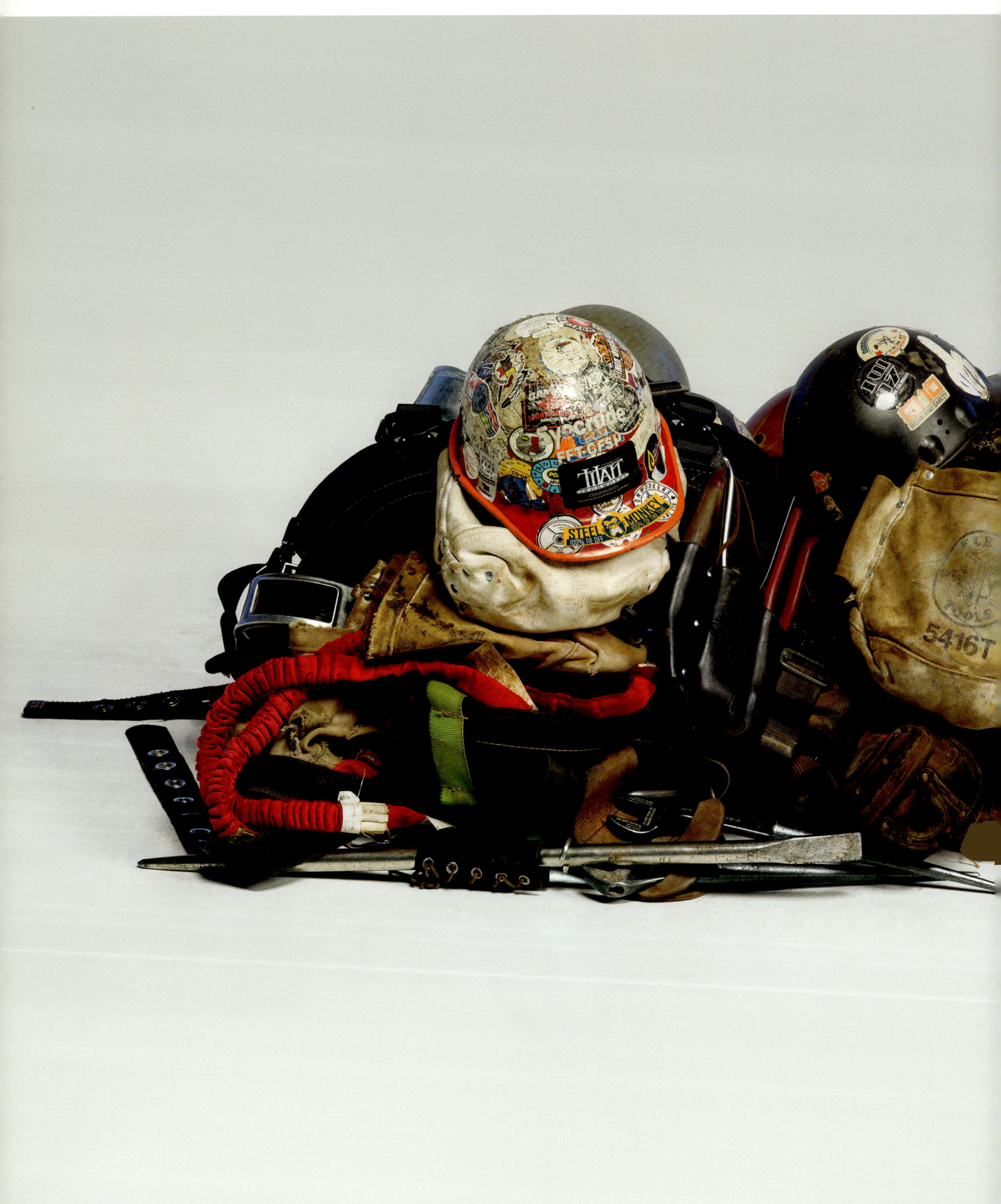
STEEL
MONKEY
100% TIE OFF
5416T

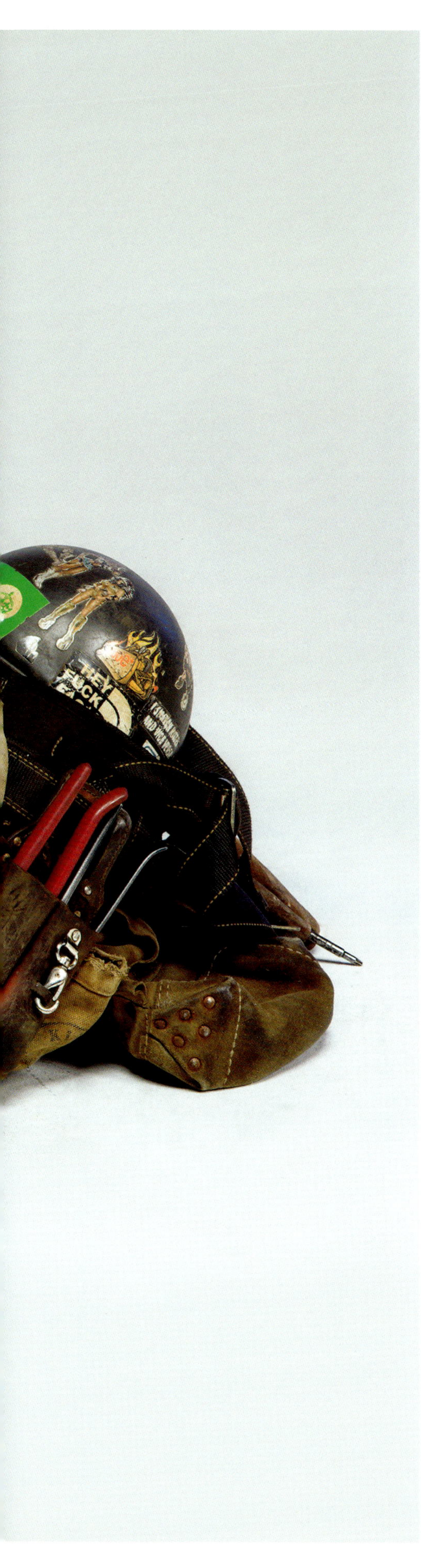

REBAR, OR SUBTERRANEAN WEAVING

The Over-Written Foundational Matrix of 21st C. Vancouver

JALEH MANSOOR

> "The city emerges in this example as a kind of meta-network, linking and assembling other principles of interconnection."
> — CAROLINE LEVINE, *Forms*[1]

A wall-scale (6' x 10') light box sits near the centre of Dana Claxton's exhibition on the second floor of the Vancouver Art Gallery. The box presents eight men—evidently "brown," in fact Indigenous—in work gear. They face the viewer, striding forward heroically, almost triumphantly. Flanking it stands another picture, smaller and a print. Construction gear comprises its content. A group portrait and a still life: what have these two objects, both summoning the spectre of "work," to do with one another?

Locked into a static mise-en-scène, the tableau is reflexively "about" the economy of vision itself; it queries the conditions that enable the containment and delivery of the image. How does that which is delivered to view, eight workers identified by their gear, summon a specific economy of vision? And in light of the failure of the politics of representation over the last decade—a failure from the point of view of Indigeneity in the aftermath of Canada's Truth and Reconciliation Commission (2008–15) as much as a failure to represent labour either politically or aesthetically—how does the representation of Indigenous labour find relevance? How does it guard against objectifying and exoticizing its content, the visually arresting men distributed over the visual field?

A video in the adjacent room functions something like an electronically mediated and time-based "flipbook" comprising seventeen hundred images generated during the photoshoot that produced the picture in the light box, or "firebox" as Claxton has identified it. A repository of the excess of production, this time-based material encompasses a kind of documentary of production itself, conjuring its metabolic through montage set to sound to effect a particular "busy" rhythm that summons the jittery tempo of creation in relationship to

NDN Ironworkers Tool Still Life, 2018

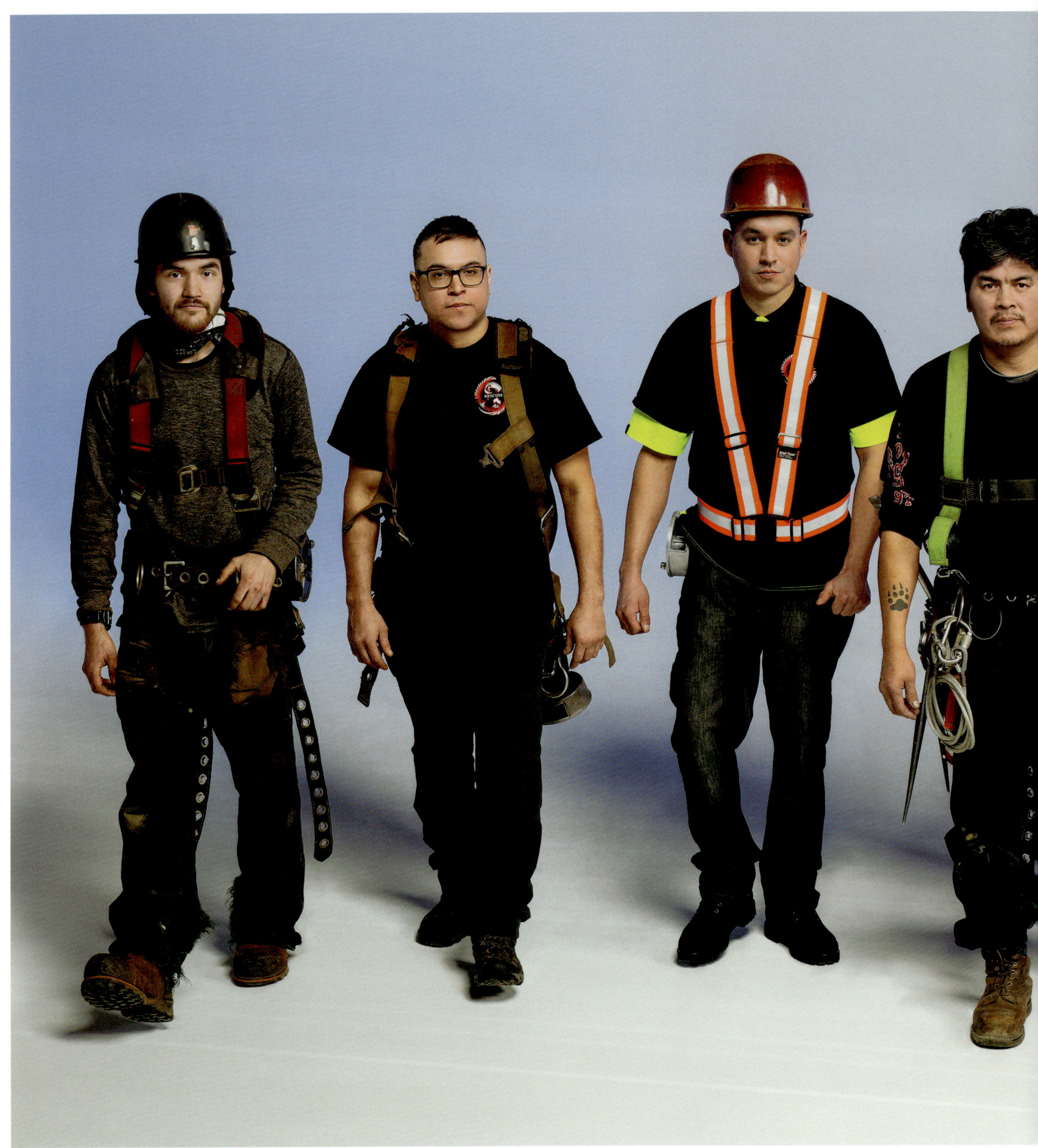

NDN Ironworkers, 2018

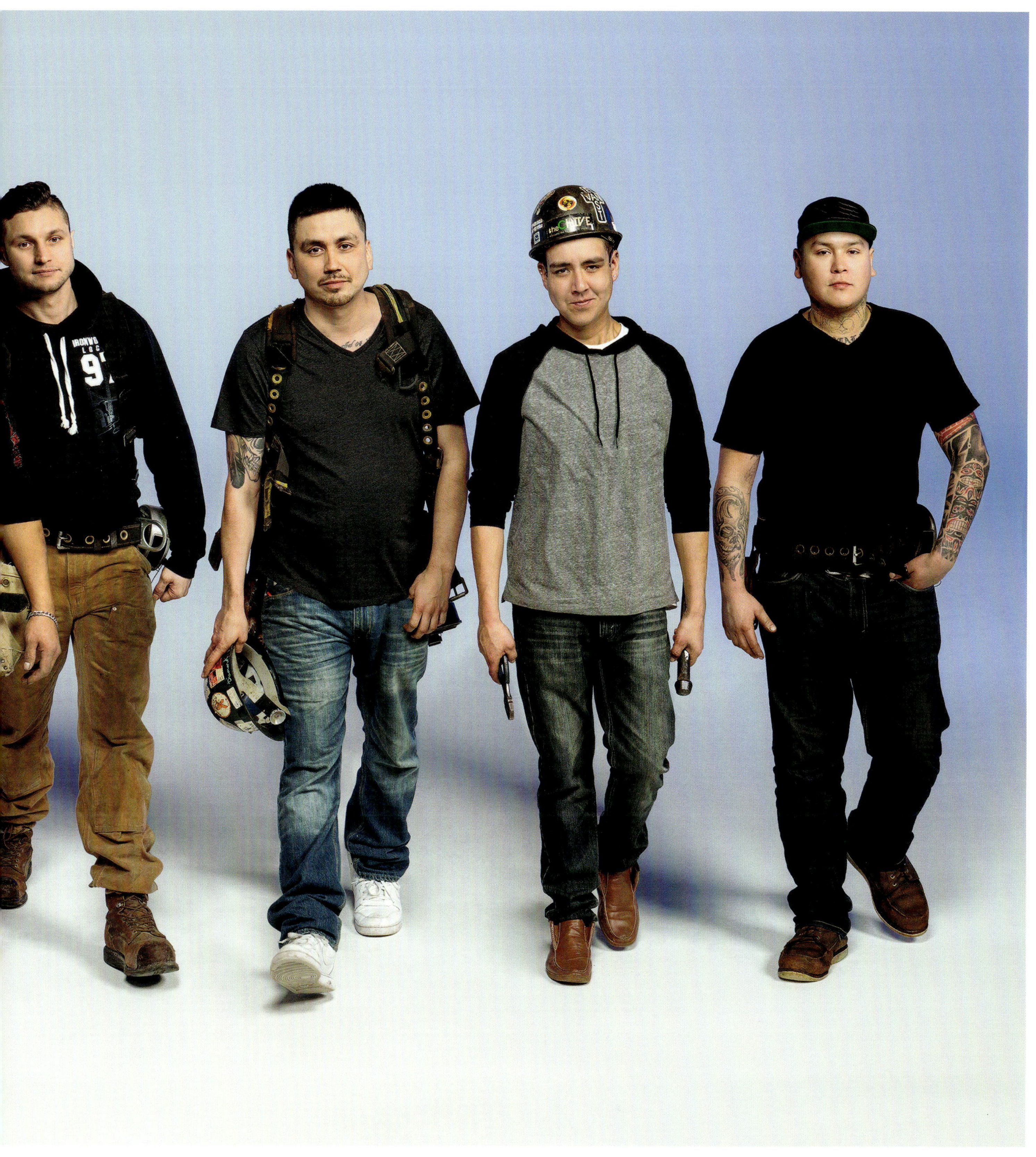
theCHIVE

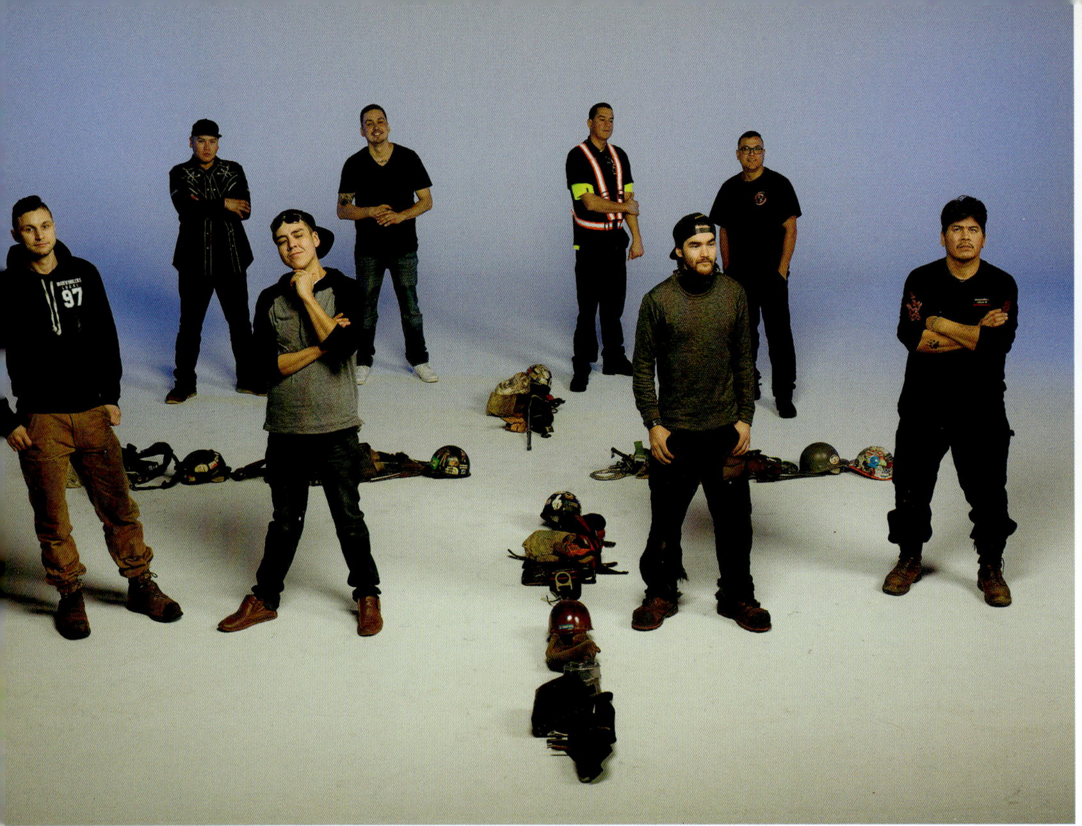

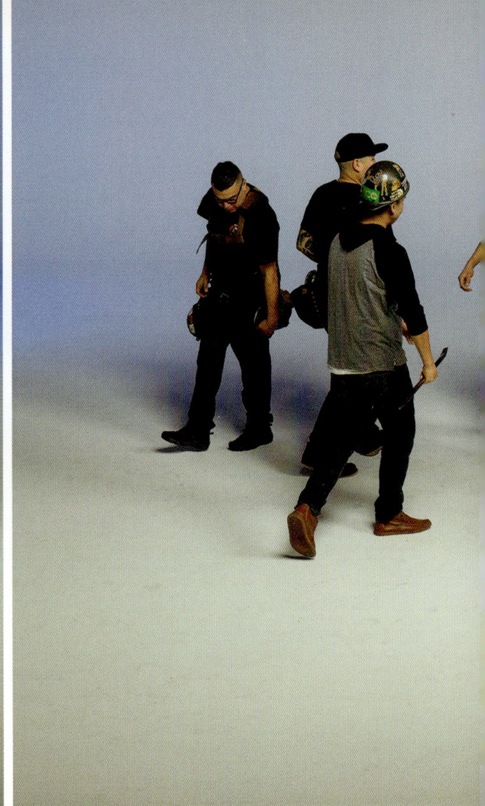

manufacture. It is set to a soundtrack mixed by Salish composers in keeping with Claxton's frequent use of the music video genre, an index of the MTV generation and a specific alignment of audio to a visual field. A time-based work, conjugate with the firebox, the video sets the unique image into the much larger accumulation of images from which it is drawn, a Brechtian nod to the conditions "behind-the-scenes." But this behind the scenes is part of the scene, suggesting once again that the image cannot be separated from its conditions of possibility.

The group portrait of striding men, among whom is implied a set of relations manifestly having to do with work and workers, is set into the structural stasis of a box, locked into a picture and aggrandized in a bright shining monument to sight. This monumentalizing and fetishistic gesture probes the (colonialist) historicity of the Vancouver School of conceptual photography and its generational iterations, mobilized here in the context of a particular contemporary condition, our present, which is poised at the intersection of the last vestiges of British Imperialism, the American cycle of capitalist accumulation that saw the greatest surge of wealth in recorded history, Pacific markets engorged by the independence of Hong Kong in 1992 with its opening onto China's exponential economic growth and, finally, an ambivalent relationship to Indigeneity and its potential insurgence as evidenced by the debates around the Truth and Reconciliation Commission.[2] But operating in a gently antagonistic countercurrent to the display structure of the medium, Claxton's mise-en-scène offers a social relation seemingly independent of these conditions of visual organization and presentation. The workers are engaged with one another, seemingly at leisure, enjoying the company of the group and the time to recharge with games, conversation, camaraderie and conviviality. At the same time, the men are clearly attuned to the conditions of the production of the image—the camera, the artist and the surroundings of the photoshoot. This awareness of the camera and the conditions of production marks an intensely present engagement with the viewer across the image; this work is more than a mere image, it "resides within the realm of visual sovereignty."[3]

NDN Ironworkers—Video Flipbook, 2018

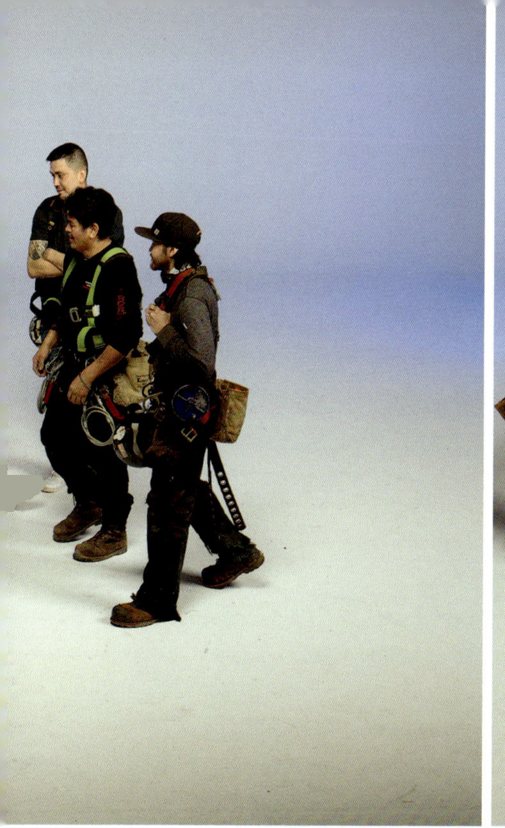
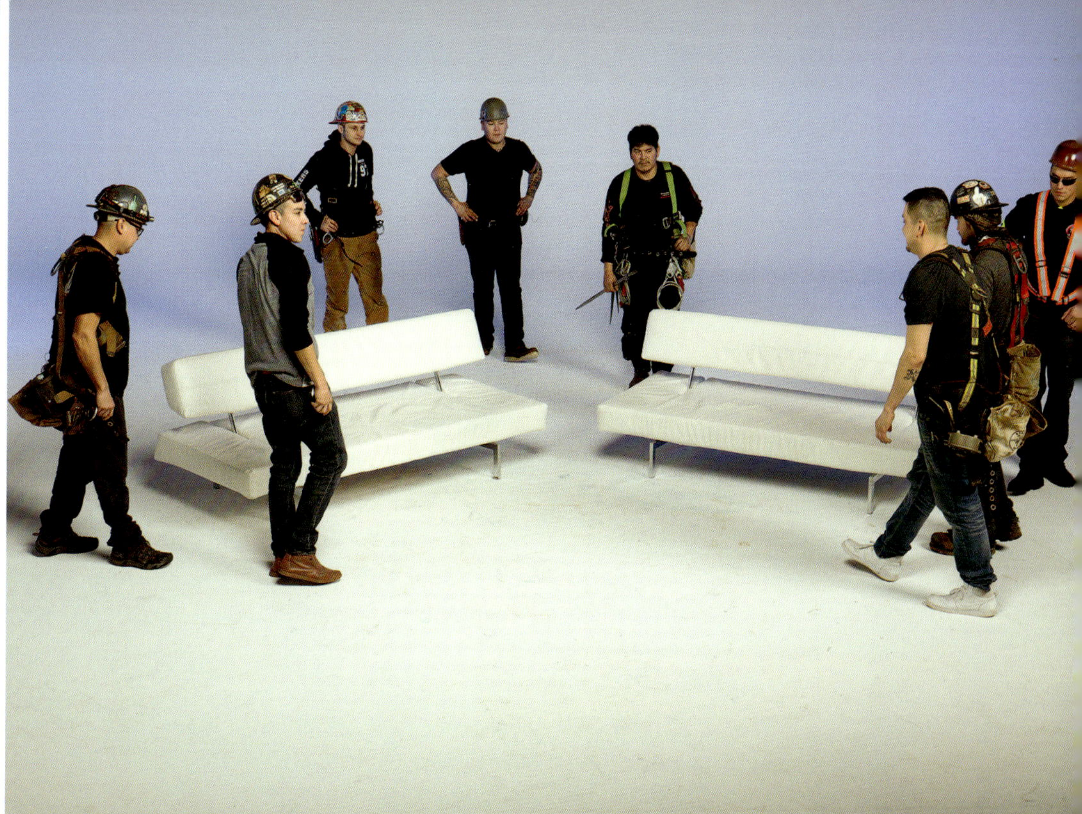

A hiatus, then, a break from the grinding work of laying the foundations of the city is shown to us, and we are drawn into the terms of the engagement.[4] But who is this "us?" What kind of work is the work doing, given that it offers a momentary suspension of labour set into another kind of labour? How to cross the different registers of labour, from the positioning of steel rebar to strengthen concrete—notoriously exhausting and dangerous work that is paid proportionately little in the hierarchy of labour—to the spectacular image that registers as so much frozen capital? The serial structure of the images in the video "flipbook" divide and isolate, then re-sutures, each grouping. This renders each scene as part of a sequence, but also emphasizes for a brief flash the individual image, situating it in a form noted for its analogy to the shop window, as though each scene (of workers at leisure, away from the scene of toil and constraint) were available for visual consumption within the parameters of the high commodity object.[5] But it quickly becomes evident that something else, something much more perverse, is at stake in the ground of the image.

Vancouver has come to be recognized as an exemplary city for three unrelated phenomena specific to contemporaneity's global and neoliberal turn. First, the "Art of Rent," the epiphenomenal soaring inflation of the market value of its otherwise standard and substandard real estate, which ramifies in every aspect of the everyday life of its occupants—be they the late-imperial landed gentry, the rentier class, or itinerant labourers (Indigenous or otherwise)—cutting through social relations on either side of a rapidly polarizing class divide like a kind of shudder haunting the present yet falling out of time, a present haunted by an unliveable future.[6] The emergent common condition of this hastened development spurred by international money in which locals, natives and foreigners panic together is said to be a new norm: the collective economically determined neurosis of the metropolis in the finally truly globalized epoch.[7]

Second, is Vancouver's entry into the theatre of rarefied culture with its lens-based image production, which began to flourish at the end of the era of Conceptual Art (1962–68) and has resonated continuously into the present, across generations of artists from Iain Baxter and N.E. Thing Co. to Jeff Wall and Stan Douglas to Evan Lee, who query the limits of opticality afforded by advanced photographic technical production. The city has come to be identified with and by its canonized visual culture, which traffics mostly in an idiom of high production values (except Lee who makes of this primitive accumulation in vision something to wager against), often to architectural scale, and often mounted in the framework associated not only with the free-standing commodity but the arena of reified vision it, the commodity, inaugurates and nurtures. The well-lit cube (or light box) summons the spectre of the shop window, now set at an interval's remove into the register of post-conceptual photography.[8]

Third, finally (and fundamentally), Vancouver is noted for its nominally "progressive" acknowledgement of the Indigenous peoples who technically and legally, even by European settler standards, have not ceded the territories in which Vancouver sits to the colonial power. A metropolis built on unceded land, the city cradles its denizens in a kind of double bind in which everyday life is lived in a kind of tense open hypocrisy. While in lived time this may contribute to a sense of contradiction and duplicity in which colonial capital repeatedly chants its contradictions and discontents, it also marks a notable margin of difference from the urban cultures, and indeed all culture, State-side. In other words, however nominal the acknowledgement, however nestled in "business as usual," the standard metabolic of constant growth, development and capitalist value extraction, this recognition is not only exceptional in North America, but contributes to a simultaneous, collective, shared sense of contradiction and even antagonism in quotidian life.

Three foundational problems, then, braid under and over the image: capitalist acceleration in twenty-first century terms, the settler-colonial matrix reiterated in daily acknowledgements that fail to curb the nihilist metabolic of capital urbanism, and a local artistic idiom gone global as one of Vancouver's greatest cultural exports. Do these developments bear any relation? Do unresolved Aboriginal sovereignty and economics; a housing crisis precipitated by tectonic shifts in global wealth distribution as the centre fails to bind and the periphery encroaches;[9] and finally culture, a genre nested within lens-based practices responsive to the collapse of medium specificity; have anything to do with one another? Does the international dispersal of swelling wealth, of surplus value generated elsewhere, have anything to do with the decomposition and re-composition of a local aesthetic? Who or what stands at the vanishing point of two seemingly unrelated phenomena that locate Vancouver on the GPS of "global" culture?

To the extent that Claxton's light box cites the local founding father of the idiom, Jeff Wall, it might be useful to remember that Wall too was preoccupied with the historical conditions making contemporary seeing possible, conditions at once offering historical continuity in how we see, and marking ruptures expressive of change. Citation of historical precedent dialectically offers up the image of rupture. As art historian Michael Newman has argued, "the self-conscious assertion of a tradition always takes place in relation to a crisis, in the form of a break. In terms of Wall's engagement with photography, the crisis was marked historically by Conceptual Art's negation of depiction. According to Wall's account, insofar as Conceptual practice relied on photography, it was unable to complete this negation, since representation is inherent to it."[10] Newman notes also that this divided relationship to representation opens onto a kind of shudder in the way the image operates: "We have already discussed the implications of mimesis being more than a representational imitation, that it is a kind of behaviour or comportment that conforms with its object, whether for the sake of adaptive self-concealment or for the sake of a non-dominating response to otherness, to the non-identical."[11] What behaviour or comportment is made available in Claxton's presentation of labour; and to what object does it "conform?" And what transition is evidenced through the economy of the image, shot through with this shudder of historicism at the level of both medium and genre? And how might this index shifts specific to this geopolitical space, at this time?

By organizing the field as a set of social relations at momentary ease, of groups of friends at play rather than as portraits or still lives—pictures of things and in the hyper scopophilic world of spectacle, people *as* things—the scene dialectically does something similar to what Marx did for commodities and for labour: it casts all social relations as a nodal points in networks (social and economic) in which invisible forces, complex and determining, cross and uncross. Summoning now the words by theorist Caroline Levine from her discussion of networks and social form that provides the epigraph to this essay, one could say that Claxton's boxes emerge as switch boxes of sorts that show the invisible cohesion of the political-economic-social conjuncture engulfing us. She does so in what is part meta-network and part subterranean network that playfully theatricalizes[12] the ways in which kinship networks find both their spur and their constraint in political economic networks: the forms of labour necessary to the physical and material structure of Vancouver's origin, growth, and maintenance as a metropolis. In other words, the warp and weft of metal that weaves a physical foundational matrix within each new concrete structure—each new condo complex or modernist home—generated of the brutally hard work of laying rebar, most frequently accomplished by Aboriginal labour, materializes the disavowed and occluded networks of socially necessary labour time that make this city un/liveable. One might take that thought—the image of social relations that constitute concrete systems comprised of foundational matter—as a metaphor or as a paradigm in the science of the social. Trope or paradigm, either way we are offered that which is rarely present to consciousness.

Nearby hang red fabric banners bearing rearranged fragments of well-known slogans by the often naïve Marxist revolutionary theorist Antonio Gramsci (1891–1937). Entitled *Red on Red: Ode to Gramsci*, the series evokes, at a formal and structural level, the text-based Conceptual Art idiom reminiscent of artists of "classical" conceptualism such as Lawrence Weiner, Edward Ruscha or Joseph Kosuth, the also canonized movement generationally preceding and understood to have opened onto the Vancouver School of lens-based practices. While citing an art movement of the sixties that is a prequel to Wall and the Vancouver School in the standard art historical narrative, the series re-situates conceptual practices in relation to that which modernism and its late iterations (Pop and Conceptualism) hoped to suspend and keep in abeyance outside the frame or the discursive structure: the historical struggles of accelerated modernity across historical periods and geopolitical contexts. The admitted failures and remaining relevance of Gramsci's historical aspirations in the terrain of class struggle, intimately entwined with the historical avant-gardes of the twentieth century, are framed anew with relevance to British Columbia now. But to say that hot new work warms up the unfinished business of the old is a tedious platitude.

Claxton's re/iteration is conjured in an altogether different key, a register of wicked humour. As Freud elaborated in *Jokes and Their Relation to the Unconscious* (1905), "a joke will allow us to exploit something ridiculous in our enemy which we could not, on account of the obstacles in the way, bring forward openly or consciously. Once again, the joke will evade restriction...it will further bribe the hearer with its yield of pleasure into taking sides with us without any very close investigation."[13] In other words, humour functions like a Trojan horse in the battlegrounds of the psyche and the social.

WHAT WAS THE POINT OF THE STRUGGLE?

UNDERSTAND YOUR HISTORICAL VALUE

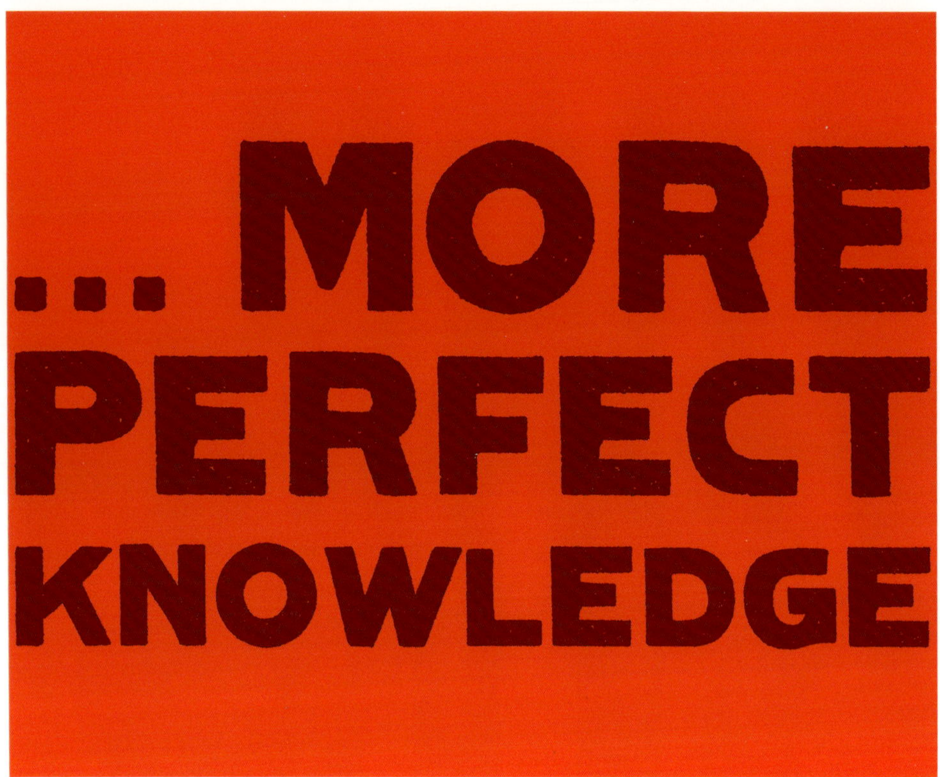

But what or who is the "enemy" at whose expense the aesthetics of administrative banality act as a kind of Trojan horse for the eruption of a humour otherwise too incendiary to unleash?

In the history of Conceptual Art, or the aesthetics of commodity administration and administration via the commodity form, from 1962 to now,[14] the photographic document is found stripped of literary, aesthetic, denotative and connotative value. Cannibalized through and through, as presciently augured by Walter Benjamin (1892–1940) in *A Short History of Photography* (1931), drafted long before the codification of this banality in aesthetic practice, Conceptualism's self-conscious summoning of banality entwined with humour found something of its apotheosis in Ed Ruscha's artist's book *Real Estate Opportunities* (1970).[15] Ruscha's work bears a strange, perverse humour: that of language folded uncomfortably into the economy of the deracinated, at an oblique remove from the picture, failing to function as informative caption; a libertarian shudder rippling through the homeless image and its institutionalization into the parameters of high art. But how does this genre, its status already belaboured by a historically determined weight and fraught with dissonance and contradiction, deliver the specific content of Claxton's practice, so far from the gloating sarcasm and intellectual irony of the academy and the privileged classes it often reflects?

In a city where the joke behind "gentrification" is "deforestation"—the absorption of endowment lands, treaty protected territories, and tribal regions—there is no lack of perverse irony in the fact that the demographic most drawn on to lay the material formation for this urban expansion, with its frenzy of construction, of cranes and forklifts, should be that same demographic that is displaced, deracinated, abstracted, and now re-imported to labour for an hourly wage to build homes for those pouring in from other countries, continents, time zones.

Classic Marxist approaches are no longer applicable, both for their myopia with regards to the forms capital has taken since contact—a racializing operation nested within colonial histories—and for the way in which any Marxian framework is being radically rewritten after the financial crisis of 2008. At the

 PREVIOUS LEFT: *Ode to Gramsci #3* (from *Red on Red*), 2017 ABOVE: *Ode to Gramsci #7* (from *Red on Red*), 2017

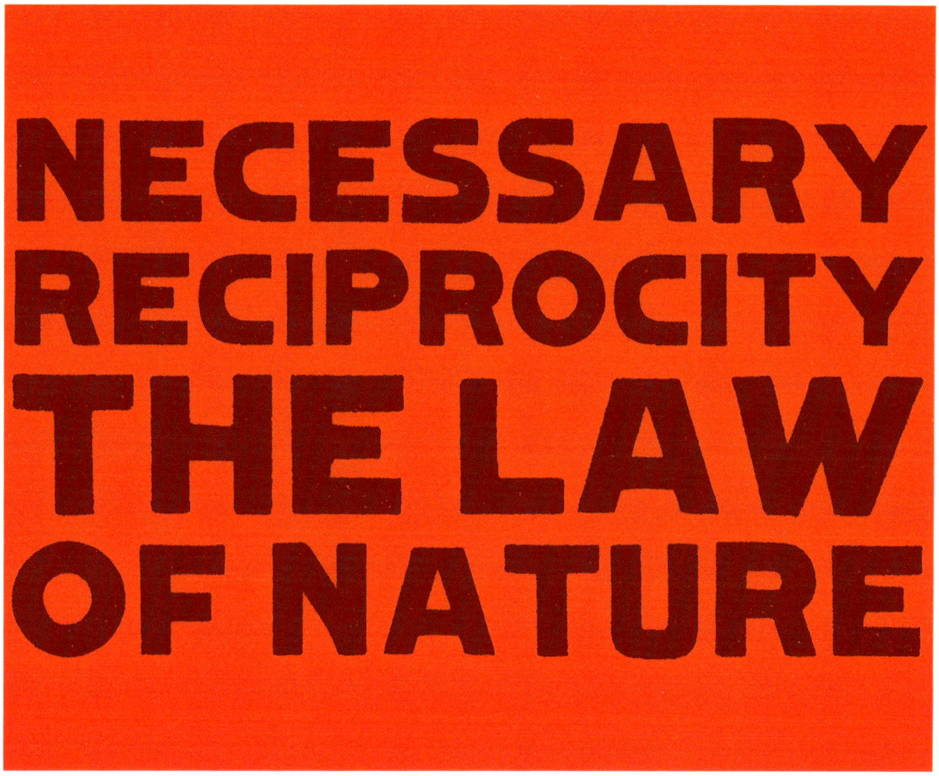

NECESSARY RECIPROCITY THE LAW OF NATURE

same time, postcolonial theories have left the way that the settler state operates via value extraction, often through the medium of the wage, out of the field of inquiry. Since contact, capitalist accumulation has produced the gendered, racialized and sexualized categories through which it manages value extraction, just as it has determined social and political trends in migration, the movement and ownership of natural resources, including the natural resources that are bodies, sources of labour power.

Neither Marxian in the classic sense nor reducible to the postcolonial theories of the past decades, our approach suspends both of those interpretive frameworks to observe anew the symptoms of the present in the interest of generating a fresh perspective with an eye to a provisional totality made up of many determining facets that are layered, networked and calcified, one over the other. Perhaps it would be useful to review here why intersectionality has proven ineffectual. As Tithi Bhattacharya, in her essay "Mapping Social Reproduction Theory," an introduction to the edited volume *Social Reproduction Theory* (2017), notes,

> intersectionality theory shows us a world where race, gender, and other oppressions 'intersect,' thereby producing a reality that is latticed—a sum total of different parts. At first glance this 'whole,' as an aggregate of different parts, may be the same as the Hegelian-Marxist conception of totality. An elementary question about the nature of intersections, however, reveals the distinction between these two concepts. If, as intersectionality tells us, race and gender (or race and class) intersect like two streets, then surely they are two separate streets, each with its own specificities. What then is the *logic* of their intersection? I suggest that the logic and conclusions of intersectional theorists actually contradict their methodology.[16]

As any survey of the extant literature on either Indigeneity and the history of the settler-colonial relationship or on local labour history will demonstrate, acknowledgements of the *mutually constitutive*

PREVIOUS RIGHT: *Ode to Gramsci #8* (from *Red on Red*), 2017 ABOVE: *Ode to Gramsci #4* (from *Red on Red*), 2017

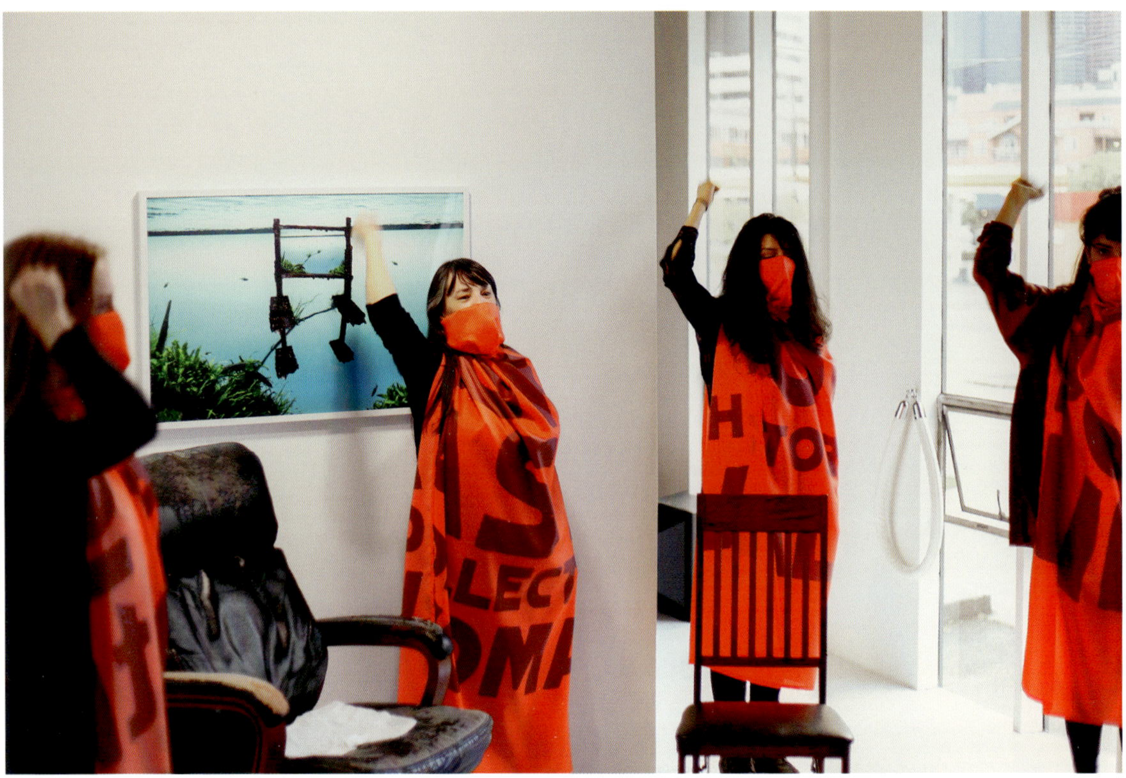

entwinement of these histories are shockingly scant. And yet the entwinement of British Columbia's labour history and its colonial legacy forms the condition for the emergence of the present conjuncture.

Instead, we turn to a more descriptive approach sensitive to the multiple relationships that comprise a social whole, and the way that fragments emerge into patterns, into a dynamic that once might have been called "totality," if the charge of the "master narrative" loathed by postcolonial theory had not compromised the drive to get a handle on the relationship between micro and macro elements of everyday life. Another way to pitch it is that it marks a link between the "real movement of history" and attempts to formalize that elusive movement. Ironically enough, this is accomplished in aesthetic form. For Levine, "a formalist method offers the tools to track the particular range of ways in which forms [and categories] run up against each other and the consequences their encounters bring into the world."[17]

The most familiar accounts of the historical emergence of the proletariat are of course from Gramsci and the British historian E.P. Thompson (1924–93). Neither acknowledge what has only just recently begun to surface in world systems theory and labour histories in relation to colonialism, namely that racialized primitive accumulation was necessary to, and the enabling condition for, the elaboration of modern capitalism from its longer historical durée from contact (1492) to the present.[18] These "organic intellectuals," Gramsci and Thompson, were Romantics who believed in national culture and autochthony. As mentioned earlier in the present essay, postcolonialism has motivated us not to turn away but to complicate and deepen labour history. Discourse moves slowly; art, always on the vanguard, holds out the articulation of history that is as yet difficult to either decipher or formalize.

Jaleh Mansoor and Dana Claxton (centre) perform *Don't Get to Work Bitch*, an intervention at the book launch for Mansoor's *Marshall Plan Modernism*, May 2017, Seattle

And yet the proper name "Gramsci" seems to function like a sign for thinking the entwined relationship of ideological oppression and material exploitation, a floating signifier for a way to rethink the complex and contradictory totality that comprises capitalism now. As such, he figures heavily in recent studies that trace the racialized composition of labour pools retroactively naturalized and justified by racism, which itself is the result of the same historical emergence. In *Colonization and Community: The Vancouver Island Coalfield and the Making of the British Columbian Working Class* (2002), John Douglas Belshaw relies heavily on Gramsci in noting the specific way in which waves of immigration from Scotland and Ireland came to squeeze out Aboriginal and Asian labour in British Columbia in the 1870s and 1880s, not least because of the primitive accumulation of women's labour in the social replication of the white worker himself, which then caused labour as such to be understood as a category of whiteness. Already a demand of the settler colonial states insatiable need for value extraction from natural resources (mining and forestry), the ossification of labour as a tendency, a characteristic, of whiteness itself, doubled back to justify the theft of resources and the second-classing of non-white labour pools.[19] Claxton's *Ode to Gramsci* finds its relevance here.

A historical matrix founded on the absorption and occlusion of Aboriginal labour, and a concomitant entwinement of blood and bodies,[20] is realized at the level of another kind of concrete abstraction.[21] I have attempted to see Claxton's boxes less as "reflections" of already constituted and ossified relationships, and more as highlighted situations of where, and how, multiple forms of relationships meet, unfold, clash and refract, enjoining the viewer to see and think about power as it is concretized in the terrain we cross, the structures we inhabit and the social relations we enjoy and dread.

How can we picture and contain, much less articulate in descriptive terms, the effects of combined and uneven development in the social and cultural fabric of local contexts? The question of a demographic's usefulness to capital, and the cultural and social dynamics brought about by the movement of capital across the globe, have recently informed a robust new discourse, as for instance Marina Vishmidt's pioneering investigation of the way in which global labour flows generate "surplus" populations and how this ramifies in culture. This growing discourse on "surplus populations" locates and identifies those not easily assimilated into the workforce or the wage system owing to the particular needs of value productive work at any given time, or, having once been useful to capital are suddenly abandoned by a given industry and at large seeking employment.[22] For instance, the demographics fuelling the automobile industry in Italy or the United States in the 1950s are not the same as those currently absorbed by technology and design in the same geopolitical locations. The former labour pool that served the industries of the immediate post-WWII era has not been able to successfully integrate into current economic needs. With changing industries come changing labour pools. But what becomes of the previously existing populations no longer necessary to value production? To this end, we look to a growing body of scholarship that acknowledges that both the historical left and established labour organizations are no longer relevant unless they reconstitute themselves to address the contingencies of the present and account for the growing existence and effect of racialized "surplus populations" set to standing reserve.

Does the racial and ethnic component of labour tell us anything about the geographies of value? Does it explain the collapse of organized labour and the historical left? Does it operate as an index of the relationship of the settler state to Aboriginal peoples? If so, which Aboriginal peoples?

How might we recognize the symptoms of an accelerated decomposition and re-composition of the labour-to-capital relationship through its resonance in local culture and local social relations? Can culture operate as a diagnostic device? For at its best, at its most opaque, art mediates form and history, coming

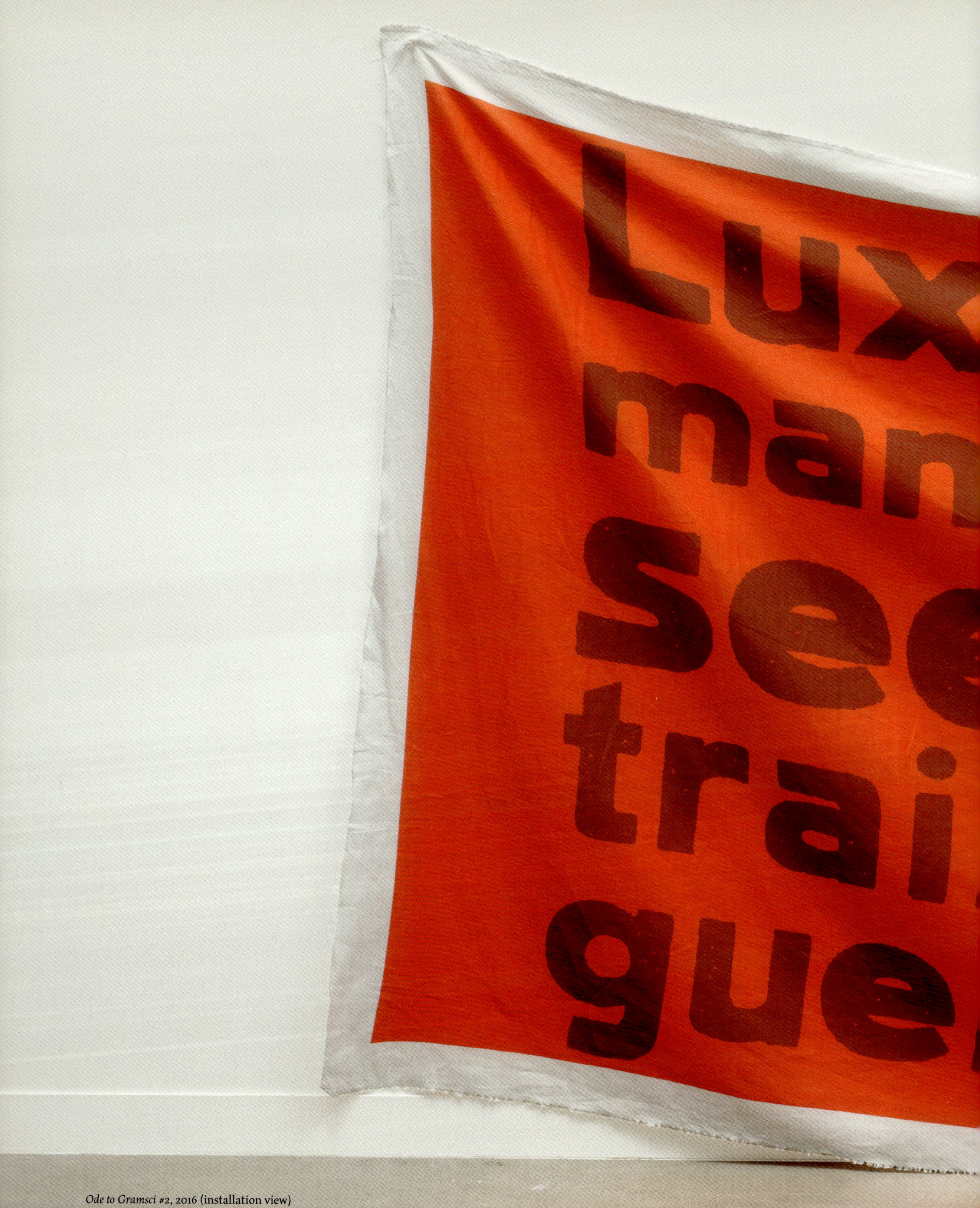

Ode to Gramsci #2, 2016 (installation view)

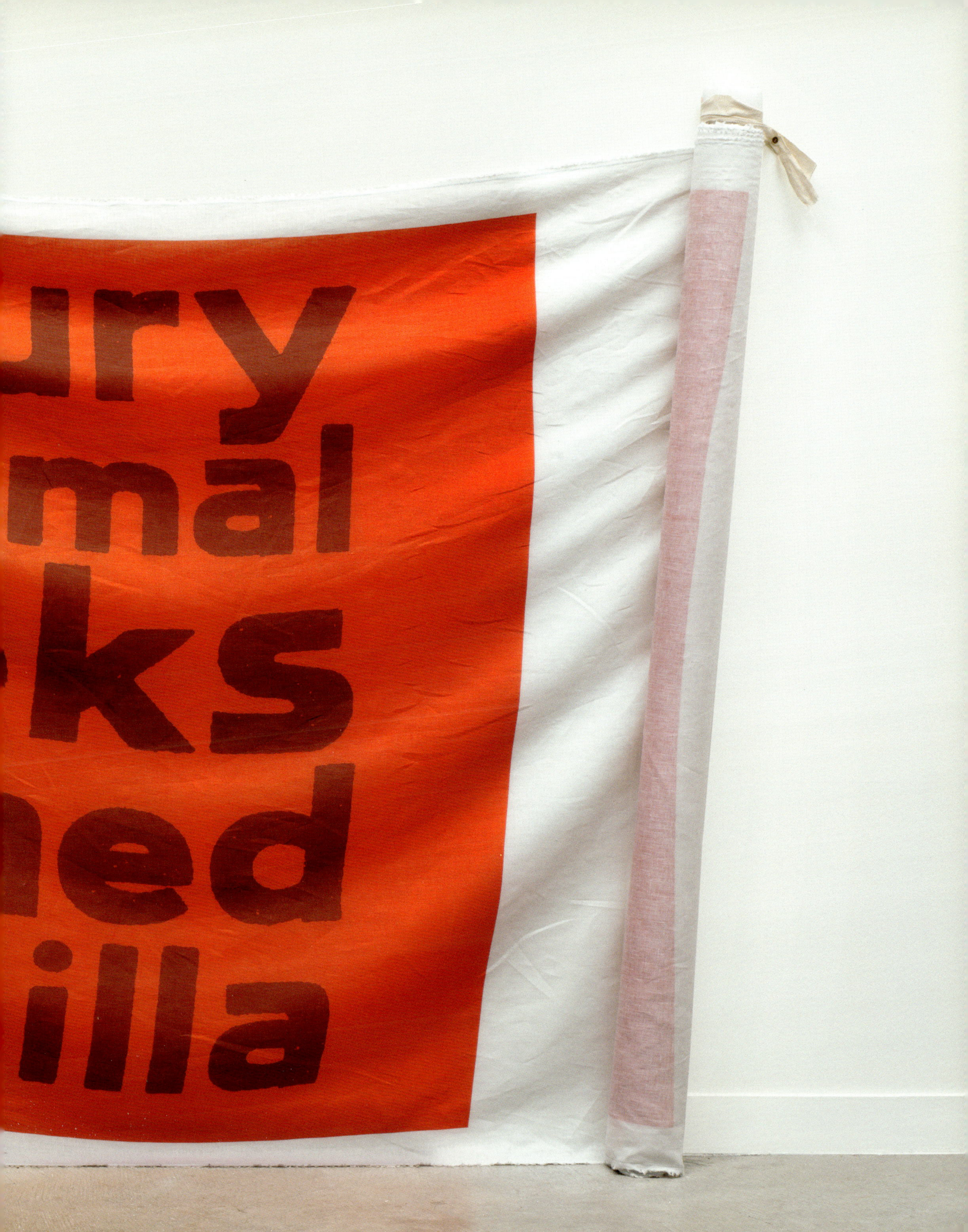
ury
mal
ks
ed
illa

as close as possible to gathering a totalizing or complete sense of dispersed social and economic relations, but only dialectically as symptom or allegory. Or as the German philosopher Theodor Adorno (1903–1969) put it, works of art are "the unconscious historiography of what is norm and what is monstrous in history."[23] The contradictions holding the social field together, a social synthesis, produce a monstrous excess. This excess operates like a repository of symptoms that cross a spectrum from critical to affirmative. Ideology is not at stake; etiology is.

Shifting labour-to-capital relationships and capital flight draw on populations in uneven ways to fuel capital's impersonal needs at any given point. Existing discourses do not, or cannot, confront the at once discursively over-determined, yet always actually occluded, fact of Aboriginal labour. Consider, then, this occlusion of the manifestly self-evident as the very platform of visibility, a kind of primitive accumulation in the field of vision that informs the economy of the image. Here, capital—frozen as image in Marxist theorist Guy Debord's famous 1967 proclamation that "value does not have its description branded on its forehead; it rather transforms every product of labour into a social hieroglyphic"[24]—is contained and set into the glossy scene of the commodity. The strangeness of the image is that this exceptionally specific commodity, *labour power*, is presented as only its product is ever presented. Labour power is the sole commodity to defy the visual economy of the commodity object; it is never seen as the things it generates—condos, townhouses, office towers—that are then offered on the market rid of any trace of production or manufacture. Claxton's gambit is to reveal primitive accumulation in the field of vision by setting workers into the honorific position of the group portrait of labour power without re-performing the exoticism and orientalism inevitably implicit in any form of framing in the society of the spectacle.

ENDNOTES

1 Caroline Levine, *Forms: Whole, Rhythm, Hierarchy, Network* (Princeton, NJ: Princeton University Press, 2015), 124. The author would like to express deepest gratitude to Katherine Eileen Neil for her research assistance.

2 Note Vancouver's inclusion in Antawan I. Byrd and Reid Shier, *Art Cities of the Future: 21st Century Avant-Gardes* (London: Phaidon, 2013). On the relationship among art, capital, and accelerated urban growth, see David Harvey, "The Art of Rent: Globalisation, Monopoly, and the Commodification of Culture." *The Socialist Register,* no. 38 (2002), 93–110. See also David Harvey, *Justice, Nature, and the Geography of Difference* (Oxford: Blackwell, 1996); and David Harvey, *The Condition of Postmodernity*, vol. 14 (Oxford: Blackwell, 1989).

3 Dana Claxton's terms, in conversation with the author.

4 Indigenous men constitute the primary labour pool to fulfill this particular skill-based demand in the feeding frenzy of construction in Vancouver, British Columbia and Canada. See Suzana Sawyer. *Crude Chronicles: Indigenous Politics, Multinational Oil, and Neoliberalism* (Durham: Duke University Press, 2004). See also *Aboriginal Ironworkers*: http://www.aboriginalironworkers.ca/sites/aboriginalironworkers/files/partners/CSC_Opportunities_e.pdf.

5 Benjamin Buchloh, Catherine David, and Jean-François Chevrier, "The Politicial Potential of Art," in *Politics-Poetics: Documenta X—The Book*, eds. Catherine David and Jean-François Chevrier (Stuttgart, Germany: Hatje Cantz, 1997), 374–403 and 624–43.

6 Agricultural workers in the Fraser River Valley or the Okanagan are frequently imported and exported on short-term notice with little in the way of a socially mandated form of organization on the part of labour. There is a growing corpus of scholarship on the recently emergent "global underclass," a demographic understood to have issued, suddenly and rapidly the world over from the seismic and profound transitions in social fabrics in many geopolitical contexts brought to bear by restructuring in the 1970s. For a classic study of earlier Indigenous labour to capital relationships in the province, see Rolf Knight, *Indians at Work: An Informal History of Native Labour in British Columbia*, 1858–1930 (Vancouver: New Star Books, 1978 and 1996). The author would like to thank Michael Turner for this invaluable reference.

7 James Surowiecki, "Real Estate Goes Global," New Yorker, May 26, 2014, https://www.newyorker.com/magazine/2014/05/26/real-estate-goes-global; Harvey, "The Art of Rent"; and Byrd and Shier, *Art Cities of the Future*.

8 Thijs Lijster, "'All Reification is Forgetting': Benjamin, Adorno, and the Dialectic of Reification," in *The Spell of Capital: Reification and Spectacle*, eds. Samir Gandesha and Johan F. Hartle (Amsterdam: Amsterdam University Press, 2016), 55–66. See also Kerstin Stakemeier and Marina Vishmidt, *Reproducing Autonomy: Work, Money, Crisis and Contemporary Art* (London: Mute, 2016). For a discussion of the Vancouver School of Photography, spearheaded by Jeff Wall, in relation to reified vision, see Benjamin H.D. Buchloh, "Readymade, Photography, and Painting in the Painting of Gerhard Richter," in *Neo-Avantgarde and Culture Industry: Essays on European and American Art from 1955 to 1975* (Cambridge: MIT Press, 2000), 365–03.

9 Aaron Benanav, "Precarity Rising," *Viewpoint*, issue 5, 2015. https://viewpointmag.com/2015/06/15/precarity-rising/; Joshua Clover and Aaron Benanav, "Can Dialectics Break BRICS?" *South Atlantic Quarterly* 113, no. 4 (Fall 2014), http://krieger.jhu.edu/arrighi/wp-content/uploads/sites/29/2014/03/Can-Dialectics-Break-BRICS_JHU.pdf, 743–59.

10 Michael Newman, "Transmission and Medium: The Economy of Photography," in *Jeff Wall: Works and Collected Writings*, ed. Michael Newman (Barcelona: Ediciones Polígrafa, 2007), 169. Newman carefully situates Wall in a long history of continuity and rupture in prevailing paradigms of pictorial construction, querying mimesis, representation and frameworks reliant on perspective. Newman's historicist-archeological project relies on Wall's own historicist-archeological project in which an interest in Manet factors heavily. Wall's writing on Manet is included in the volume. Wall identifies and admires Manet for having accomplished, in the medium of painting, the presentation of historical rupture, of the shocking newness of modernity, dialectically through historicist citation. In the same volume, which he edited, Newman includes Wall's essay "Unity and Fragmentation in Manet," where Wall notes: "The crisis is located in the interior relations of the picture, at the level of the mechanics of its concept. This level is that of the technical means by which the human figure, the human body, is established as both *painted* and *represented*...represented by means of a mechanism which inhabits it and marks its origins as modern subject: perspective."(p. 299).

11 Michael Newman. *Jeff Wall: Works and Collected Writings*. ed. Michael Newman (Barcelona: Edicions Polygrafa, 2007), 169.

12 See Michael Fried's use of the term "theatricality" with respect to nineteenth-century painting on the one hand and late twentieth century photography, notably that of Jeff Wall, on the other, in Michael Fried, *Why Photography Matters as Art as Never Before* (New Haven, CT: Yale University Press, 2008). See also his essay "Jeff Wall, Wittgenstein, and the Everyday," *Critical Inquiry* 33, no. 3 (Spring 2007): 495–526.

13 Sigmund Freud, *Jokes and Their Relation to the Unconscious*, ed. James Strachey (New York: Norton, 1960).

14 See Benjamin H.D. Buchloh, "Conceptual Art 1962–1969: From the Aesthetics of Administration to the Critique of Institutions," in *Formalism and Historicity: Models and Methods in Twentieth-Century Art* (Cambridge: MA, MIT Press, 2015).

15 Jaleh Mansoor, "Ed Ruscha's One Way Street," *October* no. 111 (Winter 2005): 127–42.

16 Tithi Bhattacharya, Introduction: "Mapping Social Reproduction Theory," *Social Reproduction Theory: Remapping Class, Recentering Oppression*, ed. Tithi Bhattacharya (London: Pluto Press, 2017), 17.

17 Levine, *Forms*, 120.

18 The only early account that does address this is Rosa Luxemburg's pioneering and ignored early work, *The Accumulation of Capital* (1913).

19 John Douglas Belshaw, *Colonization and Community: The Vancouver Island Coalfeild and the Making of the British Columbian Working Class* (Kingston, ON: McGill-Queens University Press, 2002).

20 Ann Laura Stoler, *Carnal Knowledge and Imperial Power: Race and the Intimate in Colonial Rule* (Berkeley, CA: University of California Press, 2010). See the same author's *Duress: Imperial Durabilities in Our Times* (Durham, NC: Duke University Press, 2016).

21 For a discussion of "concrete abstraction," see Sami Khatib, "'Sensuous Supra-Sensuous:' The Aesthetics of Real Abstraction," in *Aesthetic Marx*, eds. Samir Gandesha and Johan F. Hartle (London: Bloomsbury Press, 2017), 49–72.

22 Marina Vishmidt, "Human Capital or Toxic Asset: After the Wage," *Mute*, January 10, 2010, http://www.metamute.org/community/your-posts/human-capital-or-toxic-asset-after-wage. See also Bue Rübner Hansen, "Surplus Population, Social Reproduction, and the Problem of Class Formation," *Viewpoint*, October 31, 2015, https://viewpointmag.com/2015/10/31/surplus-population-social-reproduction-and-the-problem-of-class-formation/.

23 Theodor Adorno, *In Search of Wagner*, trans. Rodney Livingstone (London: Verso, 2009).

24 As elaborated on in Alfred Sohn-Rethel, "Analysis of the Exchange Abstraction," in *Intellectual and Manual Labour: A Critique of Epistemology* (London: MacMillan, 1978), 49.

Blue Headdress (from *Indian Candy*), 2013

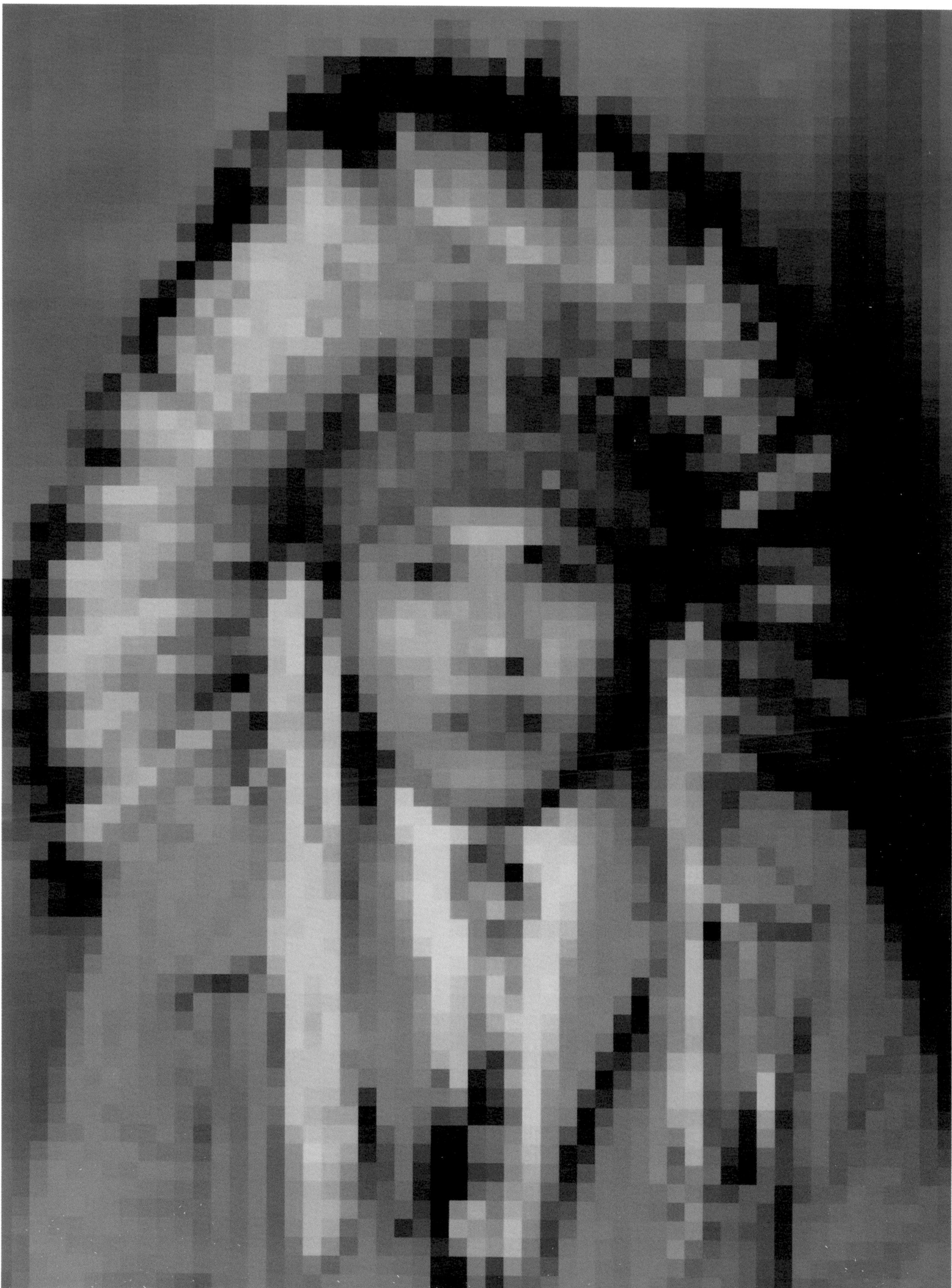

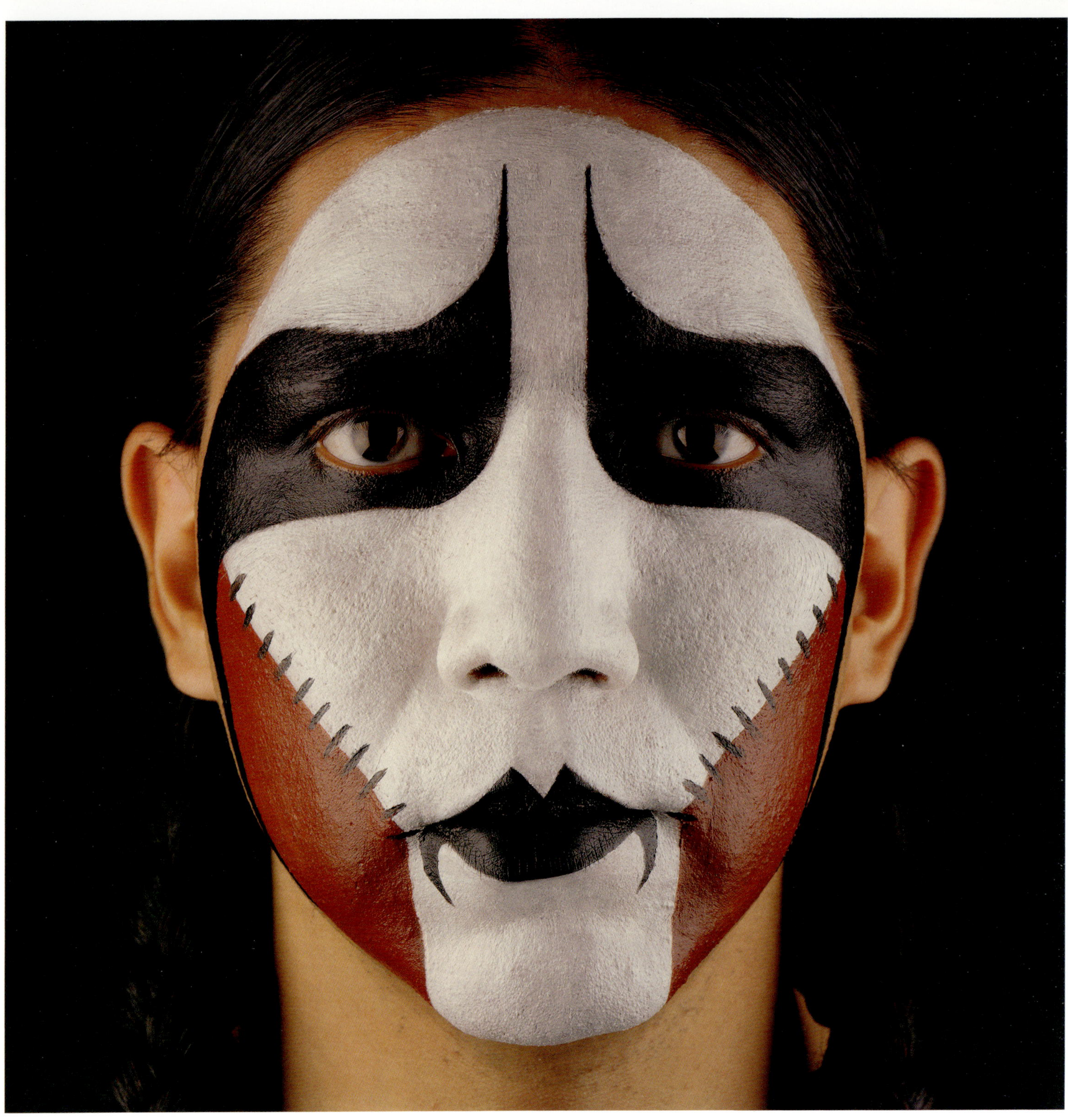

Paint Up #1, 2009

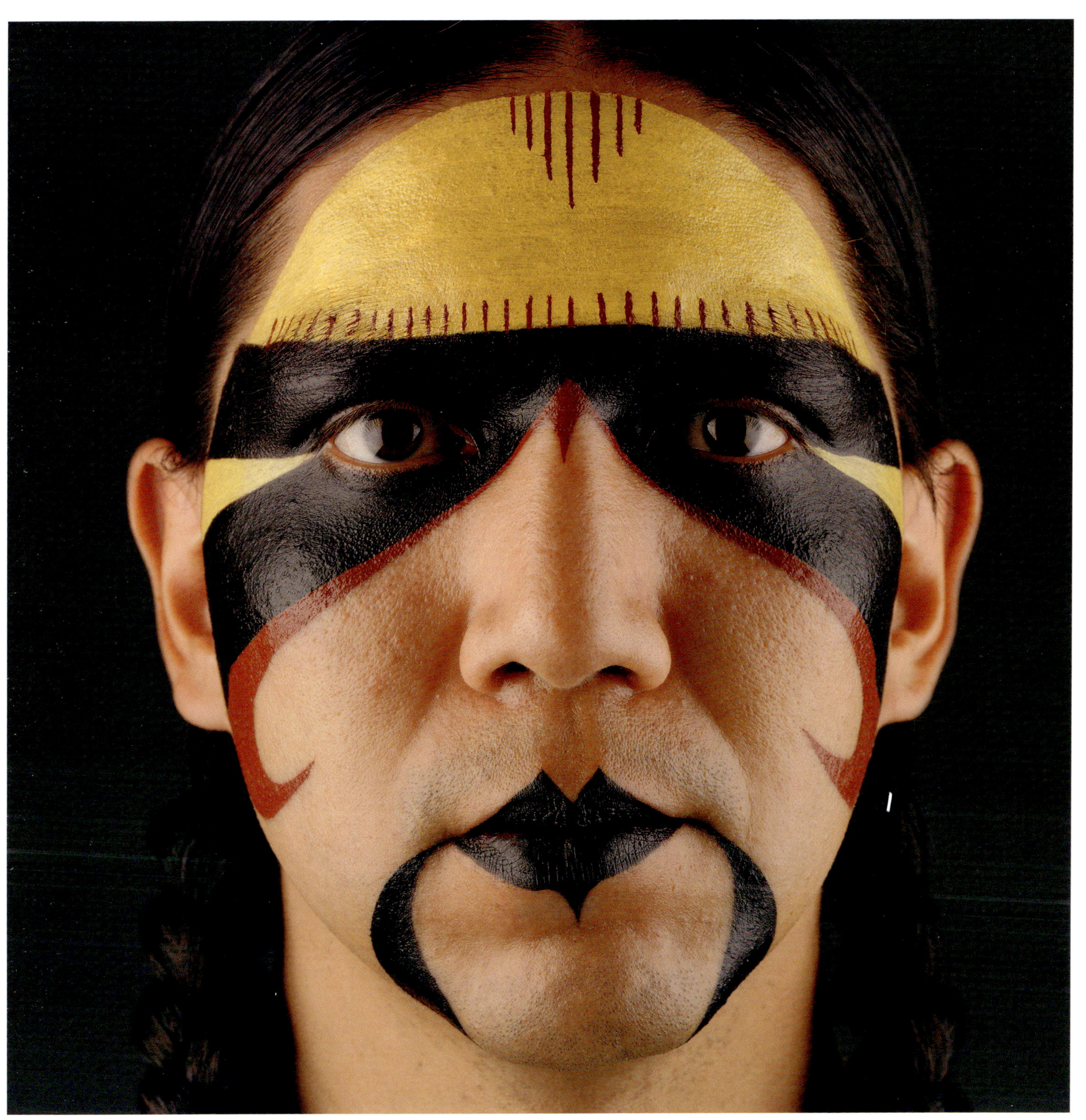

Paint Up #2, 2009

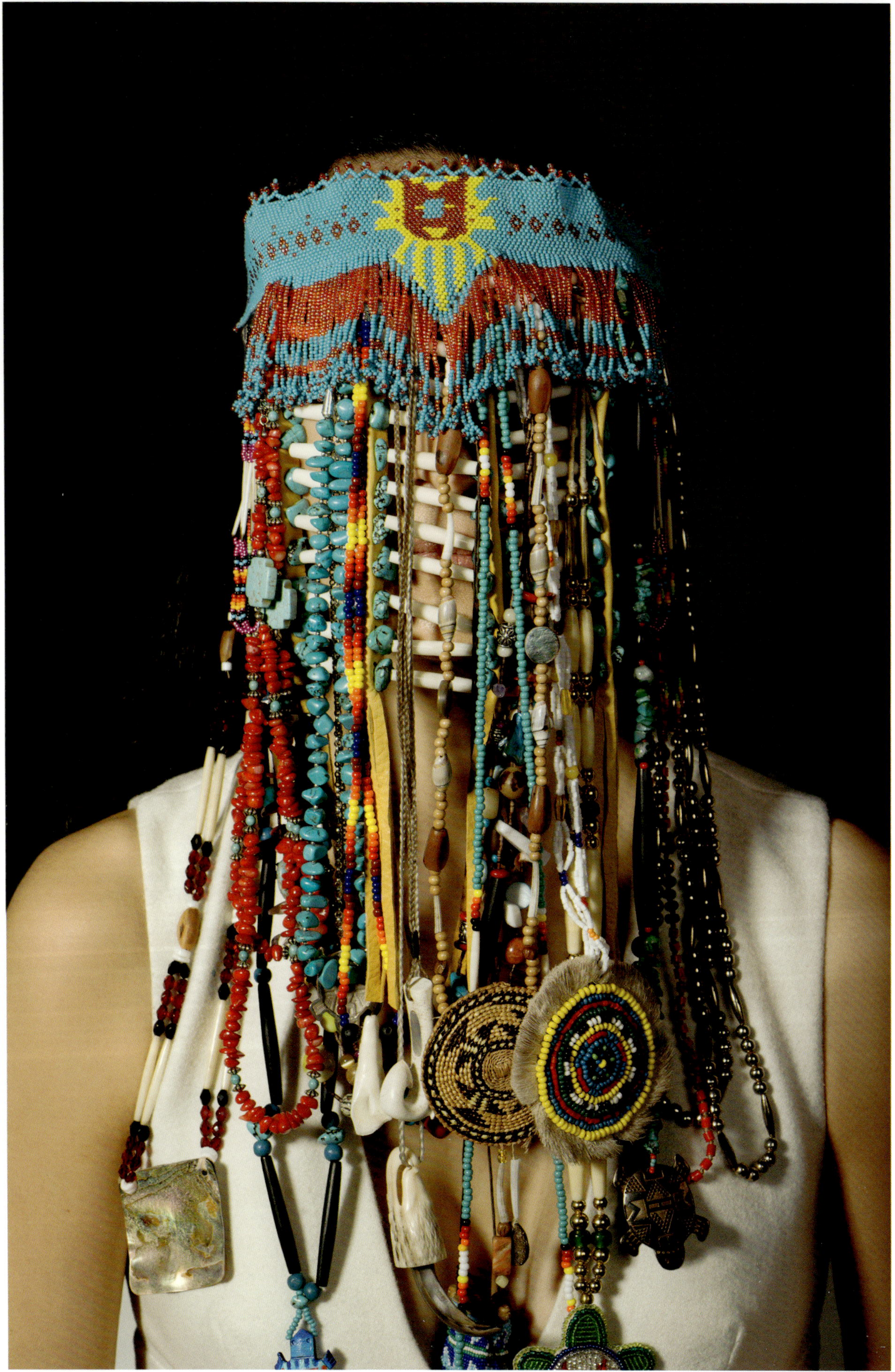

Headdress, 2015

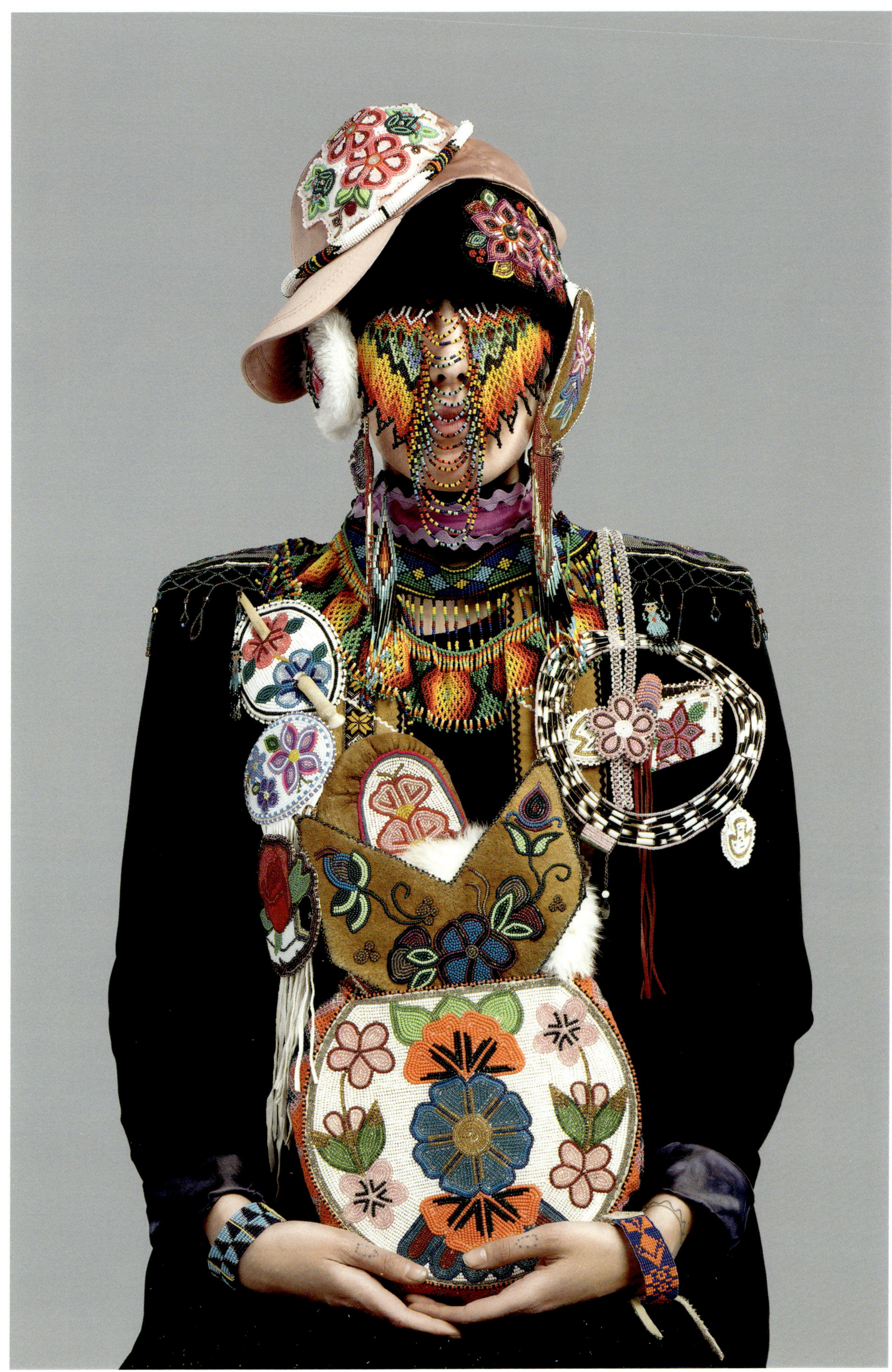

Headdress—Jeneen, 2018

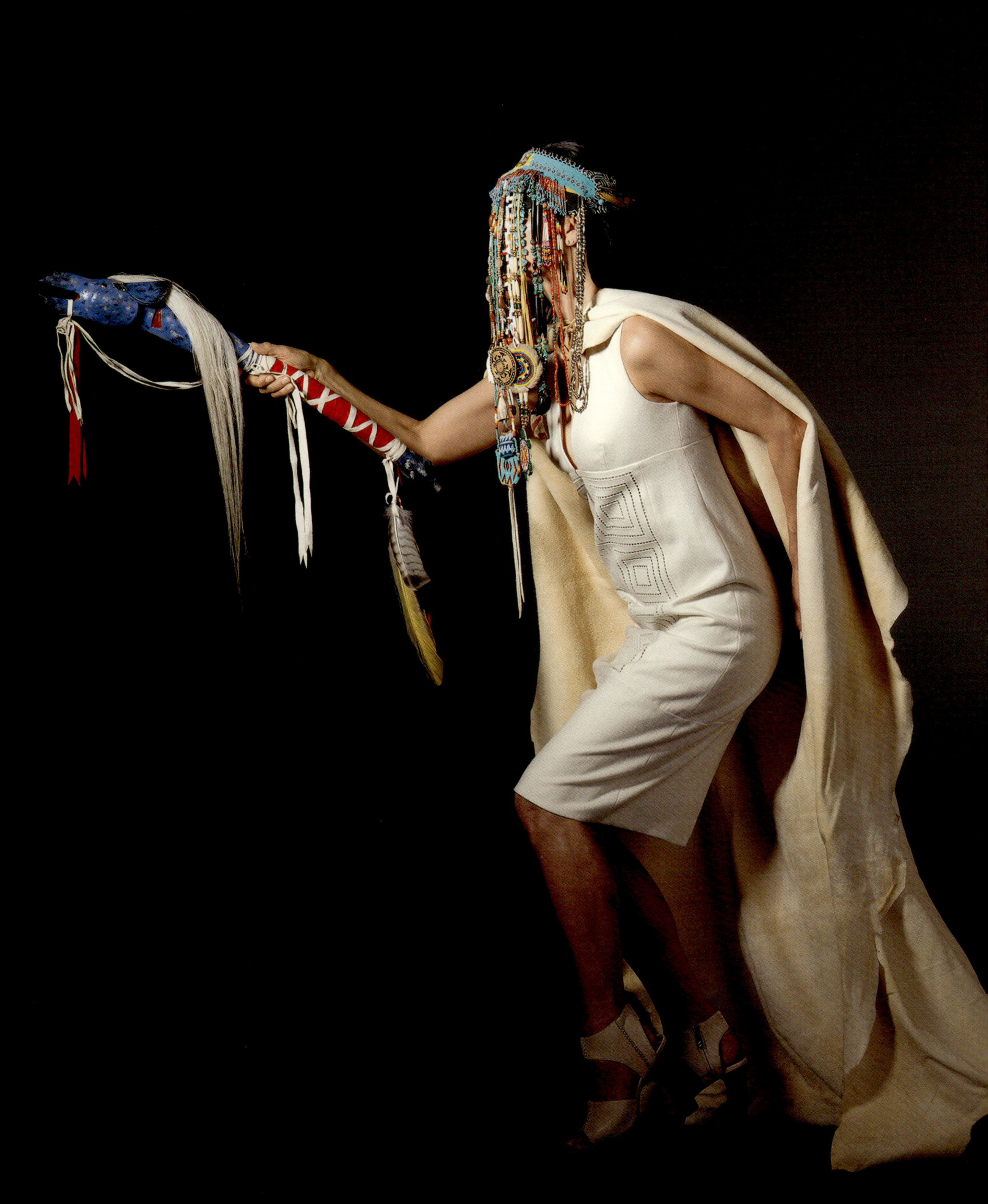

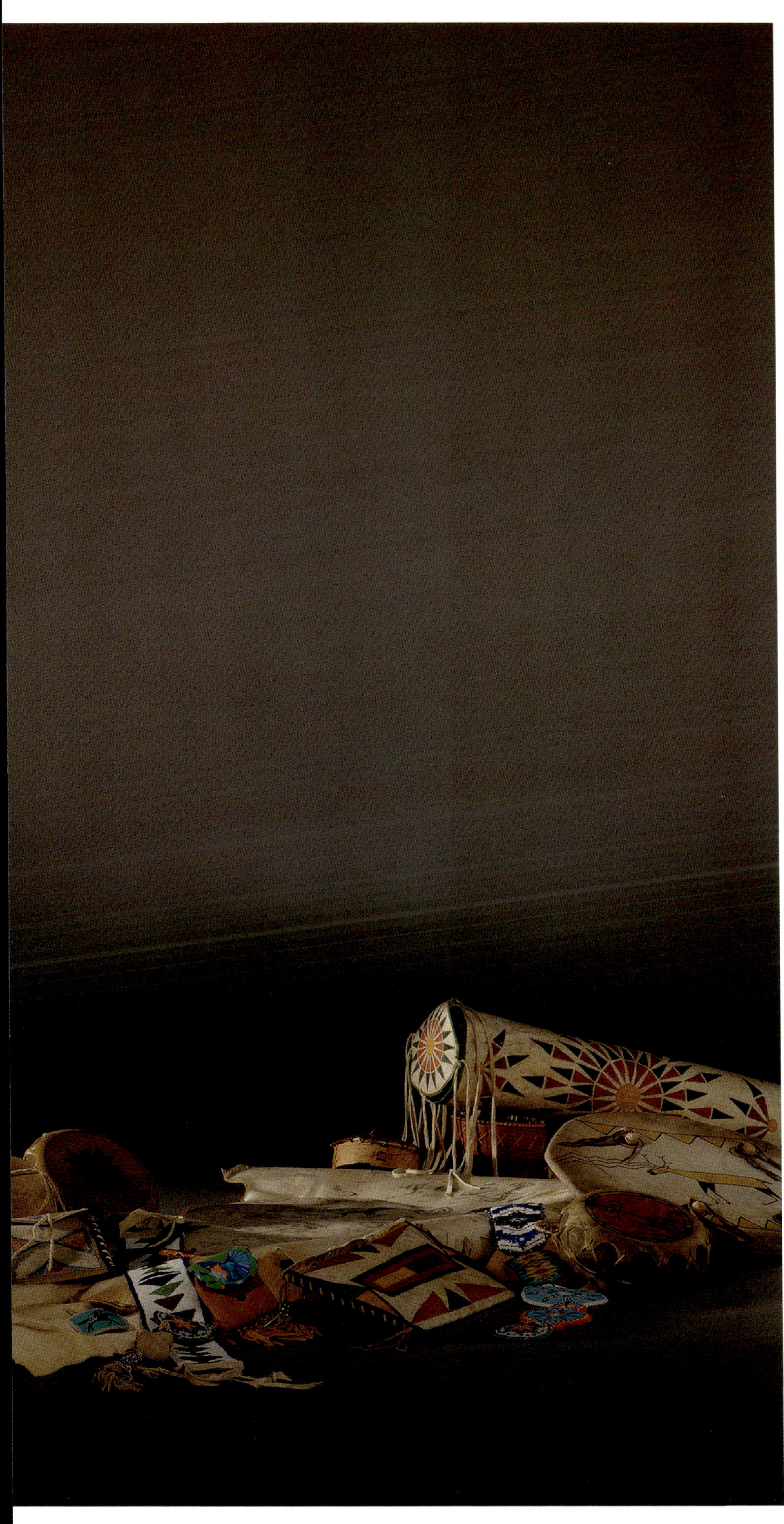

Cultural Belongings, 2016

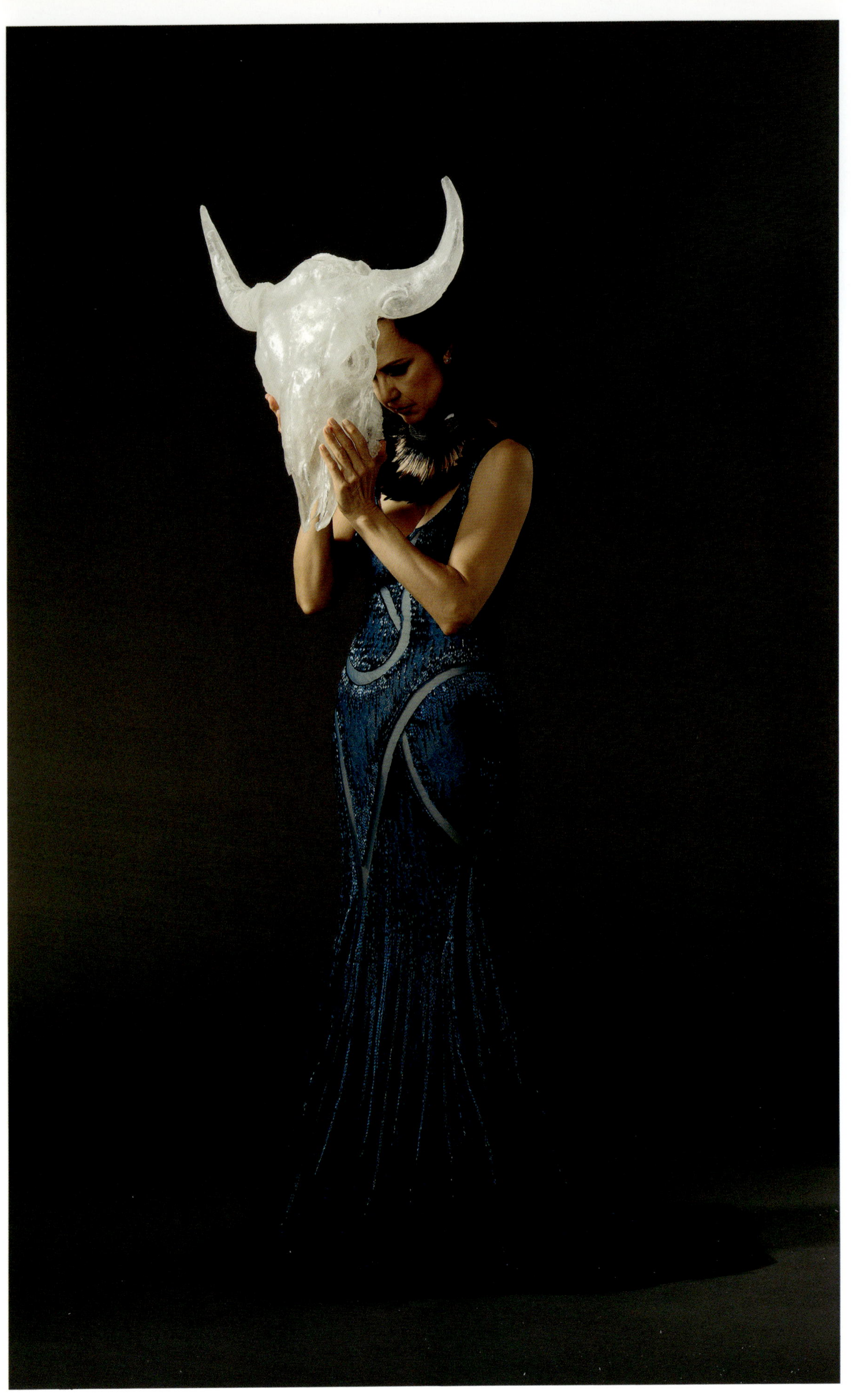

Buffalo Woman 1, 2016 (with Skull by Kevin McKenzie)

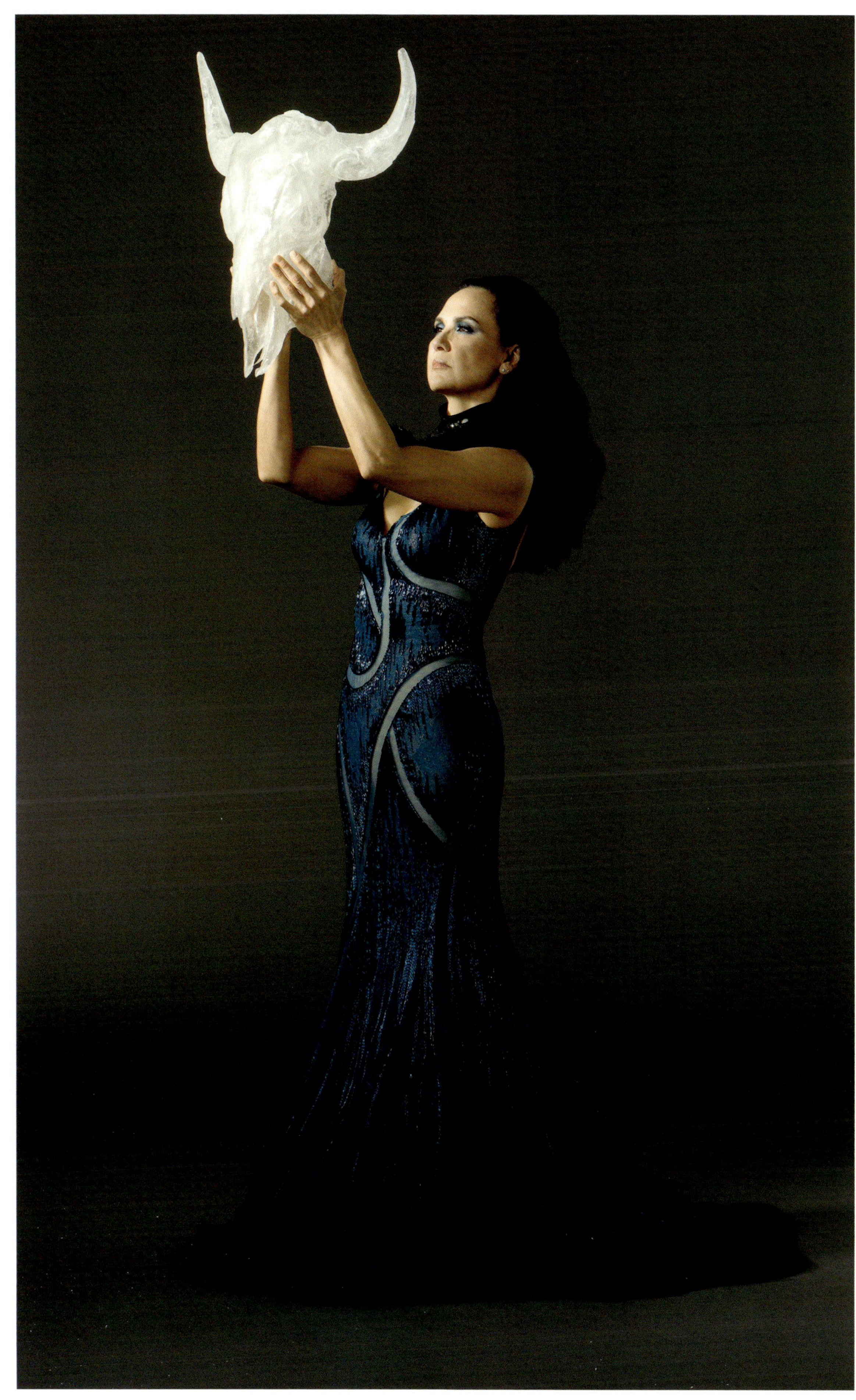

Buffalo Woman 2, 2016 (with Skull by Kevin McKenzie)

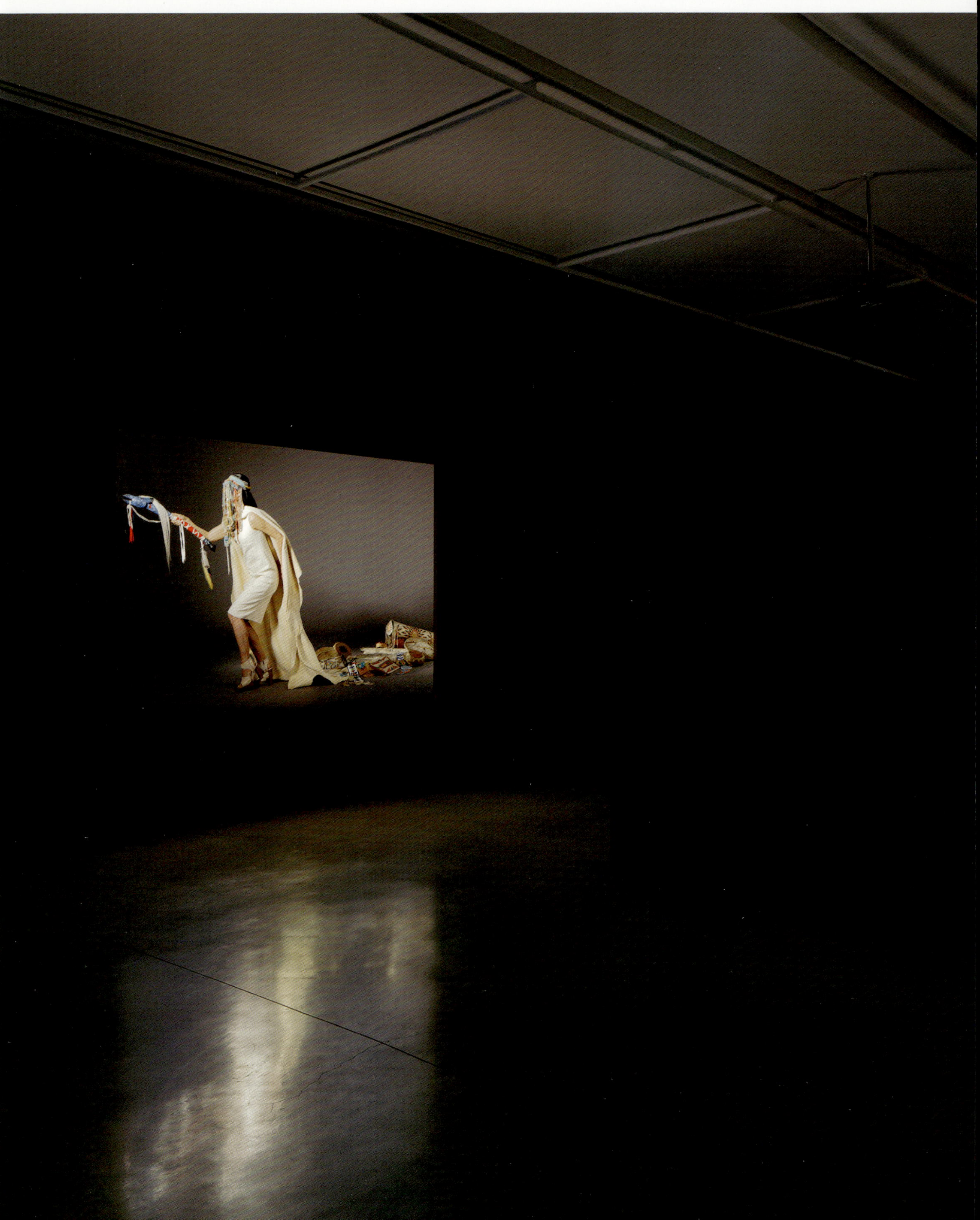

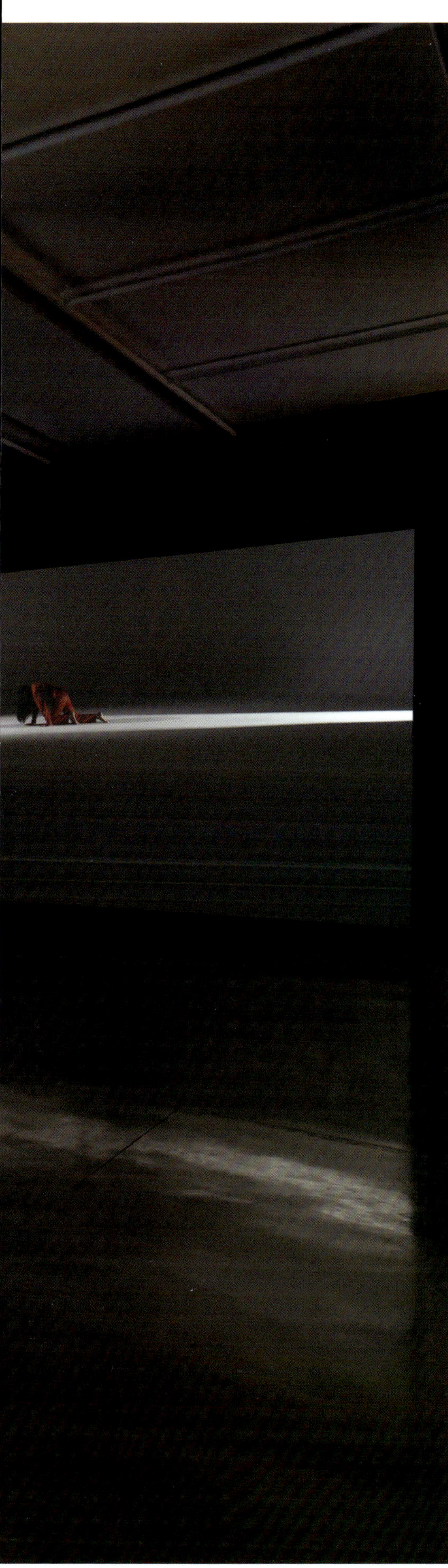

CHRONOLOGY

SIOBHAN M^c^CRACKEN NIXON

1877

Dana Claxton's maternal great-grandparents Kangi Tamaheca and Anpetu Wastewin (Good Day Woman) and their young daughter, Ayuta Najin Ktewin (Kills the Enemy that Stood Standing Woman), walk with Sitting Bull and thousands of the Hunkpapa Lakota Nation to Canada/Saskatchewan, following the defeat of General Custer of the United States Army at the Battle of Little Bighorn on June 25, 1876. The battle is commonly known as Custer's Last Stand.

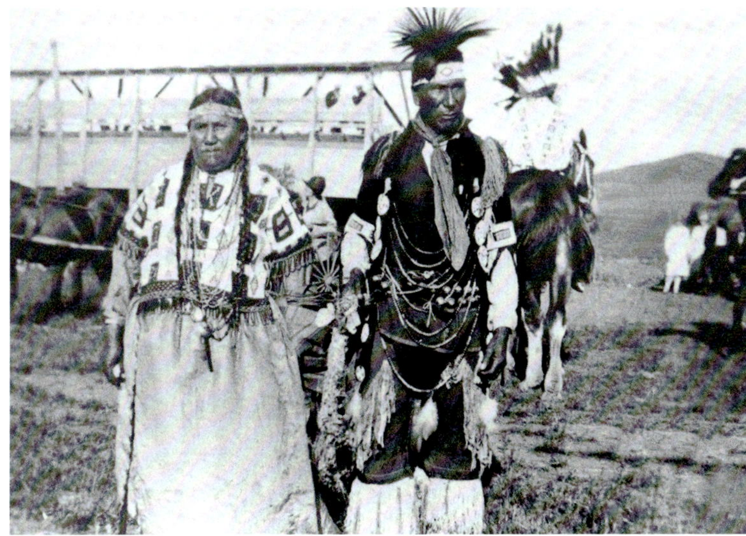

1882

While Sitting Bull eventually returned to the United States in 1881, an estimated one hundred-fifty Hunkpapa Lakota permanently settled in Saskatchewan. By 1882, an estimated one hundred lodges had been set up in Moose Jaw River Valley in the area of The Turn also known as The Sioux Camp.

OPPOSITE: *Dana Claxton: Made to be Ready*, 2016, exhibition at the Audain Gallery, Simon Fraser University, Vancouver
ABOVE: Claxton's great-grandparents, Kangi Tamaheca and Anpetu Wastewin (Good Day Woman), 1882

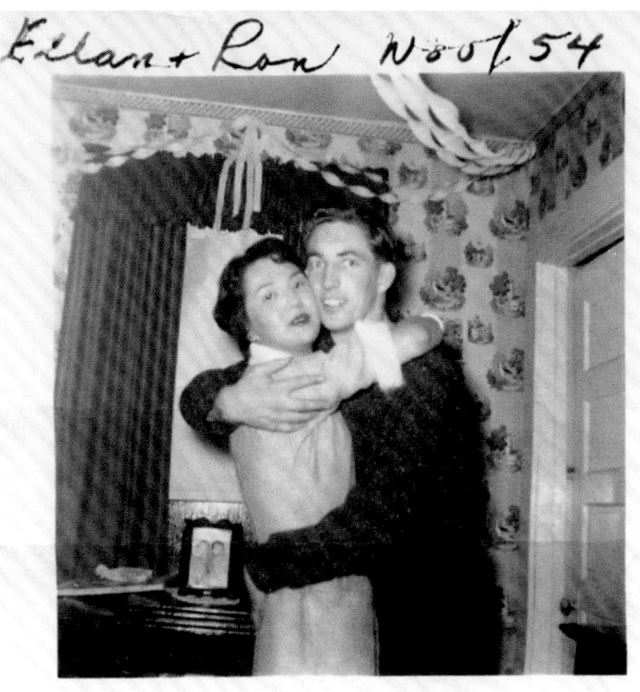

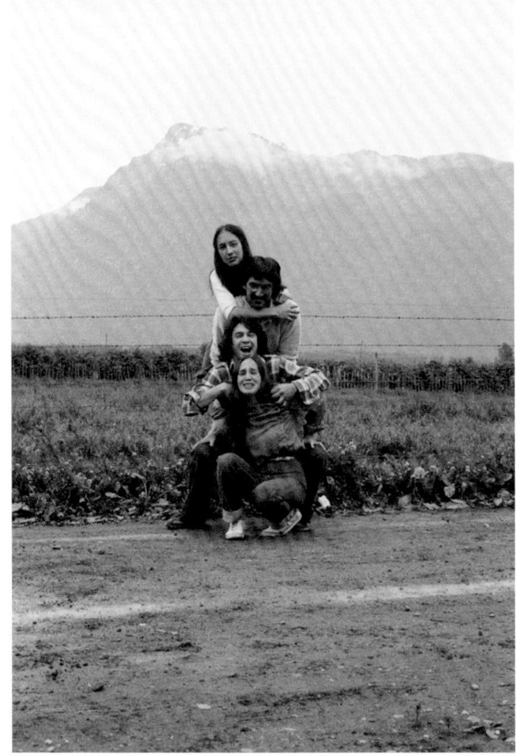

Claxton's great-grandmother Ayuta Najin Ktewin marries Oye Waste (Walks a Good Way) near Regina, Saskatchewan. Ayuta Najin Ktewin becomes known as Susan and the couple take the surname Goodtrack—which reflects Walks a Good Way.

1910–11

The Sioux encampment at Moose Jaw River Valley begins to break up as the Lakota request land to be set aside for permanent settlement. The reservation of Wood Mountain, the only Lakota Sioux reserve in Canada, is established. However, it is not until 1930 that the Wood Mountain Reserve is formally and permanently recognized by an Order-in-Council by the Canadian government. Claxton's great-grandfather is a signatory on the land agreement.

Claxton's grandmother, Pearl Goodtrack, is one of four children born in Wood Mountain. She marries Charlie Soo, a businessman of Chinese descent who owns a number of small hotels and restaurants in the Wood Mountain area.

1934

Claxton's mother, Ellen (Ella) Soo (Goodtrack), one of Pearl and Charlie's five children, is born.

1955

Ella/Ellen Soo (Goodtrack) marries Ron Claxton.

1959

Claxton is born in the small city of Yorkton, Saskatchewan. She is the youngest of four children. She grows up in Moose Jaw, Saskatchewan, and her family reserve is Wood Mountain Lakota First Nation. She spends summers in her Euro-Canadian father's hometown of Wadena with her grandmother Gladys Claxton. Of her mixed heritage the artist has remarked: "I'm influenced by my own experience as a Lakota woman, as a Canadian, a mixed-blood Canadian, and then my own relationship to the natural and supernatural world." Claxton learned how to preserve and harvest food from her paternal Euro-Canadian grandmother while she was taught to seek justice by her maternal Lakota grandmother.[1]

1970–80

Claxton lives in Moose Jaw, Saskatchewan; Williams Lake, British Columbia; Wadena, Saskatchewan; Mississauga, Ontario; Penticton, British Columbia; Rosedale, British Columbia; New Westminster, British Columbia.

ABOVE LEFT: Claxton's parents, Ellen (Ella) Soo (Goodtrack) and Ron Claxton, 1954
ABOVE RIGHT: Claxton (top) and her siblings Don, Ron and Kim, 1959

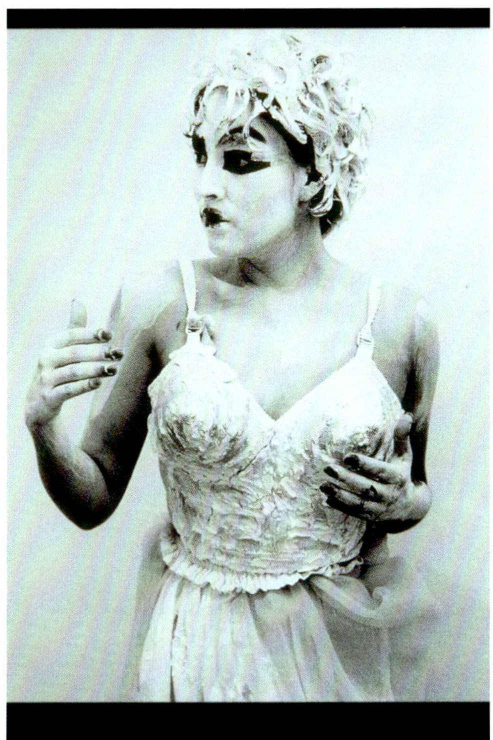

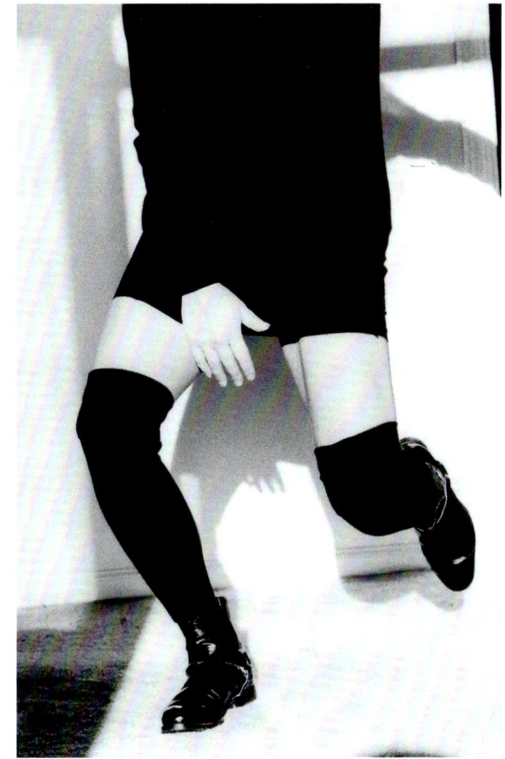

1975

Claxton obtains her first camera at the age of sixteen.

Early 1980s

Claxton observes the punk and underground art scene in Vancouver, British Columbia. She sees such acts as Tunnel Canary and AKA and attends many *Rock Against...* events.

Mid-1980s

The artist moves to Vancouver and studies theatre and arts administration at the Spirit Song Native Indian Theatre Company. Spirit Song formed in the 1980s as a training program for urban youth who had creative inclinations. Though this early experience would greatly influence the artist, the world of theatre was not entirely her place as she was drawn to more experimental forms of expression such as performance art and video. Around this time Claxton also writes an occasional fashion column, works as an art director on photo shoots and sells advertising for the Vancouver weekly newspaper *The Georgia Straight*. The artist's foray into the media also includes video training with Shelokum Television Society, founded by Larry Guno and Matthew Stewart. Claxton recalls: "In 1984, we had a show on Cable 4 here in Vancouver. We called it *The Canadian Indian Television News*. We basically tried to emulate mainstream news to talk about Indian news because we didn't see ourselves on mainstream television. We still don't see ourselves on mainstream news. There hasn't been a drastic change."[2] Claxton also works for *Kahtou*, a First Nations newspaper.

1987

Claxton performs for the first time as one of five performers in Naomi Martin's *Woman/Performance* at Artropolis' inaugural exhibition of 1987. Taking place at 788 Beatty Street, Artropolis strived to feature the works of contemporary British Columbian artists in non-traditional exhibition spaces; it took place every few years at multiple venues until 2003.

Late 1980s and early 1990s

In the late 1980s Claxton moves to the city of New York, where she lives and works for three years. The artist has commented, "I also have an interest in fashion and glamour, and purposely wanted to make Indian people glamorous. In the late 1980s I worked for *Details*, a New York–based fashion and art magazine. All of this experience comes together in the photographs. There is also a real element of the surreal. I have this innate connection with the

ABOVE LEFT: Claxton performing at Artropolis, Vancouver, 1987
ABOVE RIGHT: *Untitled*, 1991

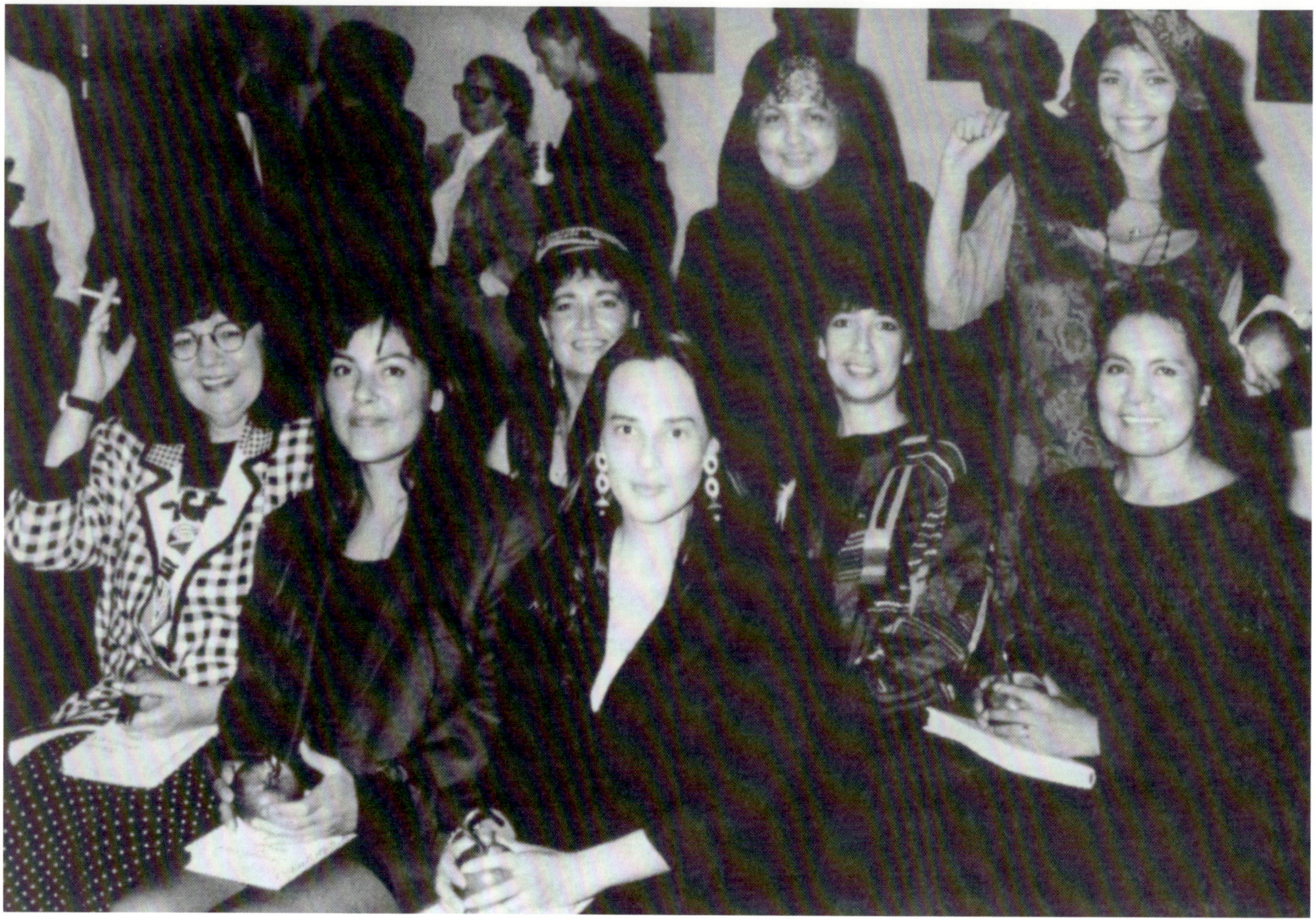

PITT GALLERY

A CENTRE FOR CONTEMPORARY MULTIDISCIPLINARY PERFORMANCE AND EXHIBITIONS

NEO-NATIVISTS

A LABORATORY OF CONTEMPORARY NATIVE ART

PRESS RELEASE **FOR IMMEDIATE RELEASE**

Once upon a time the Indians danced. Then one day a young urban Indian felt like creatively expressing himself thru multi-media-interdisciplinary performance.
He combined narration with music, video, sound and war paint.
He knew an Indian woman who created mixed media installations.
She knew an Indian poet who rhymed.
And the poet knew an Indian filmmaker.
All these Indians created great works of art which they offered to the world.
They, like their relations before them want to share their visions and tell their stories. And isn't it nice to know that they can legally share their culture. And should they want to perform the Ghost dance - they can. And should they want to hold a potlatch - they can.
Opening Monday, October 14th and 9:00pm at the Pitt Gallery - Neo-Nativiist will exhibit a mix of contemporary Native art and performance.
Teresa Macphee presents "Monopoly" a mixed media installation in the White Gallery.
Kim Soo Goodtrack will exhibit her recent water colour/India ink abstract landscapes titled "You're not Indian enough, You're too Indian, You're the wrong kind of Indian, There's no category for you" in the downstairs Black Gallery.
Rick Harry and Leonard Fisher will construct a homage to Oka installation in the performance space.
The performance series begins on Saturday, October 19, 9:00pm with Dana Claxton's multi-media poetry reading - "10 Little Poems."
Donald Morin will perform a work in progress - "Indians and Dogs" on Saturday, October 26.
Lee Maracle and Columpa Bobb give a reading performance on Saturday November 2.
Archer Pechawis presents a work in progress on Wednesday, November 6th.
Donald Ghoskeeper wraps the series up with a reading performance on Saturday, November 9th.
Doors open at 8:30pm. All performances are at 9:00pm - tickets $5 a scalp.
For additional press information call Dana Claxton 874-3464.

36 POWELL STREET VANCOUVER CANADA V6A 1E7
(604) 681.6740

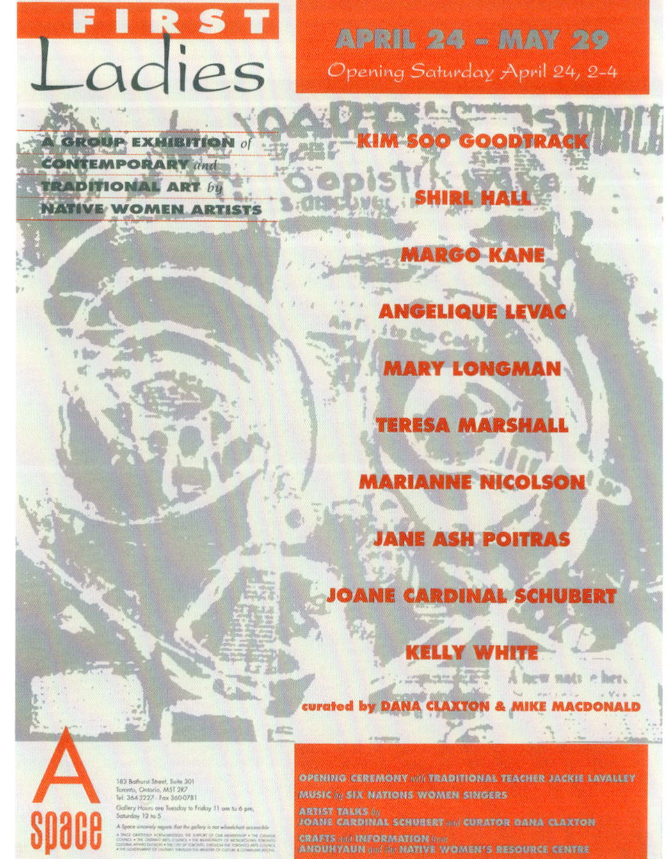

unreal—it is an Indigenous thing—the seen and the unseen supernatural in the Indian world."[3]

Alongside her magazine work, Claxton writes plays that are later turned into short films. She studies with Herbert Berghof and Uta Hagen at the HB Studio to refine her directorial skills. She also studies American Lakota Sioux history at the New York Public library, where she encounters microfiche copies of hundreds of declassified FBI documents regarding the American Indian Movement (AIM). These images would later be used in her *AIM* series in 2010. The artist recalls: "I had a great time in New York ... it brought together my creative interest, my intellectual and political interests, but also my spiritual practice. Everything sort of came together there for me..."[4]

1990

In 1990, the Oka Crisis, a land dispute in Oka, Québec, between Mohawk protesters, the Québec provincial police and the Canadian army, lasts seventy-eight days and involves one fatality and hundreds of injuries. The dispute was related to the expansion of a private golf course and condominium development onto Indigenous land that included a sacred burial ground. It is covered extensively in the media. The crisis prompts Claxton to want to foster change in Canadian society and to engage the world through the arts: "I realized there was much work to be done... Aboriginal and non-Aboriginal communities were not communicating with each other. I asked myself, how could I facilitate this huge gap, in a meaningful way?"[5] Following the Oka Crisis, Claxton works at the Pitt Gallery in Vancouver during the 1990s. She recalls: "In the early 1990s, I was thrust into the role of curator. I didn't know what a curator was! My intention was to bring contemporary Aboriginal art into the gallery space. And then it became a larger conversation of identity politics, and cultural parity."[6]

1991

From a young age Claxton was drawn to the moving image—be it film, television or music shows. The artist recalls being inspired by the enormous, cinematic scale of the Saskatchewan sky, and felt the desire to be a filmmaker from an early age.

It is not until the age of thirty-one that Claxton picks up her first film camera, a Super 8 mm bought at a thrift store for $19.95. During a trip back home to Saskatchewan, Claxton makes her first work: "The first film I ever made was called *Grant Her Restitution*, and it was just my sister and myself driving home to Saskatchewan. It was just images, no narration. I was always drawn to media but it took a while for all of the elements to come together."[7]

Claxton creates a self-portrait series that she calls the "crotch shots" that demonstrates her early interest in the female body and feminism.

As a board member of the Pitt Gallery, she curates the group exhibition *Neo-Nativists*, a visual art and poetry/performance event. A published poet who often writes Life Poems when someone goes to the spirit world, Claxton performs *10 Little Poems*—her first performance and multimedia-based work.

PERFORMANCES

10 Little Poems, as part of the exhibition *Neo-Nativists*, Pitt Gallery, Vancouver, BC

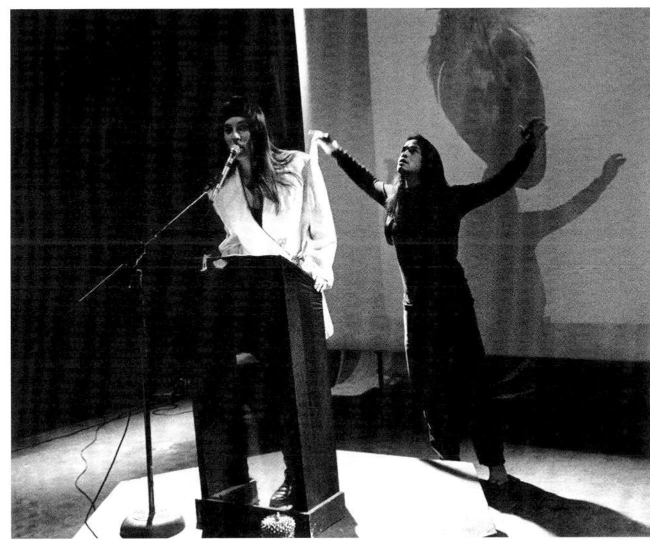

1992

Claxton becomes director of the Pitt Gallery and curates her second exhibition, *First Ladies,* which features the work of contemporary female Aboriginal artists. A star quilt by Kelly White and a birch bark biting by Angelique Merasty Levac are among the works she includes in the exhibition. The artist recollects: "It never occurred to me either prior to or during these exhibitions to really analyze what I was doing. We, as Indian women and people, were engaged in a process of articulating our own culture, our own history, as well as selecting and exhibiting what we wanted to."[8]

OPPOSITE: Claxton at the Pitt Gallery, Vancouver, 1990 ABOVE: Claxton reading *10 Little Poems* at the Pitt Gallery, Vancouver, 1991

Curation, performance, video and teaching all become important elements in Claxton's multifaceted practice: "So taking that whole bundle of experiences, it all goes into the artwork; I think that's where the multi-layering comes in because I've had a very multi-layered life. And it's all those experiences that go into the work."[9]

Claxton attends the Beyond Survival Conference in Ottawa, which brings together Indigenous artists and scholars from the Americas. She meets her relative, the renowned Lakota anthropologist Dr. Bea Medicine at the conference and spends the next thirteen years being with her.

Claxton directs her first 16 mm film, *The Red Paper*, featuring Sam Bob and Samaya Jardey.

PERFORMANCES

Tree of Consumption, grunt gallery, Vancouver, BC

1993

In the video work *Tree of Consumption*, colonialism and the treatment of women emerge as key themes in her oeuvre. The work draws a parallel between the treatment of the earth and the treatment of women through the destructive legacy of colonialism. The work depicts a woman standing amongst a devastated forest. The artist utilizes low-end video production values to produce deteriorated images that mirror the work's thematic content—splicing and manipulating images until the forest and woman dissolve and blur. Early nineties music videos very much influence the aesthetic of the artist's early single-channel works through "their use of technology, fast paced editing and pushing the genre forward, backwards, inside out."[10] Video as a whole opens up new possibilities to the artist as a relatively inexpensive, mobile and experimental medium.

Claxton begins to attend the Sitting Bull Sundance at Standing Rock, South Dakota, under the tutelage of Joe Flying Bye, Issac Dog Eagle, Bea Medicine and Sissy Goodhouse.

She travels with the Canadian Labour Congress to direct *Join the CSA*, an industrial video for a union membership drive in Dominica.

Claxton sits on the first of dozens of juries for municipal, provincial, federal and private agencies. The first is the National Aboriginal Foundation in Toronto, founded by Mohawk symphony conductor John Kim Bell.

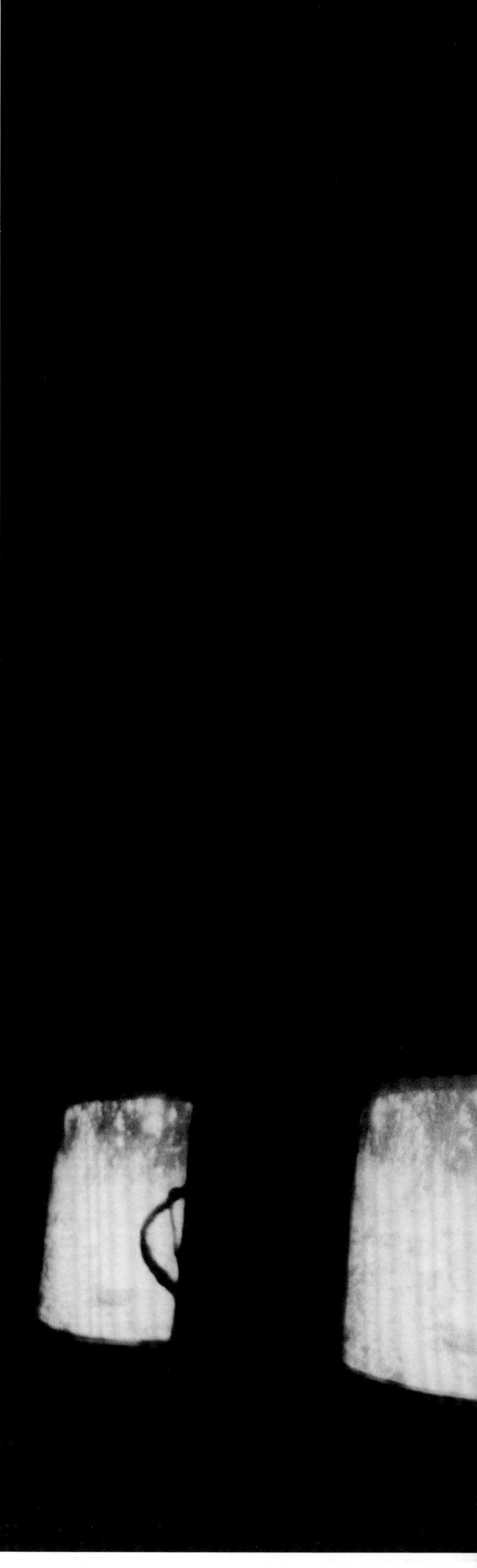

Tree of Consumption, 1992 (documentation of performance from the *First Nations Performance* series, grunt gallery, Vancouver, September 10–20, 1992)

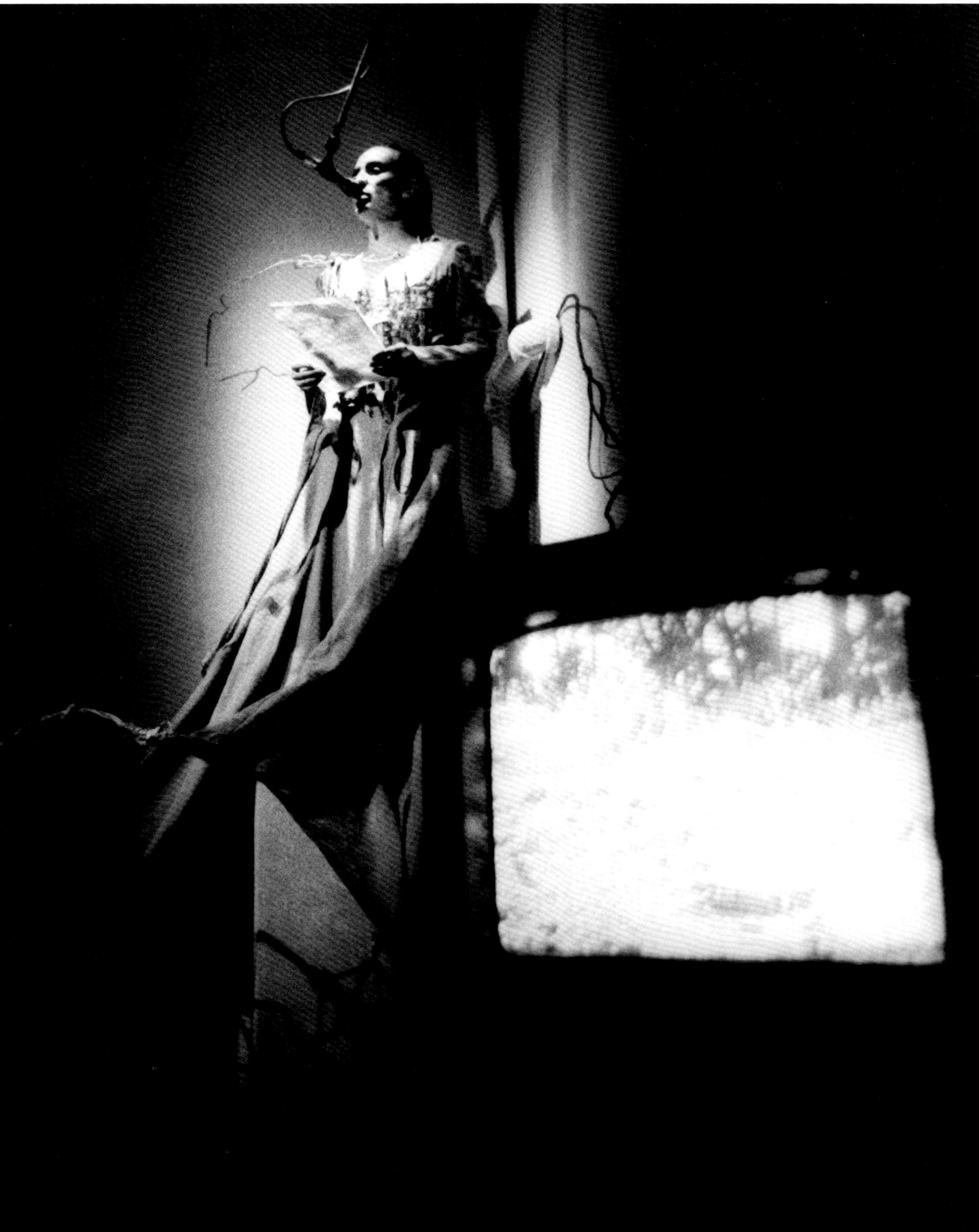

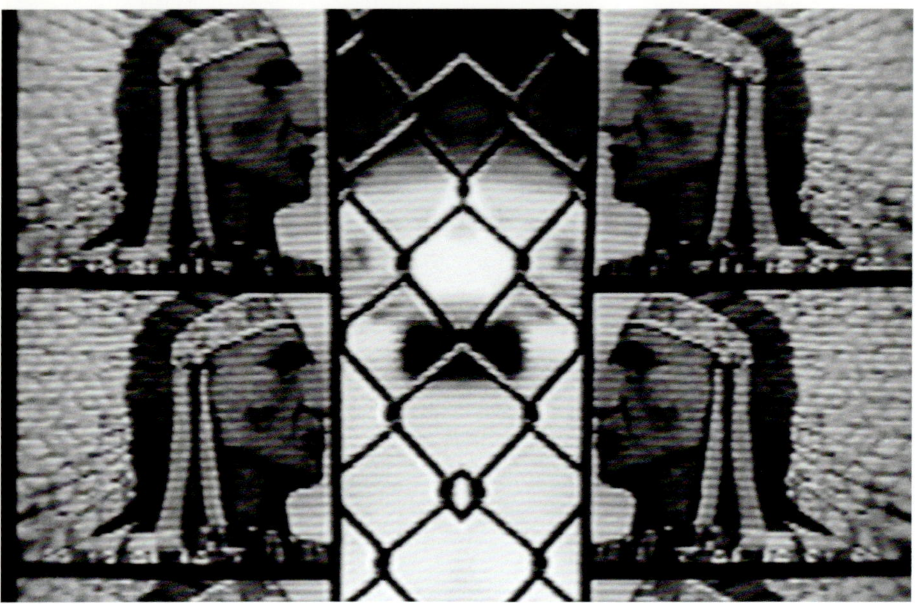

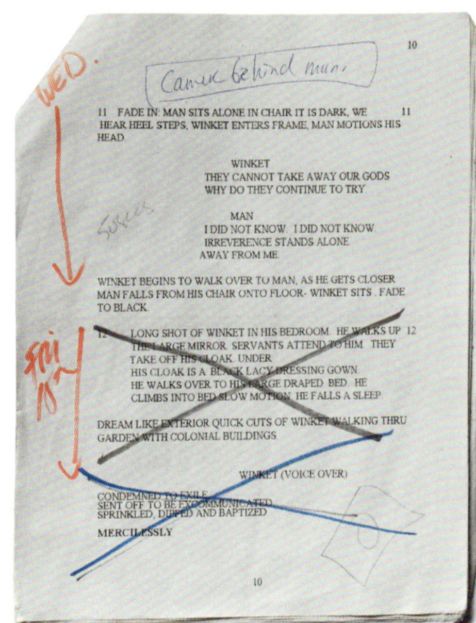

10

11 FADE IN: MAN SITS ALONE IN CHAIR IT IS DARK, WE HEAR HEEL STEPS, WINKET ENTERS FRAME, MAN MOTIONS HIS HEAD. 11

WINKET
THEY CANNOT TAKE AWAY OUR GODS
WHY DO THEY CONTINUE TO TRY

MAN
I DID NOT KNOW. I DID NOT KNOW
IRREVERENCE STANDS ALONE
AWAY FROM ME

WINKET BEGINS TO WALK OVER TO MAN, AS HE GETS CLOSER MAN FALLS FROM HIS CHAIR ONTO FLOOR- WINKET SITS . FADE TO BLACK

12 LONG SHOT OF WINKET IN HIS BEDROOM. HE WALKS UP THE LARGE MIRROR. SERVANTS ATTEND TO HIM. THEY TAKE OFF HIS CLOAK. UNDER 12
HIS CLOAK IS A BLACK LACY DRESSING GOWN.
HE WALKS OVER TO HIS LARGE DRAPED BED. HE CLIMBS INTO BED SLOW MOTION. HE FALLS A SLEEP

DREAM LIKE EXTERIOR QUICK CUTS OF WINKET WALKING THRU GARDEN WITH COLONIAL BUILDINGS.

WINKET (VOICE OVER)

CONDEMNED TO EXILE
SENT OFF TO BE EXCOMMUNICATED
SPRINKLED, DIPPED AND BAPTIZED

MERCILESSLY

10

1994

Claxton's video work, *I Want to Know Why*, examines the lasting impact of colonialism within a very personal framework. The artist continues to formally experiment with the specific character of video itself, splicing together archival imagery and personal testimony in a quickly paced format that emulates nineties music videos and powerfully threads the past into the present. As Western images of First Nations culture are interwoven with her own family history, Claxton recounts in voice-over the early deaths of her mother and grandmother and demands "I want to know why."

A new element in this work is the addition of a soundtrack by Salish artist Russell Wallace, fellow alumnus of Spirit Song Theatre. Wallace's music will play an important role in a number of Claxton's video works.

PERFORMANCES

SA – (work in progress), Western Front, Vancouver, BC

EXHIBITIONS

Walking with the Ancients, Museum of Modern Art, New York, NY

Racing Thru Space, Artspeak Gallery, Vancouver, BC

1995

I Want to Know Why is broadcast on the Women's Television Network.

1996

Claxton releases *The Red Paper*, which began as a theatre script, recalling her theatre roots. Instead it is made into a black and white film, though the work retains characteristics of theatre in its staging, pace and presentation. This is Claxton's first 16 mm film. In contrast to previous video works which used montage, repetition and image manipulation, Claxton presents a work that combines theatrical realism with a costume drama. As a result the work oscillates between a period film, art installation and theatre play. *The Red Paper* features a cast that is almost entirely Indigenous, the exceptions are two Caucasian actors who embody the "essence" of a European male and female. The work consists of a series of vignettes which play off of traditions of Shakespearean drama. Claxton employs role reversal as her First Nations actors take on the central role and tell of the arrival of the barbaric European settlers and the brutal impact of their colonialism. As a whole the work has an air of parody due to its staged look, which plays against the sombre subject matter. However, as with previous work, Claxton uses the historical to suggest the lingering presence of colonialism. The title *The Red Paper* is an inversion of the Pierre Trudeau administration's 1969 White Paper on the federal

 ABOVE LEFT: *I Want to Know Why*, 1994 (video still) ABOVE RIGHT: Script for *The Red Paper*, 1996

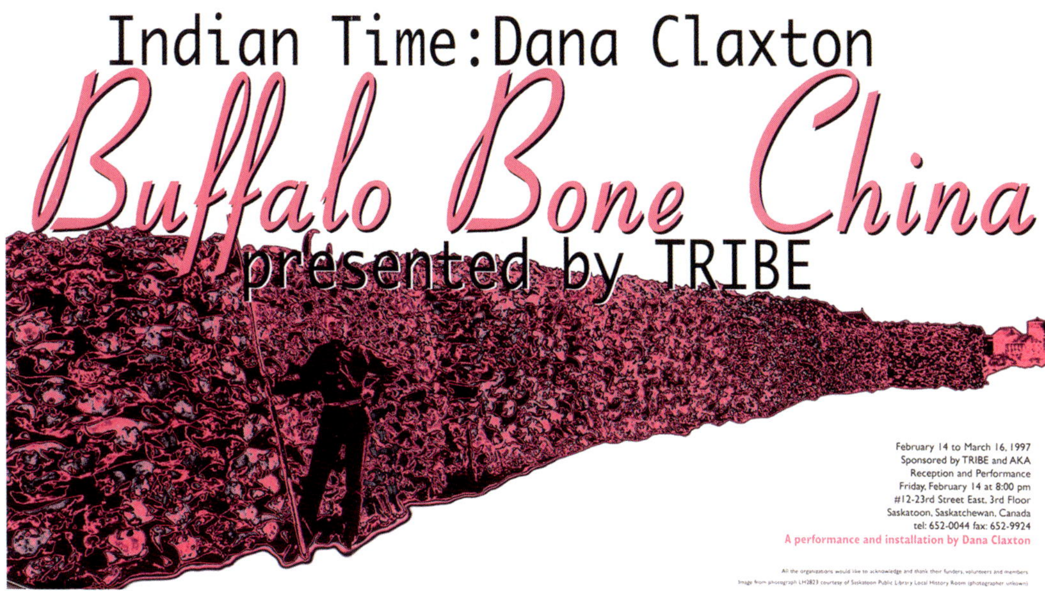

government's Indian policy, which proposed to eliminate "Indian" as a legal status, abolish the Department of Indian Affairs and repeal the Indian Act.[11]

The artist collaborates with director Jeff Bear (Maliseet) as associate producer and researcher on documentary films for television. This is the first of several documentary projects they work on together.

Claxton becomes a sundancer at the Sitting Bull Sundance Camp in Standing Rock, South Dakota.

EXHIBITIONS

topographies: aspects of recent B.C. art, Vancouver Art Gallery, Vancouver, BC

Urban Fictions, Presentation House, North Vancouver, BC

1997

Lori Blondeau curates the first solo exhibition of the artist—the installation and performance work *Buffalo Bone China*—for Tribe and AKA Gallery in Saskatoon, Saskatchewan. The work is the first in a series of ongoing projects the artist has referred to as her "Plains projects," which focus on the history, ecology, spiritual and cultural aspects of the Great Plains of North America: "It is significant how this place shapes my work. My practice has been informed by growing up in Moose Jaw, driving around the Plains, and by Lakota spiritual and cultural teachings, some of which have come to me later in life—medicine takes time to grow."[12]

Buffalo Bone China is a metaphor for the destruction of First Nations culture. The work is composed of three elements—a performance, a video and an installation. As a whole, *Buffalo Bone China* takes the historical use of buffalo bones, which were gathered and crushed en masse and then exported to England to make fine bone china, as a vehicle to explore the impact of Canadian (and by extension British and American) colonial policies, which resulted in the near extinction of the buffalo. Buffalo were central to the survival of the Indigenous peoples who had inhabited the Plains for thousands of years; they were not only sustenance to the Lakota, they held spiritual, economic and social importance to the Plains people and their way of life.

The Red Paper receives the award for Best Short Drama at the Dreamspeakers First Nations Film and Video Festival in Edmonton, Alberta.

Buffalo Bone China is the first of Claxton's film/video works to be edited by Winston Xin. He will continue to work with Claxton for more than twenty years.

Beauty and the Beast, Walter Phillips Gallery, Banff Centre, Banff, AB

Brochure for *Buffalo Bone China* performance invitation card, presented by Tribe and AKA Gallery, Saskatoon, 1997

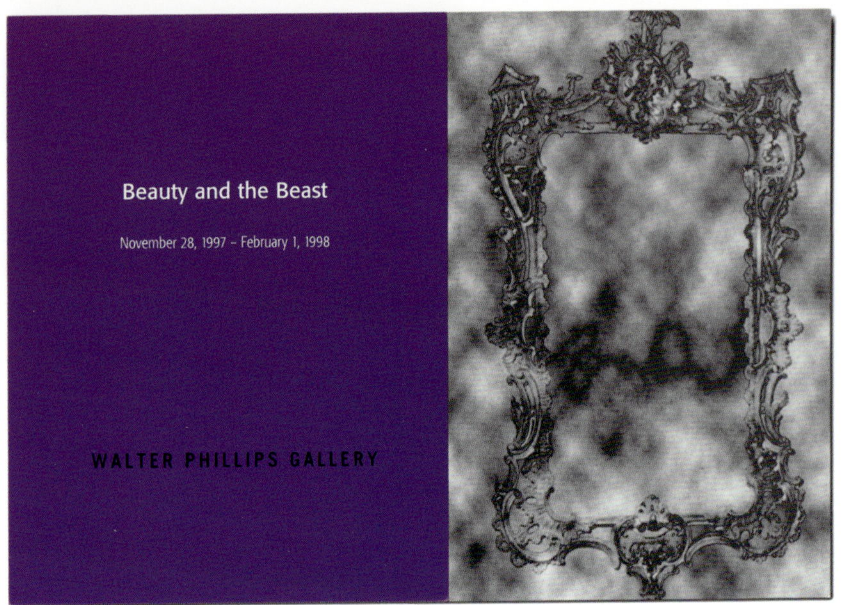

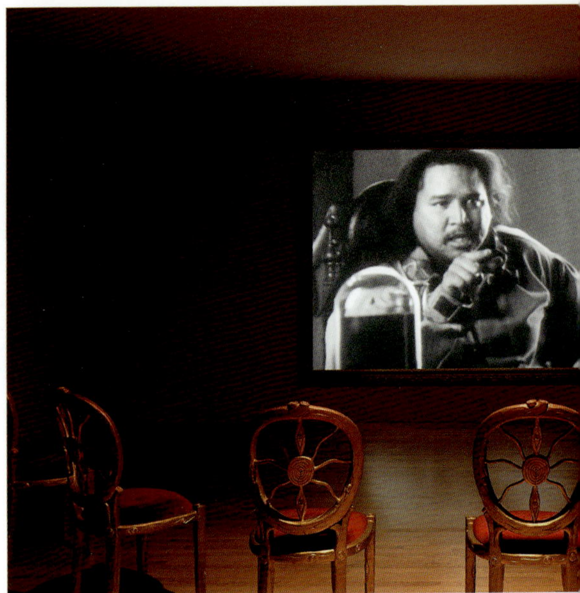

EXHIBITIONS
Buffalo Bone China, Tribe & AKA, Saskatoon, SK (solo)

1998

Claxton is a co-founder of the Indigenous Media Arts Group, a non-profit Aboriginal media resource centre whose aim was "to contribute to the cultural discourse in independent production and to disseminate Aboriginal production." This year IMAG produces Vancouver's first ever Aboriginal Film Festival. The collective members are: Marie Baker, Darryl Shawn Bird, Arlene Bowman, Thirza Cuthand, Dana Claxton, Allan W. Hopkins, Cleo Reece, Molly Morin Starlight and Cease Wyss. The organization will disband in 2007.[13]

Claxton directs *Yuxweluptun: Man of Masks*, a documentary about First Nations artist Lawrence Paul Yuxweluptun for the National Film Board of Canada.

She begins teaching at Emily Carr Institute for Art and Design (now Emily Carr University of Art + Design), where she remains on the faculty until 2003.

EXHIBITIONS
Material Zones, Walter Phillips Gallery, Banff Centre, Banff, AB

Red Interiors, Open Space, Victoria, BC; Surrey Art Gallery, Surrey, BC

1999

PERFORMANCES
Ablakela (with peyote singers Verdell Primeaux and Johnny Mike), grunt gallery, Vancouver, BC

EXHIBITIONS
Buffalo Bone China, Tranz<--->Tech: Toronto International Video Art Biennial, Toronto, ON

Taste of Landscapes, Novi Sad Cultural Centre, Novi Sad, Yugoslavia

Past Life: Future Tense, Museo Nacional de Bellas Artes, Buenos Aires, Argentina

2000

EXHIBITIONS
Waterspeak, Artspeak, Vancouver, BC (solo)

The Heart of Everything That Is, Kamloops Art Gallery, Kamloops, BC (solo)

Magnetic North: Canadian Experimental Video, Walker Arts Centre, Minneapolis, MN

From the Collection—The Red Paper, Vancouver Art Gallery, Vancouver, BC

 Poster for *Beauty and the Beast*, Walter Phillips Gallery, Banff, 1997–98

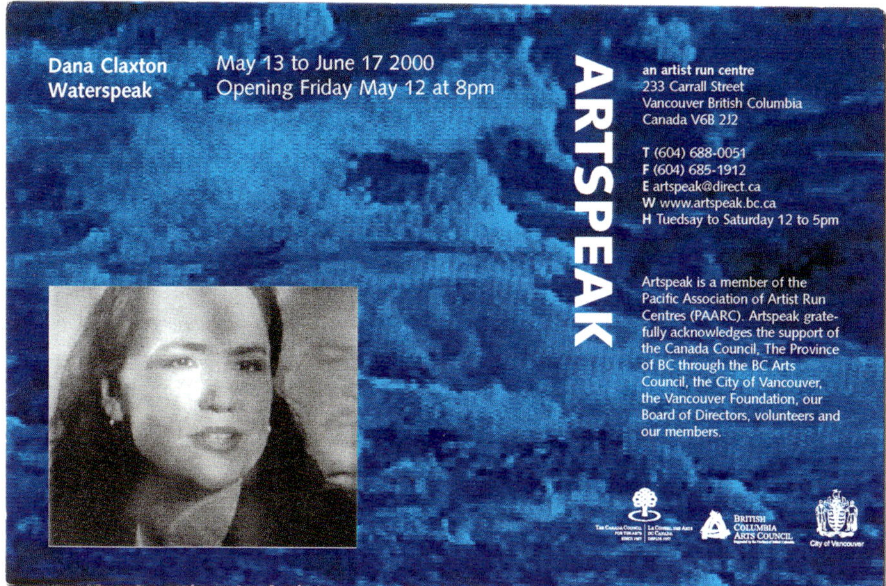

Buffalo Bone China, New Acquisitions, MacKenzie Art Gallery, Regina, SK

Centrifugal Vision: Video Circle 2000, Center for the Arts, Hong Kong University of Science and Technology, Hong Kong

2001

Claxton works on projects with the National Film Board of Canada, CBC, Vancouver Television (VTV), Aboriginal Peoples Television Network (APTN), the Canadian Labour Congress and the Government of British Columbia. She is director and producer of fifty-two episodes of *Wakanheja (Sacred One)*—a pre-school television show created by her sister Kim Soo Goodtrack, which focuses on First Nations language, culture and traditions through dance, art, storytelling and music. "Wakanheja" means sacred one, and is the word for children in the Lakota language. Regarding her broadcast television work she comments, "I don't think of this project as great cinema, but it's beautiful to think how nice it will be for all these children to be able to see themselves represented in the media."[14]

Claxton serves as executive producer and segment director of twenty-six episodes of *ArtZone*—a pre-teen program about art making, also created by Kim Soo Goodtrack.

Claxton is producer for ten episodes of *First Stories*, a program about the Indigenous community in Vancouver, for VTV.

EXHIBITIONS

Magnetic North: Canadian Experimental Video, Plug In, Winnipeg, MB; Canadian Museum of Contemporary Photography, Ottawa, ON; Art Gallery of Hamilton, Hamilton, ON; Canadian Museum of Photography, Ottawa, ON; Harvard Film Archives, Cambridge, MA; Southern Alberta Art Gallery, Lethbridge, AB

Abattoirs by Artists, Mendel Art Gallery, Saskatoon, SK

2002

Claxton and Lori Blondeau, director of the arts organization Tribe, organize *Indian Acts: Aboriginal Performance Art*, the first conference on Aboriginal performance art in North America, at the grunt gallery in Vancouver.

Claxton's *Ablakela*, a CD-ROM of the *Ablakela* performance, receives the award for Best Multimedia work at the ImagiNATIVE Film and Media Arts Festival, Toronto.

The People Dance is officially selected to screen at the Sundance Film Festival, Park City, Utah.

EXHIBITIONS

Buffalo Bone China, Estevan Art Centre, Estevan, SK (solo)

Waterspeak, Oboro, Montréal, QC (solo)

Poster for *Waterspeak*, Artspeak, Vancouver, 2000

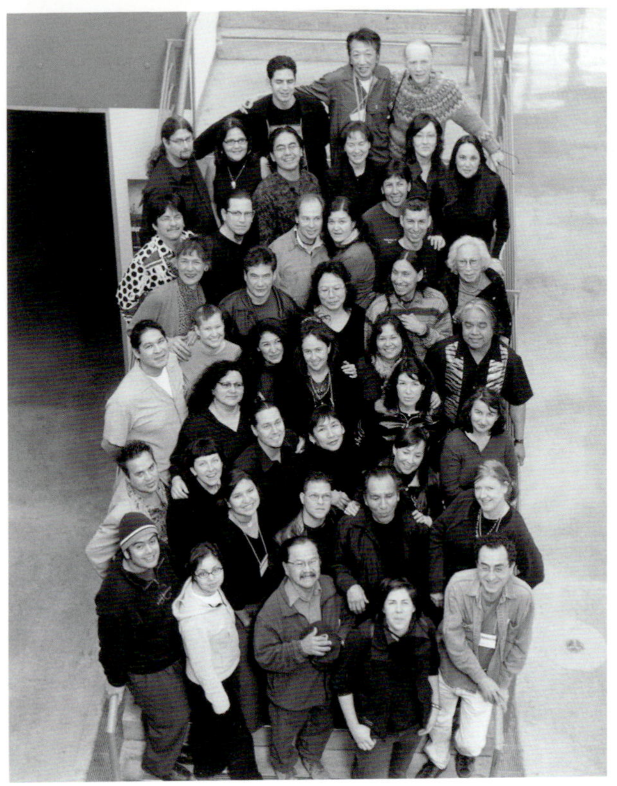

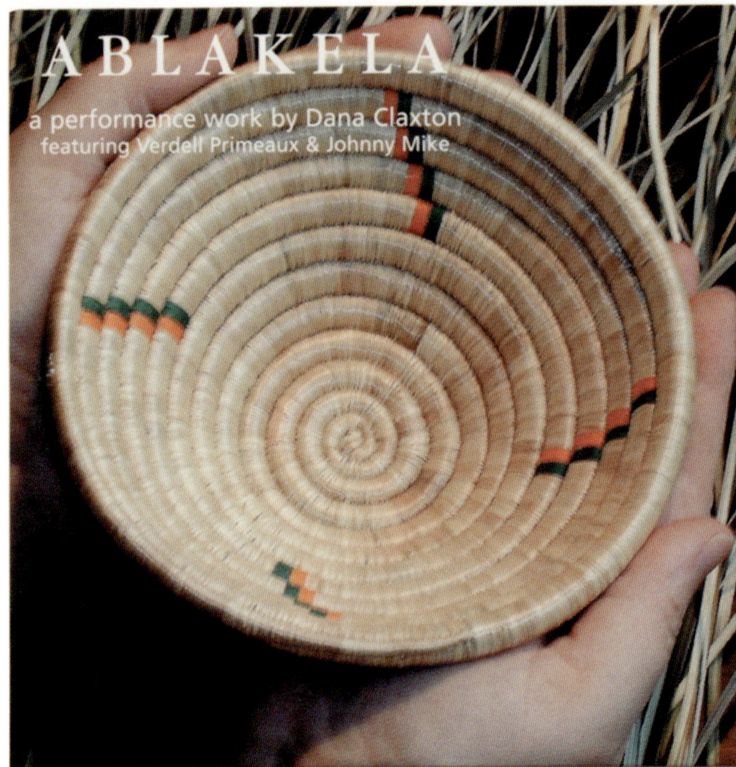

Vancouver Video, Galleria di Nuova Icona, Venice, Italy

Gatherings: Aboriginal Art from the Collection, Winnipeg Art Gallery, Winnipeg, MB

Magnetic North: Canadian Experimental Video, Huashan 1914 Creative Park, Taipei, Taiwan

2003

Claxton produces *Rattle*, a four-channel video installation. The work marks a new direction in her practice. Whereas previous work such as *I Want to Know Why* (1994) and *Buffalo Bone China* (1997), re-enacted the devastating and destructive effects of colonialism, here Claxton creates a Lakota spiritual space within the gallery through the complex interweaving of image and sound. For the piece, Claxton learned to make rattles, which have traditionally functioned to heal and connect with the spirit realm in Lakota culture. Claxton also employs blue, a colour associated with healing properties, as a recurring motif in the work. The use of four screens reflects the four directions, the four seasons and four cardinal Lakota virtues of generosity, wisdom, bravery and fortitude. Lakota cosmology is called up in other ways—the mirroring of images reflects the Lakota belief that the earth and sky in fact mirror each other. Audio is again an important element in the work, with Claxton mixing the traditional sounds of the rattles and peyote singers Verdell Primeaux and Johnny Mike with electronic music by Russell Wallace.

Claxton serves as the Global Television Chair at the University of Regina where she teaches at the School of Journalism, focussing on critical thinking and experimentation with sound and images in broadcasting.

EXHIBITIONS

Stealing to Subvert, WRO 03 International Media Arts Biennale, Wrocław, Poland (solo)

Untitled, Rialto Gallery, Venice, Italy (solo)

The Heart of Everything That Is, Change Gallery, Rome, Italy (solo)

Language of Intercession, Diazabo, Montréal, QC

BACK/FLASH, Walter Phillips Gallery, Banff Centre, Banff, AB

Gatherings: Aboriginal Art from the Collection of the Winnipeg Art Gallery, Museum of Natural History, Taipei, Taiwan

Lessons in History, MacKenzie Art Gallery, Regina, SK

ABOVE LEFT: *Indian Acts: Aboriginal Performance Art* conference participants, grunt gallery, 2002
ABOVE RIGHT: Cover for CD-ROM of *Ablakela*, 2002

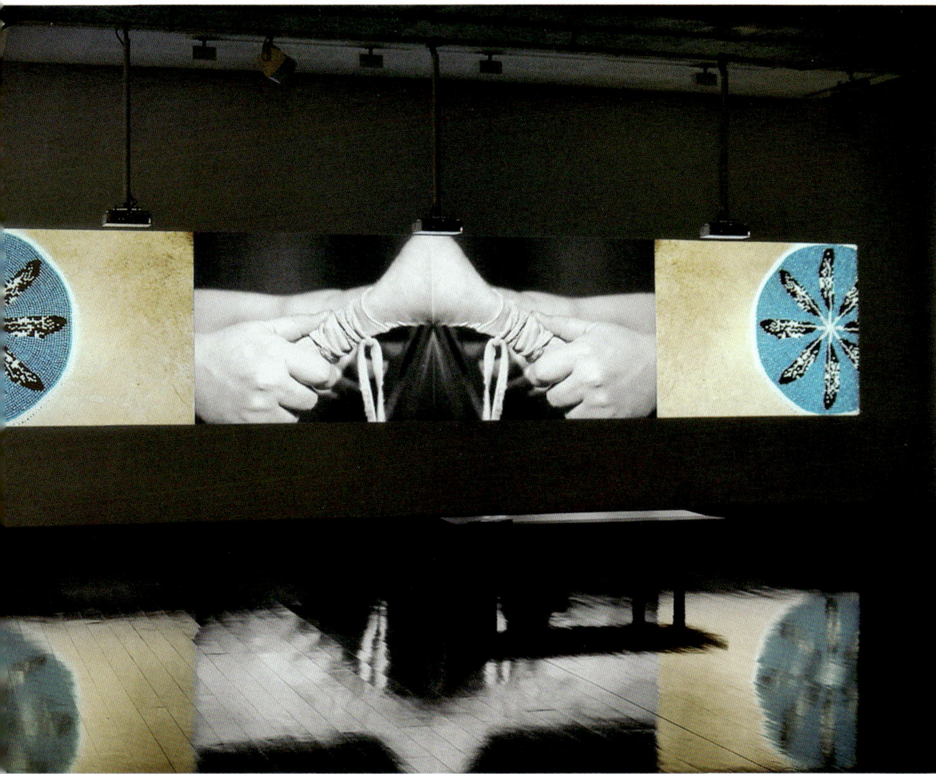

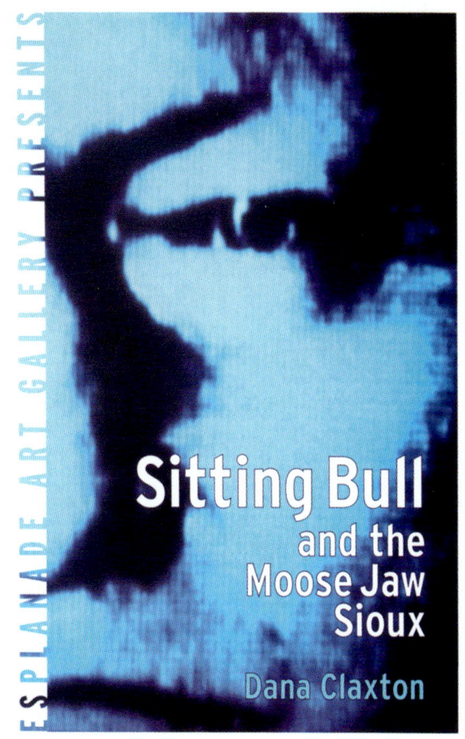

Language of Intercession, Art Gallery of Hamilton, Hamilton, ON

Vancouver Video, Folly Gallery, Lancaster, England

Photophobia, Art Gallery of Hamilton, Hamilton, ON

2004

Sitting Bull and the Moose Jaw Sioux is commissioned by the Moose Jaw Museum and Art Gallery and curated by Heather Smith. Claxton takes the city of Moose Jaw as her starting point for the work and unveils connections to its past and present through a complex interweaving of historical documents, personal stories, visual imagery, rhythmic sound, scrolling text (translations of Lakota conversations) and original footage. Across a four-screen installation Claxton unveils multiple stories and histories of place, time and people, focusing on the story of the arrival of the Sioux in Canada in 1877 and their extended relationship with the city of Moose Jaw. The main triptych is made up of three floor-to-ceiling screens which display the memory, history and story aspects of the work, while a single screen, encountered separately from the triptych, features Claxton's footage of the local Moose Jaw landscape, specifically the site of Sitting Bull's winter encampment. This footage employs a camera roaming the actual site of the camp as the filmmaker retraces the footprints of the Lakota community.

EXHIBITIONS

Sitting Bull and the Moose Jaw Sioux, Moose Jaw Art Gallery, Moose Jaw, SK (solo)

A History Lesson, MOCCA, Toronto, ON

Gatherings: Aboriginal Art from the Collection of the Winnipeg Art Gallery, Guangdong Museum of Art, Guangzhou, China

2005

Claxton co-edits *Transference, Tradition, Technology: Native New Media Exploring Visual & Digital Culture*, an anthology that explores new media work by First Nations artists in Canada, with Steve Loft and Melanie Townsend. The book is co-published by the Banff Centre, Art Gallery of Hamilton and Indigenous Media Arts Group.

Claxton receives the VIVA Award from the Jack and Doris Shadbolt Foundation.

EXHIBITIONS

Landscape #1, Surrey Art Gallery, Surrey, BC (solo)

Microwave Media Festival, Hong Kong, China (solo)

ABOVE LEFT: *Rattle*, 2003 (installation at Samstag Museum of Art, University of South Australia, Adelaide, 2011)
ABOVE RIGHT: Poster for *Sitting Bull and the Moose Jaw Sioux*, Esplanade Art Gallery, Medicine Hat, 2007

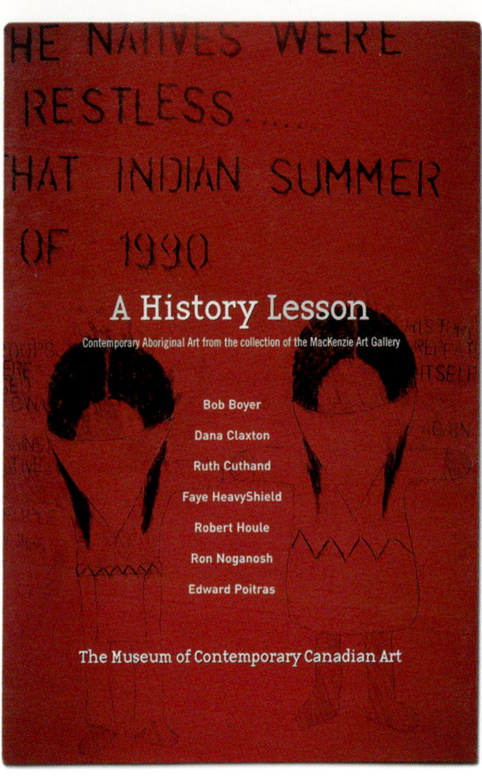

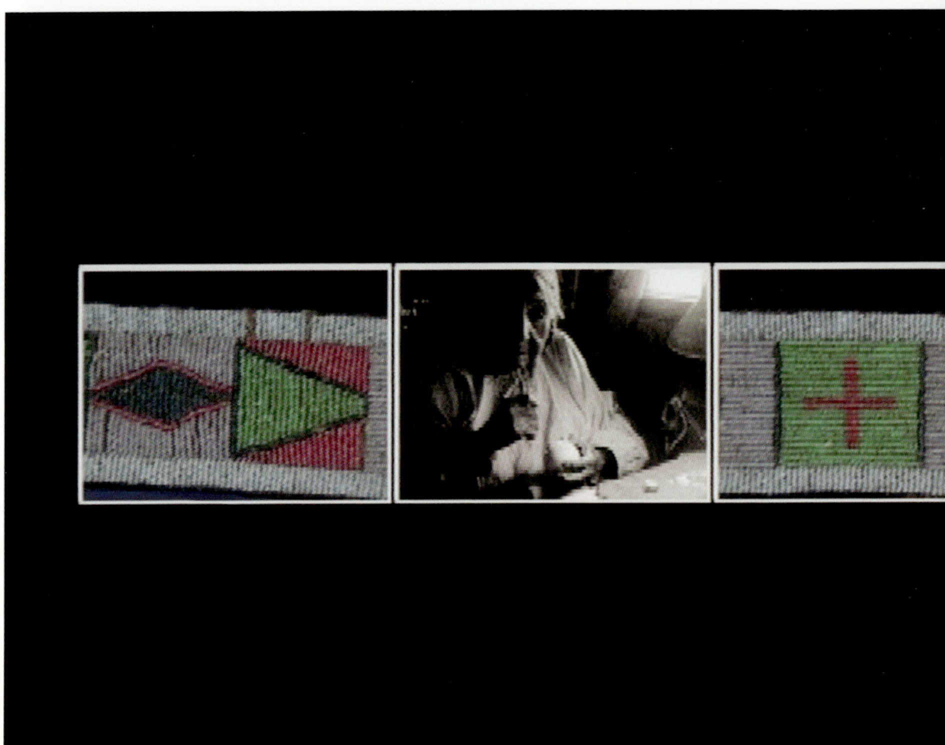

Art Start Biennale, Saw Gallery, Ottawa, ON (solo)

18 Illuminations: Contemporary Art and Light, Tom Thomson Gallery, Owen Sound, ON

Neighbourhood, Centre A, Vancouver, BC

BACK/FLASH, Winnipeg Art Gallery, Winnipeg, MB

Marking Time, Mendel Art Gallery, Saskatoon, SK

Reclamations, McIntosh Gallery, University of Western Ontario, London, ON

2006

EXHIBITIONS

Sitting Bull and the Moose Jaw Sioux, Art Gallery of Prince Albert, Prince Albert, SK; Art Gallery of Swift Current, Swift Current, SK (solo)

Red Eye, Carleton University Art Gallery, Ottawa, ON

Four Car Washes / Four Video Artists, Nuit Blanche, Toronto, ON

Canadian Video, Caixa Forum, Barcelona, Spain

Continuum, Musée Malraux, Le Havre, Biennale d'art contemporain du Havre, France

75 Years of Collecting: First Nations Myths and Realities, Vancouver Art Gallery, Vancouver, BC

BACK/FLASH, Dalhousie Art Gallery, Dalhousie University, Halifax, NS

Why I am So Unhappy, Or Gallery, Vancouver, BC

18 Illuminations: Contemporary Art and Light, Robert McLaughlin Gallery, Ottawa, ON; Art Gallery of Peterborough, ON

2007

Claxton undertakes a residency in Winnipeg, Manitoba, for six weeks as part of the MAWA—Mentoring Artists for Women's Art—programme. She would later describe the experience as both enchanting and complex. During her stay the artist chronicles daily life in the city. These original texts would later form the basis of a work shown as part of the *TXT4WPG* exhibition at Urban Shaman, Winnipeg, in 2012.

The artist is awarded the prestigious Eiteljorg Fellowship by the

ABOVE LEFT: Brochure for *A History Lesson*, Museum of Contemporary Canadian Art, Toronto, 2004
ABOVE RIGHT: *Sitting Bull and the Moose Jaw Sioux*, 2004 (video still)

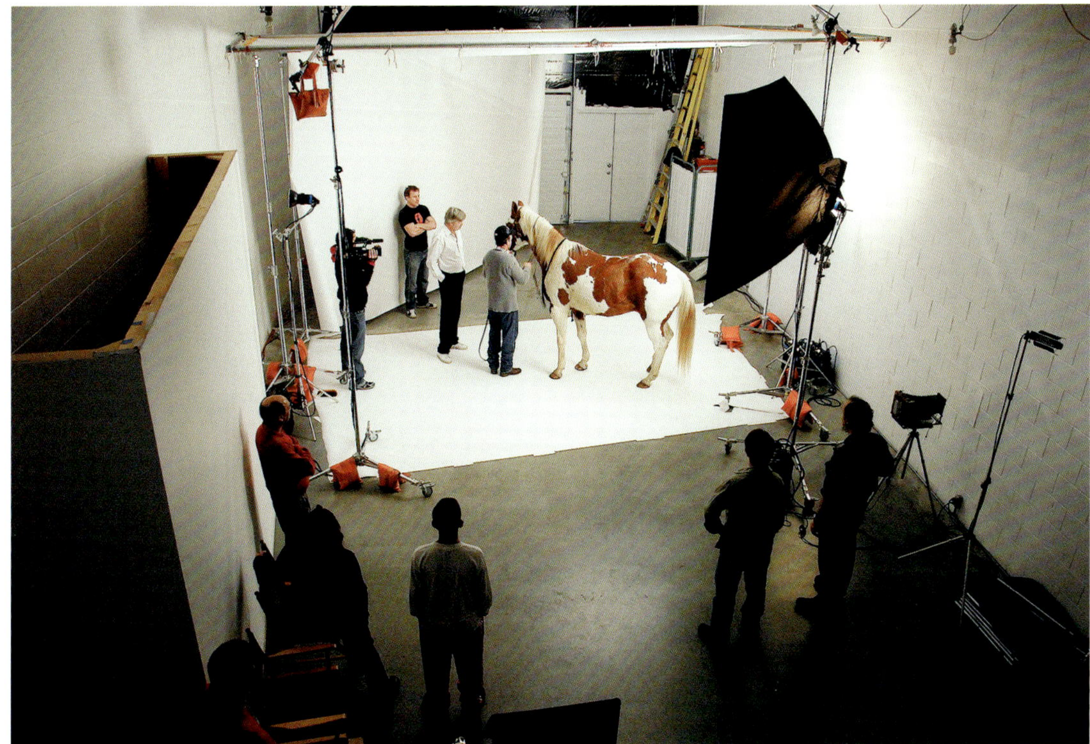

Eiteljorg Museum of American Indians and Western Art, Indianapolis, Indiana.

Claxton graduates from Simon Fraser University with a Master of Arts degree in Liberal Studies.

EXHIBITIONS

Sitting Bull and the Moose Jaw Sioux, Thames Art Gallery, Chatham, ON; Esplanade Art Gallery, Medicine Hat, AB (solo)

Starting from Home: Online Retrospective, grunt gallery, Vancouver, BC (solo)

Eiteljorg Fellowship, Eiteljorg Museum, Indianapolis, IN

Vancouver InSight, King's Lynn Arts Centre, King's Lynn, England

Rencontres Internationales, Berlin, Germany

Crack the Sky, Biennale de Montréal, Montréal, QC

Red Eye, Art Gallery of Calgary, Calgary, AB

18 Illuminations: Contemporary Art and Light, St. Mary's University Art Gallery, Halifax, NS; MacLaren Art Centre, Barrie, ON

Blink: New Commissioned Works, Winnipeg Art Gallery, Winnipeg, MB

2008

Commissioned by the Alternator Gallery in Kelowna, British Columbia, *The Mustang Suite* is a series of five large-scale staged photographic portraits of a fictional, contemporary First Nations family. Each family member is pictured with his or her own form of a "mustang" or horse—at times recast in a contemporary form such as a bicycle or car, for example. The horse has an important place in Plains culture signifying mobility and freedom. The artist was inspired by Black Elk's (a famous Lakota medicine or holy man; 1863–1950) ceremonial horse dance in which horses representing the cardinal directions joined human dancers. The recurring use of the colour red, likewise, is an important signifier in Lakota culture, denoting the direction of north and the qualities of perseverance, endurance and wisdom. The portraits portray a cultural mash-up of sorts, a family with traditional ties that undeniably hails from the contemporary world. Claxton mixes stereotypes, humour and elements of Surrealism to reclaim representations of this First Nations family from the colonial gaze. With a nod to the legacy of staged photography in both art history and contemporary art, Claxton's large-scale, visually impressive portraits play off of the conventions of popular culture while reworking old stereotypes.

Production image of *The Mustang Suite*, 2008

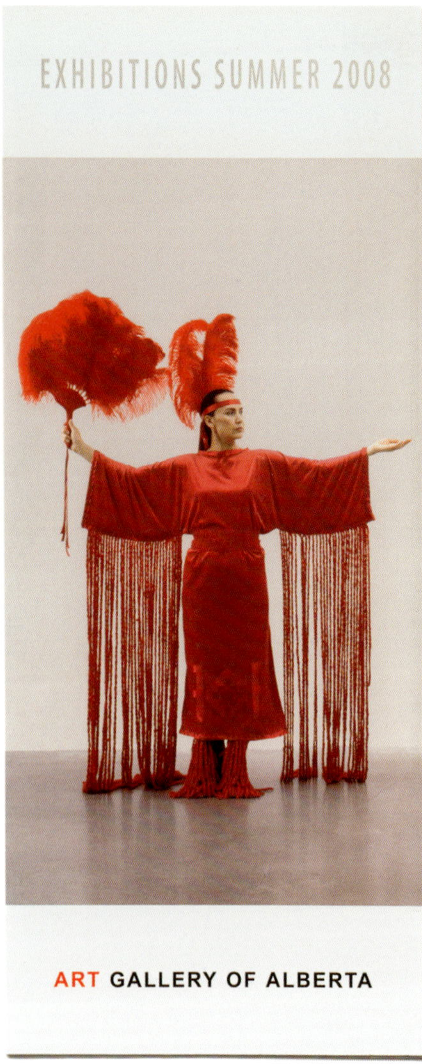

Claxton participates in the panel discussion "The Danger of Surface" at the symposium *Documents of an Encounter: Edward Curtis and the Kwakwaka'wakw First Nations*, organized by the Getty Research Institute, Los Angeles, CA.

Claxton gives an artist talk, "Placing the Real into the Imagined: Native American Art & You!" at the American College Art Association National Conference in Indianapolis, IL.

Claxton curates *The Medicine Project*, an online exhibition of visual art, performance and text for grunt gallery: www.themedicineproject.com.

EXHIBITIONS

Dana Claxton Video Art 1994–2007, Keyano Art Gallery, Fort McMurray, AB (solo)

The Mustang Suite, Alternator Gallery, Kelowna, BC (solo)

Non-Compliance (online exhibition), Urban Shaman, Winnipeg, MB

18 Illuminations: Contemporary Art and Light, Kenderdine Art Gallery, University of Saskatchewan, Saskatoon, SK; Winnipeg Art Gallery, Winnipeg, MB

Face the Nation, Art Gallery of Alberta, Edmonton, AB

Red Eye, Sir Wilfred Grenfell College Art Gallery, Corner Brook, NL

2009

Claxton undertakes a printmaking residency at Arizona State University's School of Art with F.A.R. (Future Art Research).

EXHIBITIONS

The Barbarian, On Main, Vancouver, BC (solo)

To Mark the Surface, University of Lethbridge Art Gallery, Lethbridge, AB (solo)

Cosmologies, Centre A, Vancouver, BC

Steeling the Gaze: Portraits by Aboriginal Artists, National Gallery of Canada, Ottawa, ON

Map(ing): Working Proof, Night Gallery, Tempe, AZ

Diabolique, Dunlop Art Gallery, Regina, SK

Native Visuality, C.N. Gorman Museum, University of California, Davis, CA

Buffalo Bone China, MacKenzie Art Gallery, Regina, SK (solo)

2010

Claxton is appointed as Simon Fraser University's Ruth Wynn Woodward Chair in Women's Studies. In addition to her teaching, lectures and projects undertaken this year, Claxton organizes *Unpacking the Indigenous Female Body*, a symposium and performance event at Simon Fraser University and Western Front in Vancouver.

Claxton is appointed as Assistant Professor in the faculty of Art History, Visual Art and Theory at the University of British Columbia.

 Exhibition brochure for *Face the Nation*, Art Gallery of Alberta, 2008

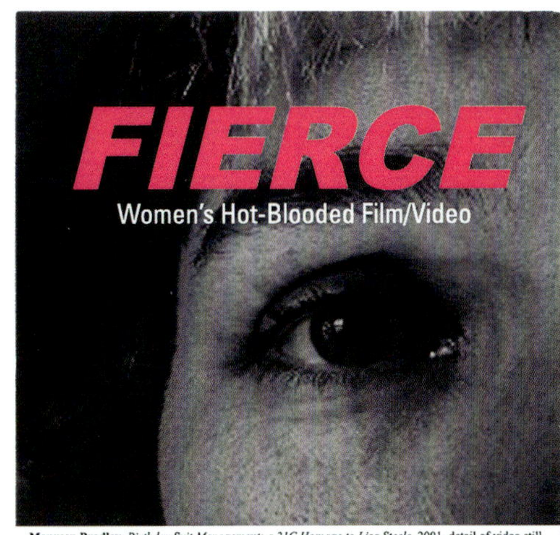

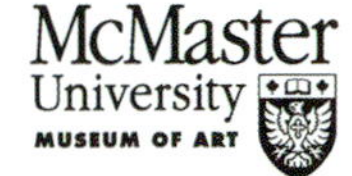

Claxton participates in the panel discussion "History, Experience, Truth and Empathy" at the 17th Biennale of Sydney, Sydney, Australia.

Claxton is a panellist for "The Politics of Hope: Contemporary Native American" at the annual College Art Association Conference in Chicago.

The artist shoots *He Who Dreams*, a fifty-one-minute experimental drama work featuring Cowboy Smithx, Sam Bob and Samaya Jardey.

PERFORMANCES

WACKO–A Disco Ceremony for Michael Jackson, Open Space, Victoria, BC

EXHIBITIONS

New Works and Then Some, Winsor Gallery, Vancouver, BC (solo)

The Beauty of Distance: Songs of Survival in a Precarious Age, 17th Biennale of Sydney, Sydney, Australia

Fierce: Women's Hot-Blooded Film/Video, McMaster Museum of Art, Hamilton, ON

Cue: Artists' Videos, Vancouver Art Gallery, Vancouver, BC

Diabolique, Galeries de l'UQAM, Montréal, QC; Oakville Galleries, Oakville, ON

Four Directions, No. 9 and Evergreen Brickworks, Toronto, ON

Endlessly Traversed Landscapes, (billboard project), Vancouver, BC

Pervasive Influence: The Mechanical Bride, MOCCA, Toronto, ON

Resistance is Fertile, A Space, Toronto, ON

2011

A new performance work, *The Elsewhere* (2011), is performed by Claxton at Western Front in Vancouver. In the work, Claxton attempts to bring Indigenous spirit into the gallery space through her actions and movements.

Claxton designs and teaches the first course in performance art to be offered by the Department of Art History, Visual Art and Art Theory at the University of British Columbia.

PERFORMANCES

The Elsewhere, Western Front, Vancouver, BC

EXHIBITIONS

Sitting Bull and the Moose Jaw Sioux, Gallery@501, Sherwood Park, AB (solo)

Faces, Morris and Helen Belkin Art Gallery, University of British Columbia, Vancouver, BC

Steeling the Gaze: Portaits by Aboriginal Artists, Thunder Bay Art Gallery, Thunder Bay ON; McMichael Canadian Art Collection, Kleinburg, ON; Dalhousie Art Gallery, Dalhousie University, Halifax, NS

Stop (the Gap): International Indigenous Art, Samstag Museum of Art, University of South Australia, Adelaide, Australia

Invitation for *Fierce: Women's Hot-Blooded Film/Video*, McMaster University Museum of Art, Hamilton, 2010

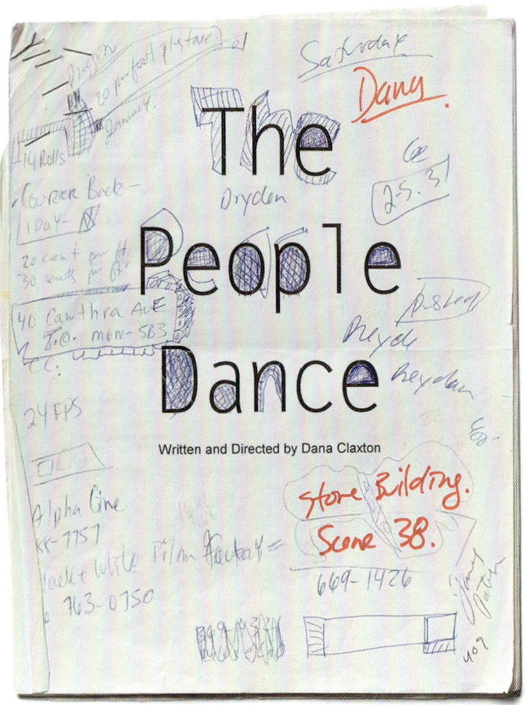

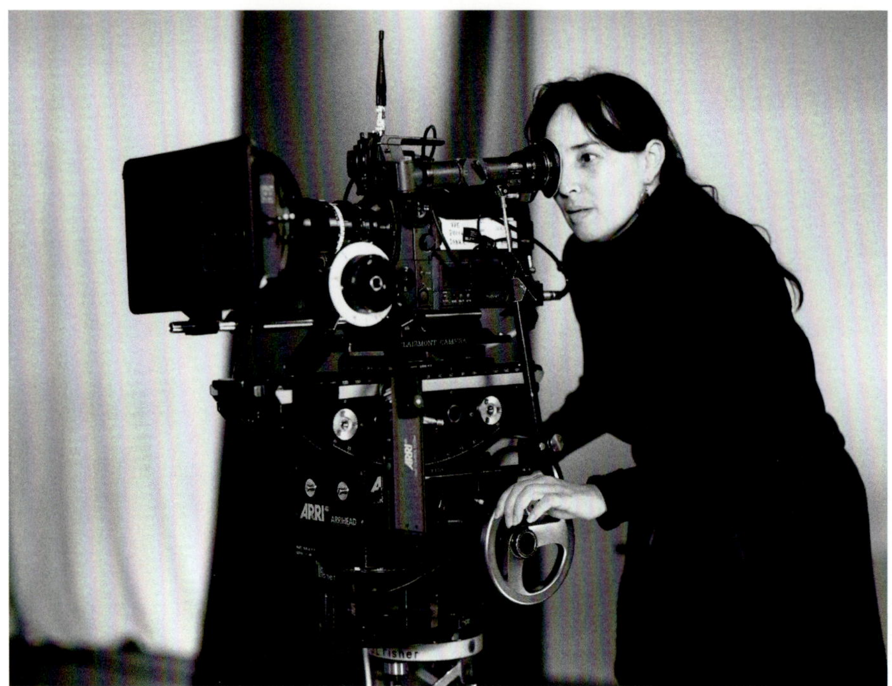

Diabolique, Founders' Gallery at the Military Museum, Calgary, AB

Fierce: Women's Hot-Blooded Film/Video, Robert McLaughlin Gallery, Oshawa, ON

Tribe Archives, Optica, Montréal, QC

2012

Alongside her early training in the theatre, Claxton has also described her roots as being based in poetry. The exhibition *TXT4WPG* at Urban Shaman, Winnipeg, marks a return to poetry in her practice. She exhibits works incorporating texts written during her extended stay in Winnipeg in 2007. The multimedia work includes digitally projected texts and watercolour paintings. The texts took the form of snippets of observations, poetry and everyday dialogue overheard by the artist during her stay in the city.

Claxton receives the Artistic Innovation Award from Women in Film and Television, Vancouver.

Claxton receives development funding for *Tipping Andy Warhol*, a feature-length script written by Claxton, Sam Bob and Courtney Crane.

PERFORMANCES

Rip, Koerner Library Gallery, University of British Columbia, Vancouver, BC

EXHIBITIONS

Beat Nation, Vancouver Art Gallery, Vancouver, BC; The Power Plant, Toronto, ON

Fashionality, McMichael Canadian Art Collection, Kleinburg, ON

In the Expanded Field: Sculptural Installations Since 1970, Winnipeg Art Gallery, Winnipeg, MB

it's fine, Faculty Gallery, University of British Columbia, Vancouver, BC

Museum at the End of the World, Nuit Blanche, Toronto, ON

SPLICE: At the Intersection of Art and Medicine, Blackwood Gallery and the University of Toronto Art Centre, Toronto, ON

Steeling the Gaze: Portraits by Aboriginal Artists, Mendel Art Gallery, Saskatoon, SK; Kelowna Art Gallery, Kelowna, BC

ABOVE LEFT: Script for *The People Dance*, 2011
ABOVE RIGHT: Dana Claxton operating a camera during the production of *The People Dance*, 2012

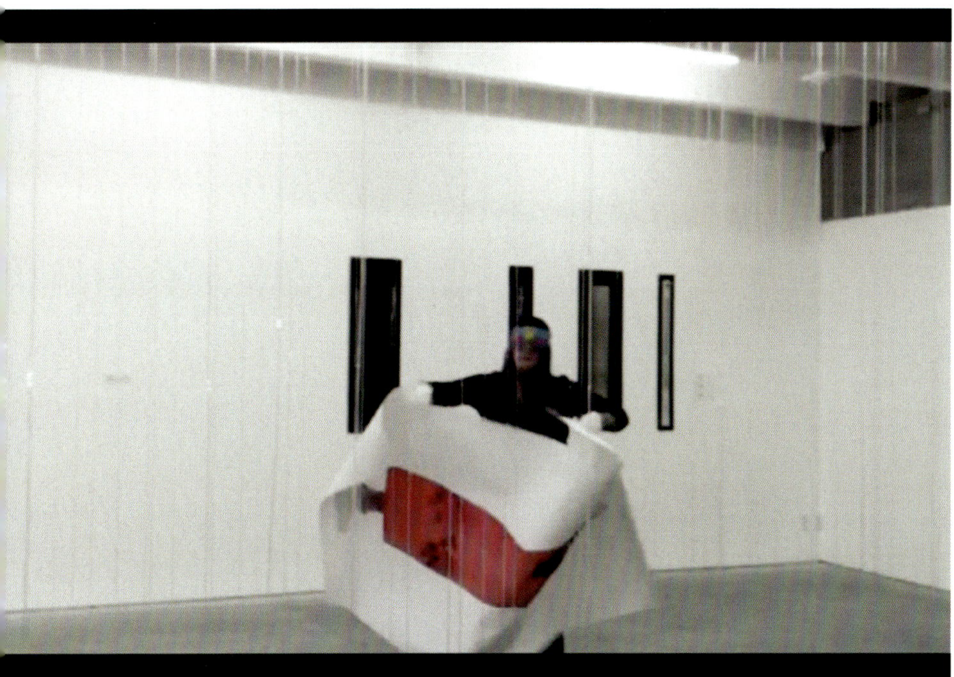

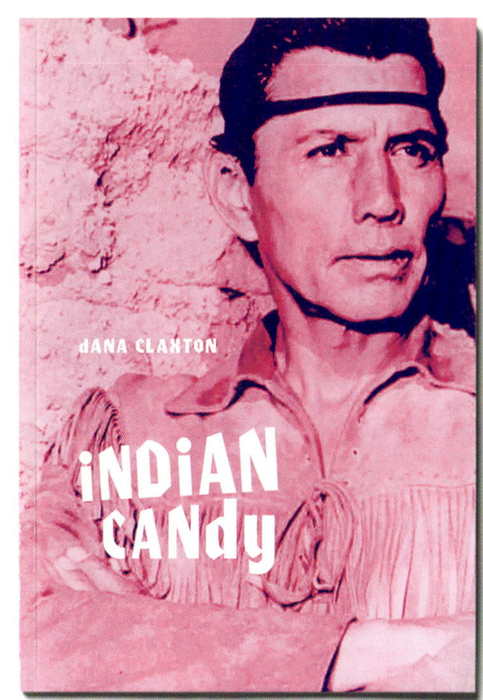

The People Dance, Wanuskewin Heritage Park Gallery, Saskatoon, SK (solo)

TXT4WPG, Urban Shaman, Winnipeg, MB (solo)

Wild New Territories, Camley Street Natural Park / The Foundling Museum, London, England

2013

Claxton produces her *Indian Candy* series. These photographic works are based on found online images associated with the idea of the Wild West and Western depictions of Indigenous culture. The artist presents the images in bright candy-coloured pinks, blues and purples, deliberately using beauty and colour to entice viewers to consider Canada's difficult history with Indigenous people, or in her in own words: "as to say—this critical knowledge is delicious and sweet!"[15] Some of the images that appear include Maria Tallchief, a Native American classical ballet dancer; Jay Silverheels, who played Tonto, the partner of the Lone Ranger in the 1950s TV series; the white buffalo, a powerful symbol for Plains Indians; and Sitting Bull. Along with the use of colour, the artist enlarges the scale of the found photograph and allows the resulting image degradation to reveal its digital origins. The resulting pixellation obscures the image, functioning to not only reveal its source but also to disrupt the gaze and thus refuse easy consumption of a pop culture image. The artist also notes the "combination of the pixel and grain, which, in some of the works, takes on an uncanny resemblance to beadwork."[16] Alongside found images from the internet, Claxton includes images she shot at the ancient site of Writing on Stone Provincial Park in south central Alberta—the site holds the largest collection of ancient rock art in Canada. The artist states these ancient images "maintain a connection to all our histories, and suggest our human collective and connectivity to the ancients, as well as a desire to visually render ourselves."[17]

Her featurette film *He Who Dreams* wins Best Experimental award at the ImagiNATIVE Film and Media Arts Festival, Toronto.

Claxton is part of the curatorial team for the exhibition *Witnesses: Art and Canada's Indian Residential Schools,* organized by the Morris and Helen Belkin Art Gallery, University of British Columbia.

PERFORMANCES

The Beat Tear Crumple, Faculty Show, University of British Columbia, Vancouver, BC

To Be With Dusk (with Bo Meyers), at the Devonian Harbour Park in association with *Wild New Territories*, Simon Fraser University Galleries, Vancouver, BC

ABOVE LEFT: *Rip*, 2011 (documentation of performance at Koerner Library Gallery, University of British Columbia, Vancouver)
ABOVE RIGHT: Catalogue for *Dana Claxton: Indian Candy*, Winsor Gallery, 2013

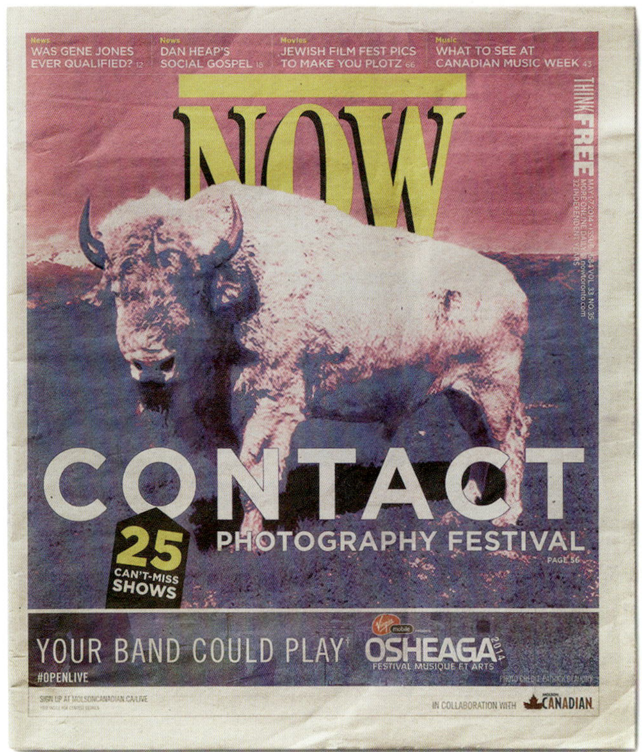

EXHIBITIONS

Beat Nation, Musée d'art contemporain, Montréal, QC

In the Flesh, Ottawa Art Gallery, Ottawa, ON

Indian Candy, Winsor Gallery, Vancouver, BC (solo)

Ghost Dance, Ryerson Image Centre, Toronto, ON

On Set: The Mustang Suite, Media Gallery, Concordia University, Montréal, QC (solo)

SPLICE: At the Intersection of Art and Medicine, Pratt Manhattan Gallery, Pratt Institute, New York, NY

Wild New Territories, Botanic Garden and Museum Berlin, Berlin, Germany; Teck Gallery, Simon Fraser University, Vancouver, BC; Kamloops Art Gallery, Kamloops, BC

2014

Curator Bonnie Rubenstein selects the *Indian Candy* series to be presented on twenty-eight billboards in Toronto, Halifax, Calgary, Montréal, Saskatoon, Winnipeg and Vancouver as part of the 2014 Scotiabank CONTACT Photography Festival. Colourful, graphic, bold and seductive—like most billboard advertising—the series is provocative in its combination of site and subject matter. Claxton states, "the work is highly political—it is very subversive. The idea was to make these glossy images that you go into. They make you realize something more is there."[18]

Dana Claxton: Paris, June Fourth, Fifth & Sixth, Two Thousand & Six, is published by Presentation House Gallery, North Vancouver.

Claxton gives the keynote speech, titled "Wisdom for All Through Identity Politics," at the *Disfiguring Identities: Art, Migration and Exile* symposium at Surrey Art Gallery.

Claxton contributes an essay titled "NWC On the Up...load" to *Native Art of the Northwest Coast: A History of Changing Ideas*, edited by Charlotte Townsend Gault, Jennifer Kramer and Ḳi-ḳe-in, published by UBC Press, Vancouver.

He Who Dreams wins the award for best cinematography at the Présence autochtone / Montréal First Peoples Festival, Montréal, QC.

Claxton has a wopila (giveaway) at the Wood Mountain Pow Wow to honour her years of sundancing in Standing Rock, South Dakota and Standing Buffalo, Saskatchewan. She then becomes a Jingle Dress dancer and is danced into the circle with her relatives and community members.

ABOVE LEFT: Poster for *On Set: The Mustang Suite*, Media Gallery, Concordia University, Montréal, 2013
ABOVE RIGHT: Cover of *Now Magazine*, May 1–7, 2014

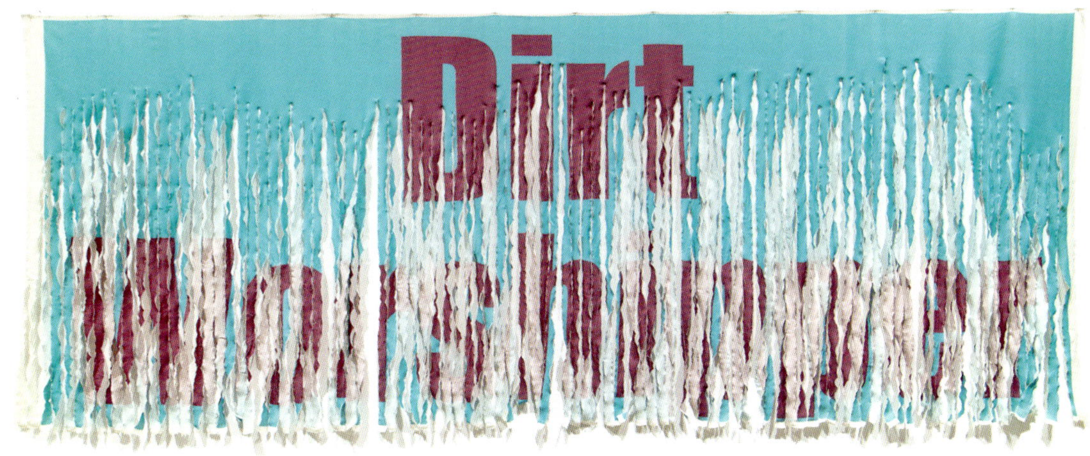

2015

Claxton produces a series of four works that explore the issues of Indigenous beauty, womanhood, sovereignty and representation. She begins working with large-scale transparencies mounted in lightboxes that she calls "fireboxes." She also begins to use ink on silk in works she identifies as "windboxes." *Headdress*, *Buffalo Woman 1* and *2*, and *Cultural Belongings* all present the life-size image of a woman played by Samaya Jardey, (Coast Salish), who Claxton works with over the span of her career. The pictured women hold, wear, or are adorned with various objects that carry Lakota associations. Together the images draw attention to the commodification of Indigenous culture. Regarding the appropriation of First Nations culture by the fashion industry and consumer culture at large, the artist explains: "You're not going to see any Indian wearing those things, but you see all those faux hippies at Coachella wearing them, right? It's insulting. But I understand why. They're beautiful. They feel amazing on. They're comforting. They have manna. They're gorgeous. They're amazing head gear, but they mean something, especially to Plains Indian people. So coming from a culture that has been oppressed and structurally dehumanized, the things that are ours, we cherish them."[19]

Claxton performs *Fringed* at the Metropolitan Museum of Art in New York as part of the exhibition *The Plains Indians: Artists of Earth and Sky*. The artist wears a garment designed by her sister, Kim Soo Goodtrack. According to the artist, in Plains culture fringe on clothing is seen to be almost alive due to the way it moves with the body and wind.[20] It serves a spiritual and practical purpose, enhancing the wearer's awareness of his or her body's relationship to the natural elements as it sweeps and sways with both bodily movement and the forces of nature.[21]

Claxton creates two installations referencing the elk for the CAPTURE Photography Festival, *Elk for c̓əsnaʔəm* and *Tatanka Wanbli Chekpa Wicincala* installed at the Marine Drive and City Centre Canada Line stations in Vancouver.

Claxton is appointed Associate Professor in the faculty of Art History, Visual Art and Theory at the University of British Columbia.

PERFORMANCES

Dirt Worshipper, AVHA Gallery, Audain Centre for the Arts, University of British Columbia, Vancouver, BC

Fringed, Metropolitan Museum of Art, New York, NY

EXHIBITIONS

Dana Claxton: Revisited, AKA, Saskatoon, SK (solo)

The Plains Indians: Artists of Earth and Sky, Metropolitan Museum of Art, New York, NY

Dirt Worshipper, 2015 (installation at AVHA Gallery, Audain Centre for the Arts, University of British Columbia, Vancouver)

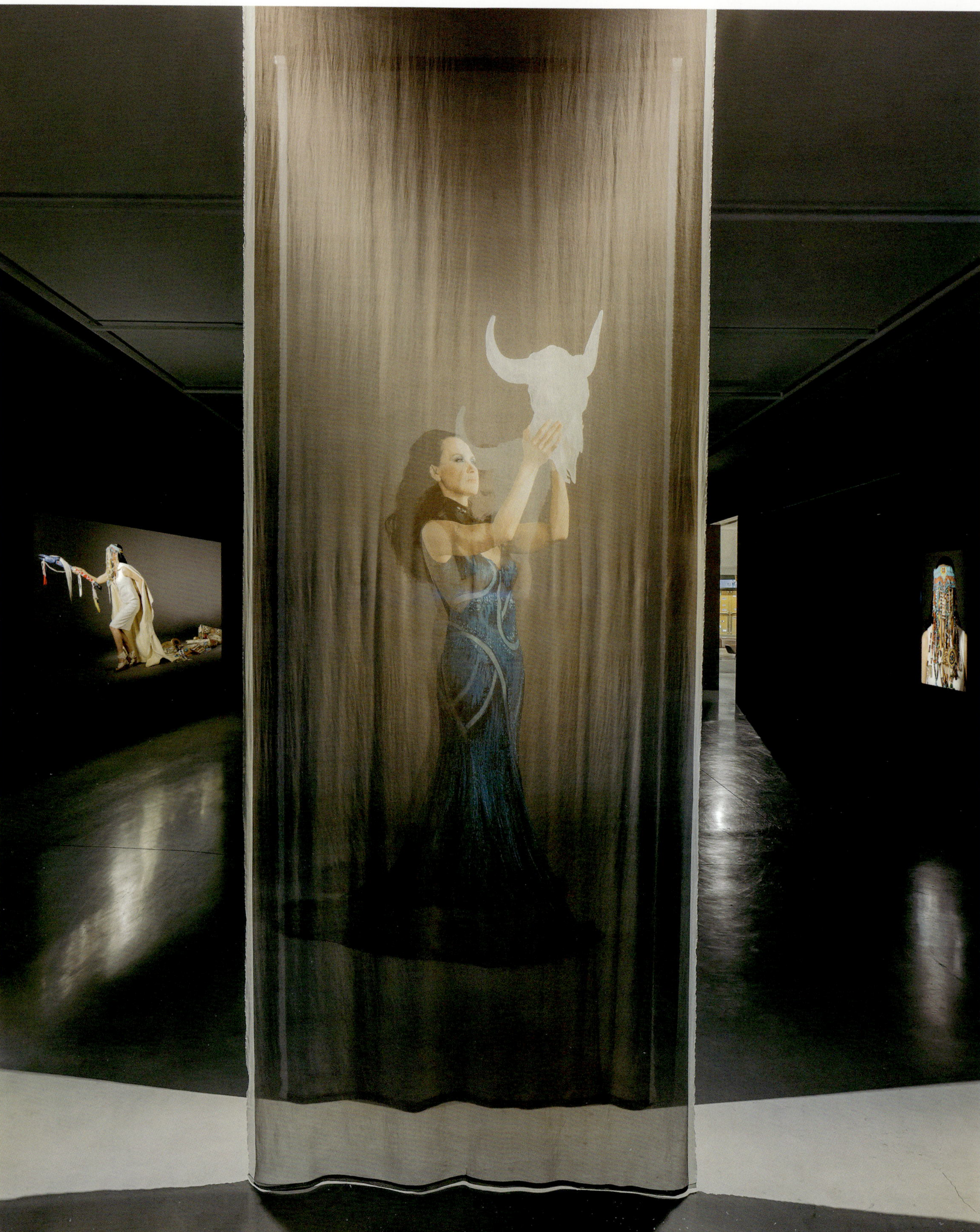

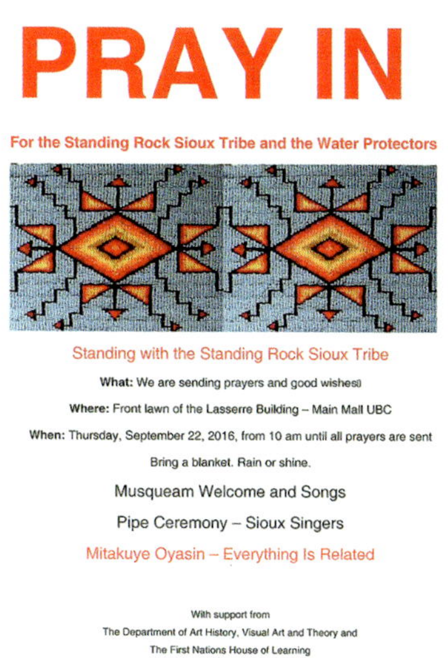

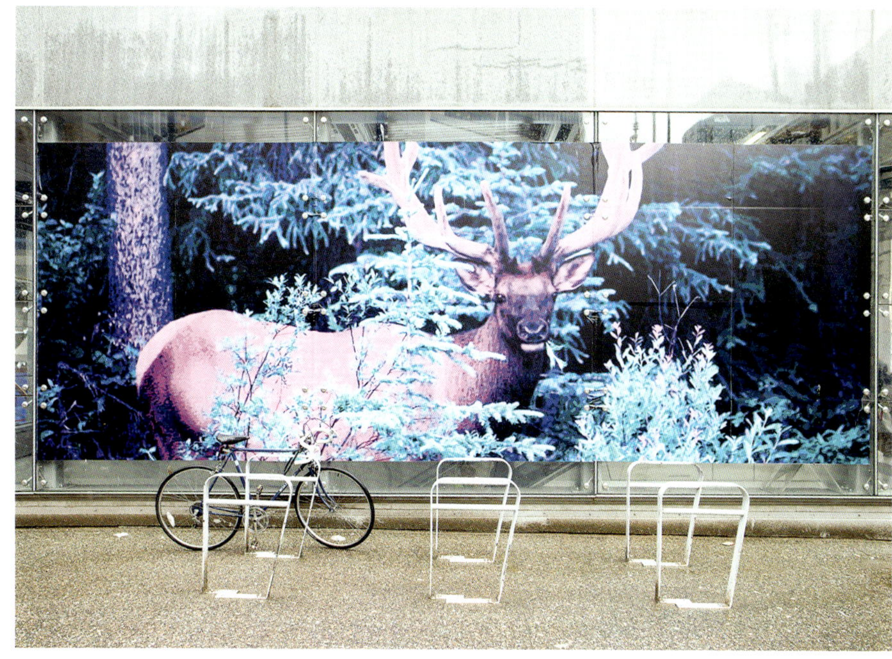

2016

The exhibition *Dana Claxton: Made to be Ready* is held at Simon Fraser University's Audain Gallery in Vancouver. The exhibition's title is a play on the modernist concept of the ready-made—taking an object from everyday life and aestheticizing it, thereby challenging what we think of as art. Here, Lakota objects such as beadwork, jewellery, dress, shields, drums, and buffalo-hide parfleche bags, are in indeed aestheticized but Claxton draws attention to the fact they also function as objects to be used; in her words they are "made to be ready." In doing so Claxton removes the objects from the category of "craft" while refuting the idea that Indigenous belongings are passive or dead artifacts.

Claxton participates in a panel discussion titled "Under Salish Influence: Vancouver as a Site of Indigenous Autonomy" in *The Concept of Vancouver* conference organized by Brock University's Centre for Canadian Studies, held at Brock University and the Niagara Artists Centre, St. Catharines, Ontario.

Claxton receives the City of Vancouver Mayor's Arts Award for Visual Arts.

On September 9, Claxton conducts a three-hour, outdoor "Pray In" at the University of British Columbia, to send good wishes to the Standing Rock Sioux in support of their opposition to construction of the Dakota Access Pipeline, which threatens the water supply to their reservation. The event contributes to the global support for the tribe's protest.

PERFORMANCES

Follow the Red Sinew, Morris and Helen Belkin Art Gallery, University of British Columbia, Vancouver, BC

EXHIBITIONS

Dana Claxton: Made to be Ready, Audain Gallery, Simon Fraser University, Vancouver, BC (solo)

"Untitled" UBC Faculty Show, AHVA Gallery, Audain Art Centre, Vancouver, BC

2017

The artist returns to her birthplace, Saskatchewan, and the subject of the Great Plains in her exhibition *The Sioux Project—Tatanka Oyate* at the MacKenzie Art Gallery in Regina. This exhibition explores contemporary Sioux aesthetics in Saskatchewan, and Sioux relationships to the notion of landscape as well as to the land itself. Claxton's work presents a video installation composed of four curved canvas screens that frame

OPPOSITE: *Buffalo Woman 1* and *2* (installation view from *Dana Claxton: Made to be Ready*, Audain Gallery, Simon Fraser University, Vancouver), 2016
ABOVE LEFT: Poster for "Pray In" to support Standing Rock Sioux in their opposition to the Dakota Access oil pipeline
ABOVE RIGHT: Elk for *č̓əsnaʔəm*, 2015 (installation at the Canada Line: Vancouver City Centre Station, CAPTURE Photography Festival)

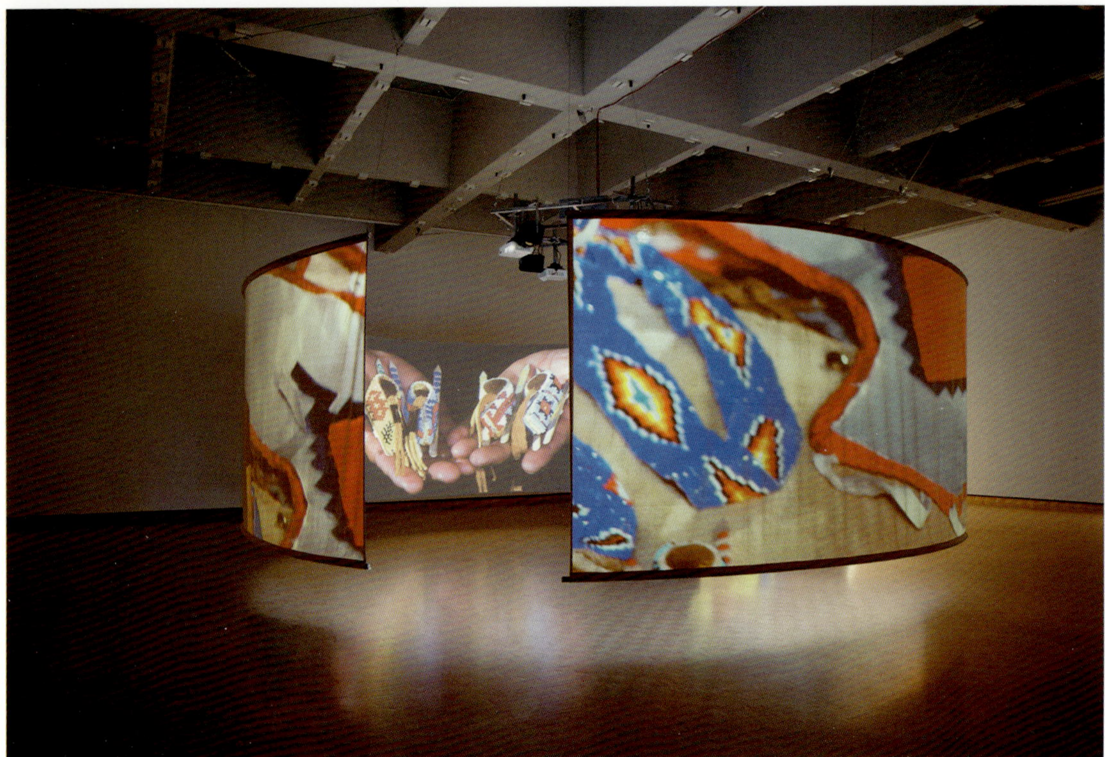

a circular space—referring to the sundance circle and the four directions—within which viewers are invited to sit. The work assembles diverse visual stories, interviews, images, dialogue and photographs, which emerged from a series of workshops Claxton and the director/actor Cowboy Smithx held with Sioux youth from the Standing Buffalo and Whitecap First Nations. Professor Lynne Bell and Gwenda Yuzicappi were also part of the team.

As part of Seattle's month-long Red May Festival, Claxton—along with Tara Bigdeli, Mitra Kazemi and Katherine Neil—performs *Don't Get to Work Bitch.* The performance is an intervention into the launch for Jaleh Mansoor's book *Marshall Plan Modernism* at the Glassbox Gallery in Seattle. The performers wear large flags that cover their bodies and half of their faces with texts based on the Italian philosopher Antonio Gramsci's writings on labour, class and gender. During the performance they fist pump to *Don't Betta Work Bitch* by Rupaul.

PERFORMANCES

Don't Get to Work Bitch, Glassbox Gallery, Seattle, WA

EXHIBITIONS

Dana Claxton: The Sioux Project–Tatanka Oyate, MacKenzie Art Gallery, Regina, SK (solo)

2018

A Forest of Canoes is exhibited along The Bentway, beneath the Gardiner Expressway in Toronto, as part of the CONTACT Photography Festival.

April 25, Claxton is appointed Chair of the Department of Art History, Visual Art and Theory at the University of British Columbia commencing January 1, 2019.

EXHIBITIONS

The Coming of Community, Arte Fiera 42, Museo d'Arte Moderna di Bologna, Bologna, Italy

Art for a New Understanding: Native Voices, 1950s to Now, Crystal Bridges Museum of American Art, Bentonville, AR

TAKUWE: An Educational Art Exhibit About the Wounded Knee Massacre, The Heritage Center at Red Cloud Indian School, Pine Ridge, SD; Akta Lakota Museum and Cultural Center, Chamberlain, SD; South Dakota Art Museum, Brookings, SD

 The Sioux Project–Tatanka Oyate, 2017 (installation at the MacKenzie Art Gallery)

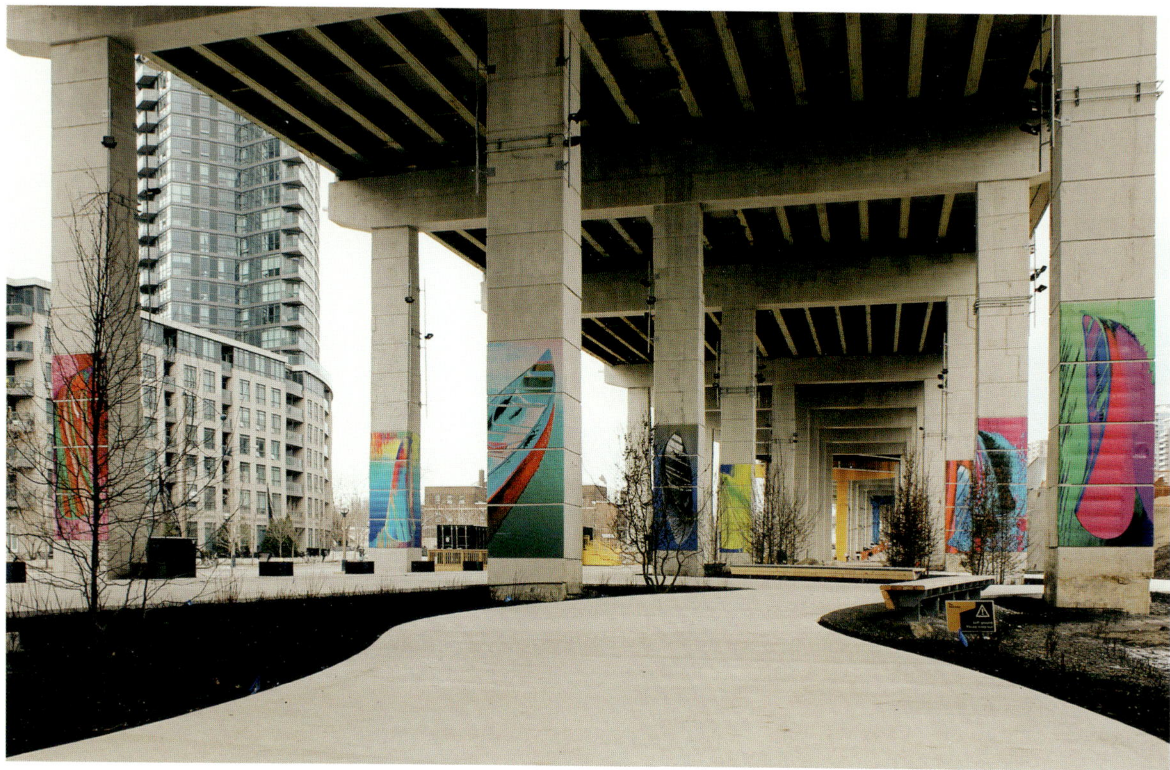

ENDNOTES

1 "Dana Claxton: Bio," *The University of British Columbia: The Department of Art History, Visual Art & Theory*, May 2018, http://ahva.ubc.ca/persons/dana-claxton/.

2 Doris Baltruschat, "Television and Canada's Aboriginal Communities Seeking Opportunities through Traditional Storytelling and Digital Technologies," *Canadian Journal of Communication* 29, no. 1 (Fall 2004), http://www.cjc-online.ca/index.php/journal/article/view/1403/1495.

3 Lynne Bell, "Dana Claxton: From a Whisper to a Scream," *Canadian Art* 27, no. 4, Winter 2010, https://canadianart.ca/features/dana_claxton/, 104.

4 Jennifer Chung, "The Story of Sitting Bull Comes Alive in Exhibit," *Saskatchewan Sage* 8, no. 11, 2004, http://www.ammsa.com/publications/saskatchewan-sage/story-sitting-bull-comes-alive-exhibit.

5 Bell, "Dana Claxton."

6 Myungsook Lee, "Dana Claxton–The Mustang Suite: Questioning Mobility, Freedom and Autonomy," *Diverse*, Summer 2011, 42.

7 Jacqueline Levitin, Judith Plessis and Valerie Raoul, eds., *Women Filmmakers: Refocusing* (Vancouver: UBC Press, 2003), 398.

8 Monika Kin Gagnon, "Framings: Dana Claxton," in Monika Kin Gagnon and Richard Fung, *13 Conversations About Art, and Cultural Race Politics* (Montréal: Artextes Editions, 2002), 35

9 "Dana Claxton: Revisited," *The University of British Columbia: The Department of Art History, Visual Art & Theory*, May 2018, http://ahva.ubc.ca/events/event/dana-claxton-revisited/.

10 Elizabeth Neal, "Dana Claxton – Hunkpapa Lakota Sioux" *Contemporary North American Indigenous Artists*, December 29, 2012, http://contemporarynativeartists.tumblr.com/post/39159194194/dana-claxton-hunkpapa-lakota-sioux.

11 Levitin et al., *Women Filmmakers*, 416.

12 Bell , "Dana Claxton."

13 Levitin et al., *Women Filmmakers*, 404, 414

14 Jackie Bissley, "Dana Claxton." *Indian Cinema Entertainment*, Winter 2001.

15 Dana Claxton, "Artist Statement," in *Dana Claxton: Indian Candy* (Vancouver: Winsor Gallery, 2013), 6.

16 Ibid.

17 Ibid.

18 Kevin Griffin, "Goes National for CONTACT," *Vancouver Sun*, April 26, 2014, http://vancouversun.com/news/staff-blogs/dana-claxton-indian-candy-goes-national-for-contact.

19 Leah Collins, "Dana Claxton Wants to Change the Way You Think About Indigenous Women," *CBC Arts*, January 14, 2016, http://www.cbc.ca/arts/dana-claxton-wants-to-change-the-way-you-think-about-indigenous-women-1.3403600.

20 Kevin Griffin, "Dana Claxton to Perform New Work at The Metropolitan Museum," *Vancouver Sun*, March 9, 2015, http://vancouversun.com/news/staff-blogs/dana-claxton-to-perform-new-work-at-the-metropolitan-museum.

21 Amanda Malcolm, "Dana Claxton to Perform Original Piece, Fringed at the Met," *The Met*, March 12, 2015, https://www.metmuseum.org/blogs/now-at-the-met/2015/dana-claxton-performs-fringed/.

A Forest of Canoes, 2018 (installation along The Bentway, CONTACT Photography Festival, Toronto)

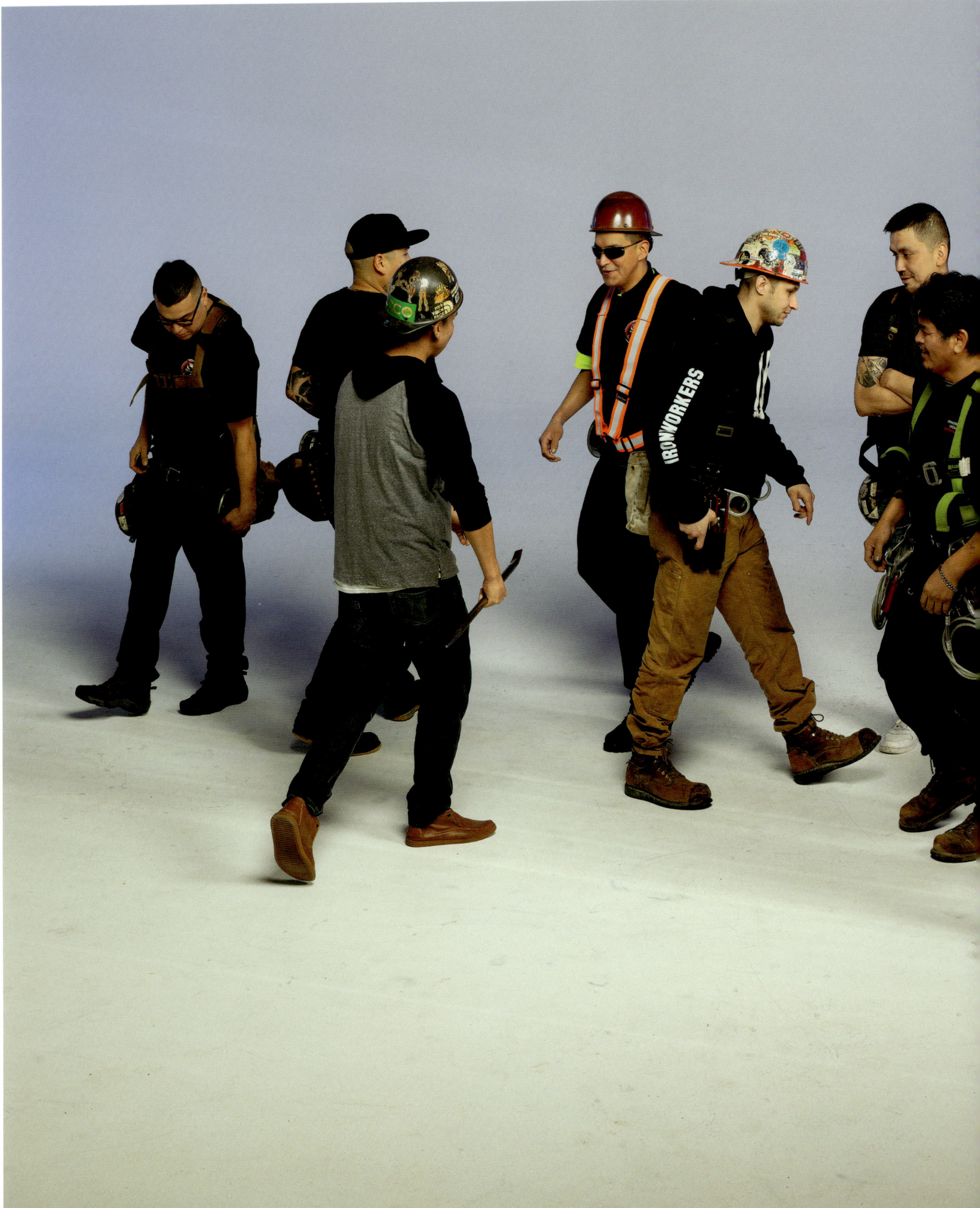
IRONWORKERS

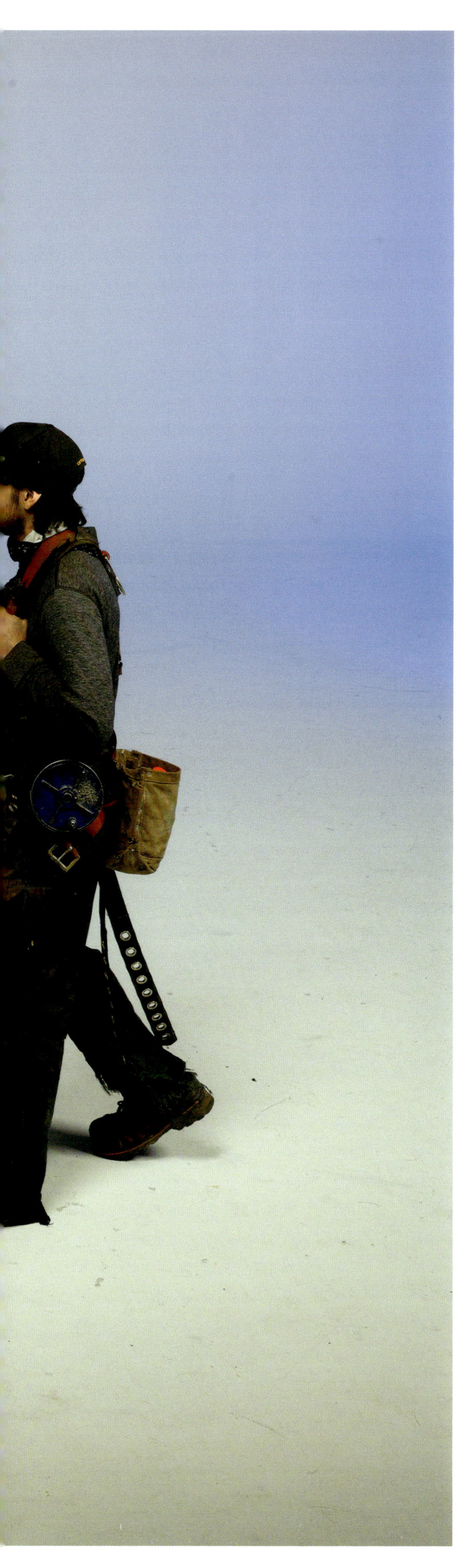

SELECT BIBLIOGRAPHY

EXHIBITION CATALOGUES AND ARTIST BOOKS

Arnold, Grant. "Photoconceptual Art and Vancouver." In *Shore, Forest and Beyond: Art from the Audain Collection,* edited by Grant Arnold and Ian M. Thom, 101–4. Vancouver: Vancouver Art Gallery, Douglas & McIntyre, 2011.

Baerwaldt, Wayne. *Remuer ciel et terre / Crack the Sky: la Biennale de Montréal 2007.* Montréal: Centre international d'art contemporain de Montréal, 2007.

Barnett, Derek, Dana Claxton and Reid Shier, eds. *Dana Claxton: Paris, June Fourth, Fifth, & Sixth, Two Thousand & Six.* North Vancouver: Presentation House Gallery, 2014.

Bell, Lynne. "Taking a Walk in the City." In *Urban Fictions,* by Rosa Ho and Lynne Bell, 43–56. North Vancouver: Presentation House Gallery, 1996.

Cachia, Amanda. "Map of Blood," in *Diabolique.* Regina: Dunlop Art Gallery, 2009.

Crowston, Catherine. *Beauty and the Beast. Dana Claxton, Isaac Julien and Alison Murray.* Banff: Walter Phillips Gallery, 1997.

Deadman, Patricia. "Dana Claxton: Sitting Bull and the Moose Jaw Sioux." In *Dana Claxton: Sitting Bull and the Moose Jaw Sioux.* Moose Jaw: Moose Jaw Museum & Art Gallery, 2007.

Elliott, David, ed. *17th Biennale of Sydney, The Beauty of Distance: Songs of Survival in a Precarious Age.* Sydney: Biennale of Sydney, 2010.

Gagnon, Monika Kin. "Moving Ground Underfoot." In *topographies: aspects of recent B.C. art,* 47–82. Vancouver: Vancouver Art Gallery, Douglas & McIntyre, 1996.

Gale, Peggy. "Dana Claxton: In Search of Sitting Bull." In *Dana Claxton: Sitting Bull and the Moose Jaw Sioux.* Moose Jaw: Moose Jaw Museum & Art Gallery, 2007.

Jessup, Lynda, and Shannon Bagg. *On Aboriginal Representation in the Gallery.* Gatineau: Canadian Museum of Civilization, 2002.

Kunard, Andrea, and Steve Loft. *Steeling the Gaze: Portraits by Aboriginal Artists.* Ottawa: Canadian Museum of Contemporary Photography, 2011.

Lion, Jenny, ed. *Magnetic North.* Minneapolis: University of Minnesota Press, 2000.

Rice, Ryan. "Turn the Beat Around." In *Face the Nation.* Edmonton: Art Gallery of Alberta, 2008.

Ritter, Kathleen, "What is an Archive?" In *Dana Claxton: Indian Candy.* Vancouver: Winsor Gallery, 2013.

Ritter, Kathleen, and Tania Willard. *Beat Nation.* Vancouver: Vancouver Art Gallery, 2012.

NDN Ironworkers—Video Flipbook, 2018 (video still)

Todd, Jeremy. "The Ongoing Powers of Dana Claxton." In *Fierce: Women's Hot-Blooded Film/Video*, edited by Janice Hladki, 28–31. Hamilton, ON: McMaster Museum of Art, 2010.

Wlusek, Ola, and Ariel Smith. *In The Flesh: Lance Belanger, Dana Claxton, Brad Isaacs, Meryl McMaster.* Ottawa: Ottawa Art Gallery, 2013.

Zimmerman, Patricia R., "Ardent Spaces, Formidable Environments." In *Fierce: Women's Hot-Blooded Film/Video*, edited by Janice Hladki, 41–46. Hamilton: McMaster Museum of Art, 2010.

REVIEWS, ESSAYS AND ARTICLES

"The Plains Indians: Artists of Earth and Sky." *USA Today Magazine*, April 15, 2015.

Abramson, Stacey. "In the Blink of an Eye." *C Magazine* 94, Summer 2007.

Allen, Christopher. "Inventive, Despite the Preaching." *The Australian*, March 4, 2011.

Alteen, Glenn. "Liturgy for a New Secular World." *Ablakela*. CD-ROM. Vancouver: grunt gallery, 1999.

Anderson, Jack. "Diabolique." *Canadian Art* 26, no. 4, Winter 2009.

Baltruschat, Doris. "Television and Canada's Aboriginal Communities: Seeking Opportunities through Traditional Storytelling and Digital Technologies." *Canadian Journal of Communication* 29, no. 1 , January 2004. http://www.cjc-online.ca/index.php/journal/article/view/1403/1495.

Battiste, Marie, Lynne Bell, Isobel M. Findlay, Len Findlay and James (Sákéj) Youngblood Henderson."Thinking Place: Animating the Indigenous Humanities in Education." *The Australian Journal of Indigenous Education* 34, (2005): 7–19.

Bell, G.J. "Dana Claxton." *Canadian Art* 31, no. 1, Spring 2014.

Bell, Lynne. "Dana Claxton: From a Whisper to a Scream." *Canadian Art* 27, no. 4, Winter 2010.

———. "The Post/Colonial Photographic Archive and the Work of Memory." In *Image and Inscription: an Anthology of Contemporary Canadian Photography*, edited by Robert Bean, 151–65. Toronto: YYZ Books, 2005.

Berson, Amber. "Dana Claxton, The Mustang Suite and Hybrid Humour." *St. Andrews Journal of Art History and Museum Studies* 14 (2010): 77–83.

Bissley, Jackie. "Dana Claxton." *Indian Cinema Entertainment*, Winter 2001.

Brophy, Sarah and Janice Hladki. "Visual Autobiography in the Frame: Critical Embodiment and Cultural Pedagogy." In *Embodied Politics in Visual Autobiography (Cultural Spaces)*, edited by Sarah Brophy and Janice Hladki, 3–28. Toronto: University of Toronto Press, 2014.

Burnham, Clint. "Dana Claxton: Made to be Ready." *Espace* 113, Spring–Summer 2016.

Dahle, Sigrid. "Negative Space: Abattoirs by Artists and the Representation of Trauma." In *Obsession, Compulsion, Collection: On Objects, Display Culture, and Interpretation*, edited by Anthony Kiendl, 133–145. Banff: Banff Centre Press, 2004.

Dowell, Kristin L. "Exploring the Sacred in Aboriginal Performance Art." *E-Misferica* 2, no. 1 (Spring 2005). http://hemisphericinstitute.org/journal/2_1/dowell.html

——— "Performance and 'Trickster Aesthetics' in the Work of Mohawk Filmmaker Shelley Niro." In *Native American Performance and Representation*, edited by S.E. Wilmer, 207–21. Tucson: University of Arizona Press, 2011.

———. "Pushing Boundaries, Defying categories." In *Native Art of the Northwest Coast: A History of Changing Ideas*, edited by Charlotte Townsend-Gault, Jennifer Kramer, and Ki-ke-in, 828–863. Vancouver: UBC Press, 2013.

———. *Sovereign Screens: Aboriginal Media on the Canadian West Coast.* Lincoln: University of Nebraska Press, 2013.

———. "The Future Looks Rad from Where I Stand: A Review of Claiming Space: Voices of Urban Aboriginal Youth at the UBC Museum of Anthropology." *Anthropologica* 57, no. 1 (2015): 239–46.

Durand, Guy Sioui. "Look-facebook-auto'ado texto-photo ! totem hypermoderne." In *Rebelles*, edited by Ève Cadieux. Québec: J'ai VU, 2012.

———. "Regards d'acier, Portraits par des artistes autochtones," *Ciel variable* 82, Summer 2009.

Fitzpatrick, Blake. "Four Directions." *Ciel variable* 88, Spring–Summer 2011.

Fuglerud, Øivind. "Art and Ambiguity: An Extended Review of Border Zones at the Museum of Anthropology, British Columbia." *Museum Anthropology* 35, no. 2 (Fall 2012): 170–84.

Gagnon, Monika Kin. *13 Conversations Art & Cultural Race Politics*. Montréal: Artextes Editions, 2002.

———. "Worldviews in Collision: Dana Claxton's Video Installations." In *Other Conundrums: Race, Culture and Canadian Art*, edited by Monika Kin Gagnon, 33–48. Vancouver: Arsenal Pulp Press, 2000.

Garneau, David. "Dana Claxton's Patient Storm," *Storm Spirits: Aboriginal New Media Art* (October 2006). http://www.stormspirits.ca/English/Storm/essay.html.

———. "Dana Claxton: Sitting Bull and the Moose Jaw Sioux," *Vie des Arts* 197, Winter 2004.

———. "Western Canada in Brief: Fall 1996 and Winter 1997." *C Magazine* 52, February–April 1997.

Garneau, David and Margaret Farmer. "Little Distance Between Us." *Fuse Magazine* 33, no. 4, Fall 2010.

Gillespie, James L. "Language of Intercession." *Canadian Art* 22, no. 2, Summer 2005.

Guglietti, Maria Victoria. "Imagining Drumbytes and Logging in Powwows: A History of Community Imagination in Canadian-based Aboriginal New Media Art." PhD diss., Carleton University, May 2010.

Hill, Richard William. "*Before and after the Horizon: Anishinaabe Artists of the Great Lakes*, Art Gallery of Ontario, Toronto July 26–Nov 23, 2014 & *The Plains Indians: Artists of Earth and Sky*, Metropolitan Museum of Art, New York City, March 9–May 10, 2015." *C Magazine* 128, Winter 2016.

Hladki, Janice. "Decolonizing Colonial Violence: The Subversive Practices of Aboriginal Film and Video." *Canadian Woman Studies* 25, no. 1–2 (Winter/Spring 2006): 83–88.

———. "'Remembering Otherwise': Counter-Commemoration and Re-Territorialization in Indigenous Film and Video Art." *Revisita de Estudios Globales y Arte Contemporáneo* 2, no. 1 (2014): 93–116.

Hood, Mary. "Map(ing): Multiple Artists Printing (Indigenous and Native Geographies)." *American Indian Art Magazine* 38, no. 4, Autumn 2013.

Hubbard, Tasha. 'The Buffaloes are Gone' or 'Return: Buffalo'?—The Relationship of the Buffalo to Indigenous Creative Expression.' *The Canadian Journal of Native Studies* 29, 1–2 (2009): 65–85.

Hunkpapa Woman: Dana Claxton. DVD. Directed by Marianne Jones and Jeff Bear. Urban Rez Productions, 2007.

Isaac, Jaimie and Leah Decter. "(Official Denial) Trade Value in Progress: Unsettling Narratives." *West Coast Line* 74 vol. 46, no. 2 (Summer 2012): 162–78. http://journals.sfu.ca/line/index.php/wcl/issue/archive.

Kelsey, Penelope Myrtle. "Condolence Tropes and Haudenosaunee Visuality." In *American Indian Studies: Visualities*, edited by Denise K. Cummings, 119–130. East Lansing: Michigan State University Press, 2011.

Korniakova, Elena. "Canadian and Russian Animation on Northern Aboriginal Folklore." MA thesis, Concordia University, 2014.

Krivdova, Zofia. *Steeling the Gaze: Collaborative Curatorial Practices and Aboriginal art*. MA thesis, Concordia University, 2014.

Kunard, Andrea and Carol Payne. *The Cultural Work of Photography in Canada*. Montréal: McGill-Queen's University Press, 2011.

La Flamme, Michelle. "Dana Claxton: Reframing the Sacred and Indigenizing the White Cube." In *Diversity and Dialogue: The Eiteliorg Fellowship for Native American Fine Art*, edited by James H. Notage, 49–57. Indianapolis: Eiteljorg Museum of American Indians and Western Art; Seattle: University of Washington Press, 2008.

———. "Unsettling the West: First Nations Films in BC." In *Women Filmmakers: Refocusing*, edited by Jacqueline Levitin, Judith Plessis, Valerie Raoul. Vancouver: UBC Press, 2003.

LaPensée, Elizabeth and Jason Edward Lewis. "Timetraveller™: First Nations Nonverbal Communication in Second Life." In *Nonverbal Communication in Virtual Worlds: Understanding and Designing Expressive Characters*, edited by Joshua Tanenbaum, Magy Seif El-Nasr and Michael Nixon, 94–107. Pittsburgh: ETC Press, 2014.

Laurence, Robin. "Dana Claxton." *Canadian Art* 17, no. 3, Fall 2000.

Lee, James Jason. "Urban Fictions (Vancouver School, Exhibition)." *Parachute: Contemporary Art Magazine* 51, no. 3, July/September 1996.

Lin, Brian. "*Ablakela* Invokes Calm and Innovation." *Windspeaker* 19, no. 10 (February 1, 2002).

Lindner, Markus H. „WE ALL HAVE TO PAY BILLS": Zeitgenössische Sioux-Künstler und der Markt." *Paideuma* 57 (2011): 135–59.

Marubbio, M. Elise. "Introduction to Native American/Indigenous Film." *Post Script* 29, no. 3 (2010).

Mastai, Judith. "The Elevation of BC Art." *C Magazine* 52, February–April 1997.

———. "The Post-Colonial Landscape." *Blackflash* 14, no. 2 (Summer 1996): 10–13.

Mathur, Ashok. "Arts, Activism and the Academy: Resistance is Fertile." *Fuse Magazine* 33 no. 4, Fall 2010.

Mathur, Ashok, Jonathan Dewar, and Mike DeGagné. *Cultivating Canada: Reconciliation Through the Lens of Cultural Diversity*. Ottawa: Aboriginal Healing Foundation, 2011.

Mathur, Ashok and Rita Wong. "Employing Equity in Post-Secondary Art Institutes." In *Retooling the Humanities: The Culture of Research in Canadian Universities*, edited by Smaro Kamboureli and Daniel Coleman, 113–31. Edmonton: University of Alberta Press, 2011.

Mattes, Catherine. *Gatherings: Aboriginal Art from the Collection of the Winnipeg Art Gallery*. Winnipeg: Winnipeg Art Gallery, 2002.

McKegney, Sam. *Masculindians: Conversations about Indigenous Manhood*. Winnipeg: University of Manitoba, 2014.

McLeod, Dayna. "Dana Claxton and the Graceful Art of Rage."

No More Potlucks, no. 12 (November 2010). http://www.vtape.org/critical-writing-index-article?id=4526.
Methot, Suzanne. "Artists Explore Contemporary Idioms and Media." *Ontario Birchbark* 3, no. 8 (2004): 9.
Milroy, Sarah. "Primeval Meets Postmodern in BC Art." *Globe and Mail*, September 28, 1996.
Oh, Susan. "Soaring Beyond the Totem Poles." *Maclean's*, May 7, 2001.
O'Reilly, Finbarr. "A New Wave of Aboriginal Filmmakers is Determined to Leave Portrayals of Natives as Victims Where They Feel They Belong—in the Past." *National Post*, June 18, 1999.
Perron, Annie. "La photographie comme territoire identitaire: l'autoreprésentation photographique et les technologies web comme médium de déploiement identitaire et de rencontre dans le contexte communautaire des jeunes des Premières Nations." MA thesis, Université du Québec à Chicoutimi, 2010.
Pourtavaf, Leila. "Biennale de Montréal 2007. Can Art Exhibitions Have Upsets, Just Like a Sports Competition?" *C Magazine* 95, Fall 2007.
Ramde, Bénédicte. "Do the Clothes Make the Man?" *Ciel variable* 101, Fall 2015.
Redwood, Tom. "Indigenous Media Art: Complex Visions." *Real Time* 102, April–May 2011.
Robinson, Tim. "Native Artists, New Media." *The Silhouette* 74, no. 2, June 27, 2003.
Rondeau-Hoekstra, Cheryl. *Sharing the Cultural Experience: A Comprehensive Guide to First Nations Film and Video*. Montréal: Artexte, 1996.
Roy, Marina. "Corporeal Returns: Feminism and Phenomenology in Vancouver Video and Performance, 1968–1983." *Canadian Art* 18, no. 2, Summer 2001.
Ruiz, Cristina. "The European Enlightenment is Over." *Art Newspaper* 19, no. 214, 2010.
Rushing, W. Jackson. "Manifest Sovereignty: 'Diversity and Dialogue' at the Eiteljorg Museum."*American Indian Art Magazine* 33, no. 3, 2008.
Sepsi, Enikö, Judith Nagy, Miklós Vassányi and János Kenyeres. *Indigenous Perspectives in North America: A Collection of Studies*. Newcastle upon Tyne: Cambridge Scholars Publishing, 2014.
Smith, Charles C. *Pluralism in the Arts in Canada: A Change is Gonna Come*. Ottawa: Canadian Centre for Policy Alternatives, 2012.
Steel, Lisa. "Appropriate Behaviours." *Toronto International Video Art Biennial* (1999).
Stimson, Adrian A. "Two Spirited For You: The Absence of 'Two Spirit' People in Western Culture and Media." *West Coast Line* 40, no. 1, 2006.
St-Jean Aubre, Anne-Marie. "L'art contemporain Amérindien s'expose." *Inter Art Actuel* 104 (Winter 2009–10): 70–72.
St-Laurent, Jason. "*History in Parts: The Work of Dana Claxton*." Ottawa: SAW Gallery, 2005..
Sugrue, Meagan. "Humour in Contemporary Indigenous Photography: Re-focusing the Colonial Gaze." *Arbutus Review* 3, no. 2, 2012.
Tanzer, Ivan. "*Ghost Dance: Activism. Resistance. Art.* Ryerson Image Center, Toronto, 18 September to 15 December 2013." *Ciel variable* 97, Spring–Summer 2014, 92–93.
Taunton, Carla. "PUSHING BOUNDARIES: 'Non Compliance' Short experimental program at imagineNATIVE Film + Media Arts Festival." *Fuse Magazine* 33, no. 1, Winter 2010.
———. "(Re)memory and Resistance: Video Works by Dana Claxton." In *Native Americans on Film: Conversations, Teaching, and Theory*, edited by Eric L. Buffalohead and M. Elise Marubbio, 116–34. Lexington: University of Kentucky, 2013.
Townsend-Gault, Charlotte. "Let X = Audience." In *Reservation X: The Power of Place in Aboriginal Contemporary Art*, edited by Gerald McMaster, 41–51. Hull: Museum of Civilization, 1998.
———. "Topographies: Aspects of Recent BC art." *Canadian Art* 14, no. 1, Spring 1997.
Walker, Morley. "Poetry in Motion Pictures: WAG Exhibit Strives to Open Winnipeggers' Eyes to Avant-garde Filmmaking." *Winnipeg Free Press*, January 15, 2007.
Weder, Adele. "The Art of Medicine." *CMAJ* 184, no. 15 (October 16, 2012): 1717–18.
Wemigwans, Jennifer. "Indigenous Worldviews: Cultural Expression on the World Wide Web." *Canadian Woman Studies* 26, no. 3–4 (Winter/Spring 2008): 31–38.
Willard, Tania. "Beginning from Home." Online curatorial essay, 2007. www.danaclaxton.com.

ARTIST WRITINGS

Claxton, Dana. "3 Performance Works and Other Thoughts." *Canadian Theatre Review* 146, Spring 2011.

———. *Aboriginal Screen Culture: Celebrating 10 Years of ImagiNATIVE*. Toronto: Vtape, 2009.

———. "A Decade in Retrospect: 10 Years of Dramatic Programming at ImagineNATIVE." In *ImagineNATIVE: Aboriginally Produced Film & Video*, edited by Lisa Steele, 52. Toronto: imagineNATIVE, 2009.

———. "Embellished Indigeneity: The Art Making of Skeena Reece." *OBORO* (2017). http://www.oboro.net/sites/www.oboro.net/files/pdf/opuscules/opuscule-reece-web-en.pdf.

———. "Going to the Centre: Performance Works and Other Thoughts." *Canadian Theatre Review* 146 (Spring 2011): 28–31.

———. "Lawrence Paul Yuxweluptun: Master Mixer, Man of Many Colors." In *Red: The Eiteljorg Contemporary Art Fellowship*, edited by Jennifer Complo and Ashley Holland, 21–41. Indianapolis: Eiteljorg Museum of American Indians and Western Art, 2013

———. "Making Medicine." *The Medicine Project*. (n.d.) http://www.themedicineproject.com/curatorial-essay.html.

———. "My Best Shot: 'Aim #1'." *Blackflash* 29, no. 2, 2012.

———. "NWC on the Up...Load: Surfing for Northwest Coast Art." In *Native Art of the Northwest Coast: A History of Changing Ideas,* edited by Charlotte Townsend-Gault, Jennifer Kramer, and Ḳi-ḳe-in. Vancouver: UBC Press, 2013.

———. "*Ode to Gramsci #1, #2, #3, #8*, from *Red on Red*. As reproduced in *GRAMSCIANA: Rivista Internazionale di Studi su Antonio Gramsci* no. 2 (2016): 201.

———. "Red Woman White Cube: First Nations Art and Racialized Space." MA thesis, Simon Fraser University, 2007.

———. Review of *Ceremony, Spirituality, and Ritual in Native American Performance: A Creative Notebook*, by Hanay Geiogamah, *American Indian Culture and Research Journal* 38, no. 4 (2014).

———. "Re:Wind." In *Transference, Tradition, Technology: Native New Media Exploring Visual & Digital Culture*, edited by Dana Claxton, Melanie A. Townsend and Steve Loft, 14–41. Banff, AB: Walter Phillips Gallery, 2005.

———. "Together Doings: Presence in the Work of Guadalupe Martinez." In *Supermoon: UBC Master of Fine Arts Graduate Exhibition 2014*. Vancouver: Belkin Art Gallery/Brick Press, 2014.

———. "Wisdom for All Through Identity Politics: A Hopeful Idea." In *In the Wake of the Komagata Maru: Transpacific Migration, Race and Contemporary Art: Voices from the Exhibition Ruptures in Arrival and the Symposium Disfiguring Identity,* edited by Lisa Marshall with Jordan Strom, 44–48. Surrey: Surrey Art Gallery, 2015.

Claxton, Dana, and Tania Willard. "Imperfect Compliance: A Trajectory of Transformation." *ArcPost*, Institutions by Artists: Vol. Two,, 2013. http://arcpost.ca/articles/imperfect-compliance.

———. "NDN AXE/IONS—A Collaborative Essay." *Indian Acts: Aboriginal Performance Art*. (n.d.) http://indianacts.gruntarchives.org/essay-ndn-axe-ions-claxton-and-willard.html

AUTHOR BIOGRAPHIES

DAVID GARNEAU (Métis) is Professor of Visual Arts at the University of Regina. His practice includes painting, curation and critical writing. He recently co-curated *Transformer: Native Art in Light and Sound*, with Kathleen Ash Milby, at the National Museum of the American Indian, New York; *Moving Forward, Never Forgetting*, with Michelle LaVallee, an exhibition concerning the legacies of Indian Residential Schools, other forms of aggressive assimilation, and (re)conciliation, at the MacKenzie Art Gallery in Regina; and *With Secrecy and Despatch*, with Tess Allas, an international exhibition about massacres of Indigenous people and memorialization, for the Campbelltown Art Centre in Sydney, Australia. Garneau has recently given keynote talks in Australia, New Zealand, the United States, and throughout Canada. He is part of the five-year, SSHRC-funded curatorial research project, "Creative Conciliation," and is working on a public art project in Edmonton. His paintings are in numerous public and private collections.

JALEH MANSOOR is Associate Professor of Art History at the University of British Columbia. Her areas of teaching and research include modernism and the avant-gardes, European art since 1945, formalism, Marxist feminism, and social reproduction theory. Mansoor's current project traces the historical and structural entwinement of aesthetic and real (or concrete) abstraction, the latter understood as the extraction of labour power valorized by exchange on the market. She co-edited an anthology of essays addressing Jacques Rancière's articulations of politics and aesthetics entitled *Communities of Sense: Rethinking Aesthetics and Politics* (Duke UP, 2010). Mansoor's first monographic book, *Marshall Plan Modernism: Italian Postwar Abstraction and the Beginnings of Autonomia* was published by Duke University Press in September 2016. She has been a frequent contributor to *October* and *Texte Zur Kunst*, writes reviews for *Artforum* and is the recipient of a three-year SSHRC Insight grant with her collaborator, artist Dana Claxton.

MONIKA KIN GAGNON is Professor of Communication Studies and a Research Fellow at Concordia University. She has published on cultural politics and the visual and media arts since the 1980s, including *Other Conundrums: Race, Culture and Canadian Art* (2000); *13 Conversations about Art and Cultural Race Politics* (2002), with Richard Fung; and *Reimagining Cinema: Film at Expo 67*, co-edited with Janine Marchessault, (2014), with whom she is co-director of CINEMAexpo67. Her current research is on cultural memory, creative archiving, and experimental media arts, and has included curating and creative alternatives to conventional archiving of experimental media. She was co-curator of *In Search of Expo 67* with Lesley Johnstone at the Musée d'art contemporain de Montréal for the 50th anniversary of Expo 67. She curated *La Vie polaire /Polar Life* at the Cinémathèque québécoise in 2014, and *Theresa Hak Kyung Cha | Immatérial* for DHC Art at Centre Phi in 2015. She is currently working on a book entitled *Posthumous Cinema: Unfinished Films in the Archives*.

OLIVIA MICHIKO GAGNON is a PhD candidate in Performance Studies at New York University. Her dissertation, *Archival Entanglements: Re/Encountering History in Contemporary Feminist, Queer, and Decolonial Art & Performance*, explores how the archive is taken up in contemporary feminist, queer, and decolonial art and performance in ways that enact modes of feeling historical and historical feeling predicated upon entanglement. Her writing has appeared or will appear in *Women & Performance: a journal of feminist theory*, *emisférica*, *Canadian Theatre Review* and *Undercommoning*. She is currently Managing Editor of *Women & Performance*, where she is co-editing a special issue of co-authored articles about the capaciousness of couple forms with James McMaster. She is also Managing Editor of HemiPress at the Hemispheric Institute of Performance and Politics.

GRANT ARNOLD is Audain Curator of British Columbia Art at the Vancouver Art Gallery, where he contributes to the exhibition program and development of the collection. He was previously Senior Curator at the Art Gallery of Windsor and Extension Coordinator at the Mendel Art Gallery in Saskatoon. Recent exhibition projects include *Kevin Schmidt: We Are the Robots*; *Pictures From Here*; *Susan Point: Spindle Whorl* (with Ian Thom); *Stephen Waddell: Dark Matter Atlas*; *Harry Callahan: The Street*; *Jerry Pethick: Shooting the Sun/Splitting the Pie*; *Residue: The Persistence of the Real*; *Emily Carr and Landon Mackenzie: Wood Chopper and the Monkey*; *Myfanwy MacLeod, or There and Back Again* (with Cassandra Getty); *In Dialogue with Carr—Gareth Moore: Allochthonous Window*; *Rodney Graham: Canadian Humourist*; and *SPIRITLANDS: t)/HERE: Marian Penner Bancroft, Selected Photo Works 1975—2000*. In 2017 Arnold was the recipient of the Alvin Balkind Curator's Prize.

LAYLI LONG SOLDIER holds a BFA from the Institute of American Indian Arts and an MFA from Bard College. Her poems have appeared in *POETRY Magazine, The New York Times, The American Poet*, *The American Reader*, *The Kenyon Review Online*, *BOMB* and other publications. She is the recipient of an NACF National Artist Fellowship, a Lannan Literary Fellowship, a Whiting Award and was a finalist for the 2017 National Book Award. Most recently, she received the 2018 PEN / Jean Stein Award and the 2018 National Book Critics Circle Award. She lives in Santa Fe, New Mexico.

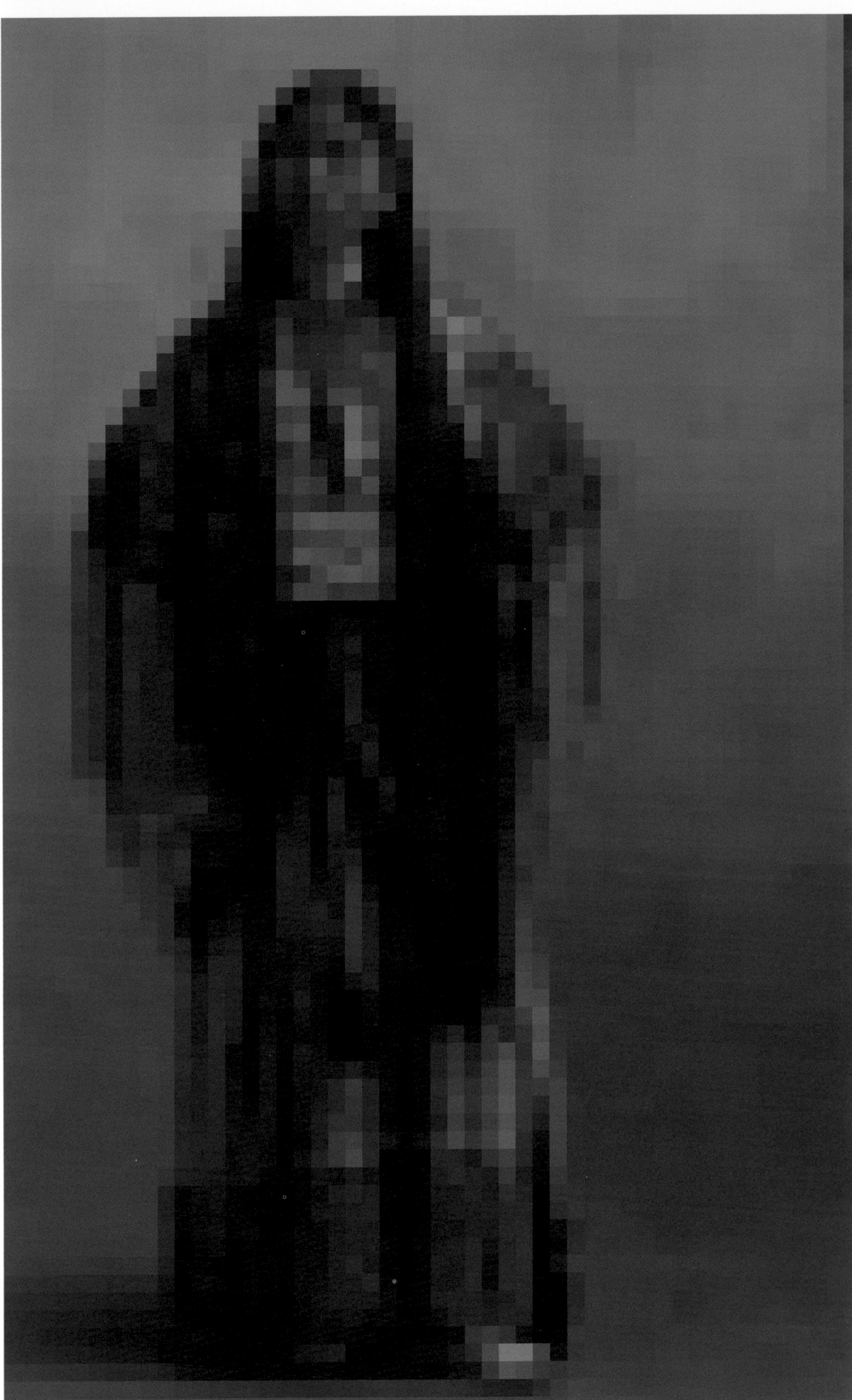

LIST OF WORKS

Dimensions are in centimetres and are listed as height x width x depth

Untitled, c. 1990
3 silver gelatin prints
200 × 120 (each)
Courtesy of the Artist

I Want to Know Why, 1994
single-channel video with audio
6:20 min.
Courtesy of Video Out Distribution / VIVO Media Arts

Sa, 1994
single-channel video with audio
39:48 min.
Courtesy of the Artist and Western Front, Vancouver, BC

The Red Paper, 1996
single-channel video with audio
13:30 min.
Collection of the Vancouver Art Gallery, Vancouver Art Gallery Acquisition Fund with the financial support of the Canada Council for the Arts Acquisition Assistance Program

Buffalo Bone China, 1997
mixed media installation with single-channel video, broken china, stanchions and rope
12:00 min., dimensions variable
Collection of the MacKenzie Art Gallery, Purchased with financial support of the Canada Council for the Arts Acquisition Assistance Program

Jingle Dress #1, 1998–2011
chromogenic print (black and white)
84 × 117
Private Collection

Jingle Dress #2, 1998–2011
chromogenic print (black and white)
84 × 117
Private Collection

10, 2003
single-channel video with audio
8:00 min.
Courtesy of Video Out Distribution / VIVO Media Arts

Rattle, 2003
4-channel video installation with audio
5:37 min.
Collection of John Cook

Sitting Bull and the Moose Jaw Sioux, 2004
4-channel video installation with audio
34:10 min.
Collection of the Moose Jaw Museum & Art Gallery

Onto the Red Road, 2006
5 chromogenic prints
183 × 152 (each)
Courtesy of the Eiteljorg Museum of American Indians and Western Art, Indianapolis

Paris, June Fourth, Fifth, & Sixth, Two Thousand & Six, 2006
20 silver gelatin prints
22 × 33 (each)
Courtesy of the Artist

The Patient Storm, 2006
single-channel video with audio
8:00 min.
Courtesy of Video Out Distribution / VIVO Media Arts

Baby Boyz Gotta Indian Pony (from *The Mustang Suite*), 2008
chromogenic print
127 × 157.7 × 5.3 (framed)
National Gallery of Canada, Ottawa, Purchased 2009

Longhair Blue Woman (from *Indian Candy*), 2013

Baby Girlz Gotta Mustang
(from *The Mustang Suite*), 2008
chromogenic print
127 × 157.7 × 5.3 (framed)
National Gallery of Canada, Ottawa, Purchased 2009

Daddy's Gotta New Ride
(from *The Mustang Suite*), 2008
chromogenic print
127 × 157.7 × 5.3 (framed)
National Gallery of Canada, Ottawa, Purchased 2009

Family Portrait (Indians on a Blanket)
(from *The Mustang Suite*), 2008
chromogenic print
127 × 157.7 × 5.3 (framed)
National Gallery of Canada, Ottawa, Purchased 2009

Momma Has a Pony Girl…(named History and sets her free) (from *The Mustang Suite*), 2008
chromogenic print
127 × 157.7 × 5.3 (framed)
National Gallery of Canada, Ottawa, Purchased 2009

Paint Up #1, 2009
chromogenic print
183 × 183
Audain Collection, Promised Gift
to Audain Art Museum

Paint Up #2, 2009
chromogenic print
183 × 183
Collection of Neil Chrystal

AIM #1, 2010
chromogenic print
152.4 × 106.7
Collection of John Cook

AIM #2, 2010
chromogenic print
152.4 × 106.7
Collection of John Cook

AIM #3, 2010
chromogenic print
152.4 × 106.7
Collection of John Cook

AIM #4, 2010
chromogenic print
152.4 × 106.7
Collection of John Cook

Blue Headdress (from *Indian Candy*), 2013
chromogenic print mounted on aluminum
61 × 46
Collection of Robert Watson

Blue Horse Man (from *Indian Candy*), 2013
chromogenic print mounted on aluminum
86 × 154
Courtesy of the Artist

Buffalo Bill Purple (from *Indian Candy*), 2013
chromogenic print mounted on aluminum
60 × 38
Collection of the Art Gallery of Greater Victoria, Purchased with the support of the Canada Council for the Arts Acquisition Grants program and the George and Lola Kidd BC Art Acquisitions Fund

Diefenbaker Blue Letter
(from *Indian Candy*), 2013
chromogenic print on mounted aluminum
32 × 27
Collection of John Cook

Geronimo in Pink (from *Indian Candy*), 2013
chromogenic print mounted on aluminum
61 × 122
Courtesy of the Artist

Longhair Blue Woman
(from *Indian Candy*), 2013
chromogenic print mounted on aluminum
61 × 41
Private Collection

Maria Tallchief in Turquoise (from *Indian Candy*) 2013
chromogenic print mounted on aluminum
155 × 121
Collection of Lauren Victoria Armstrong

Sitting Bull Blue (from *Indian Candy*), 2013
chromogenic print mounted on aluminum
13.3 × 41.3
Collection of John Cook

Sitting Bull Centennial Train
(from *Indian Candy*), 2013
chromogenic print mounted on aluminum
38 × 27
Collection of John Cook

Sitting Bull Draws the Dandy
(from *Indian Candy*), 2013
chromogenic print mounted on aluminum
102 × 138
Collection of Westport Fuel Systems Inc.

Tatanka (Buffalo) (from *Indian Candy*), 2013
chromogenic print mounted on aluminum
114 X 152
On Loan from Mary Wesik

Tonto Prayer (from *Indian Candy*), 2013
chromogenic print mounted on aluminum
22.4 × 17.7 cm
Collection of the Art Gallery of Greater Victoria, Purchased with the support of the Canada Council for the Arts Acquisition Grants program and the George and Lola Kidd BC Art Acquisitions Fund

Wild Red Envelope (from *Indian Candy*), 2013
chromogenic print mounted on aluminum
122 × 51
Collection of Jennifer Winsor

Writing on Stone Headdress (from *Indian Candy*), 2013
chromogenic print mounted on aluminum
61 × 106
Courtesy of the Artist

Headdress, 2015
LED firebox with transmounted chromogenic transparency
122 × 81
Collection of the Vancouver Art Gallery, Purchased with the support of the Canada Council for the Arts Acquisition Grants program and the Vancouver Art Gallery Acquisition Fund

Buffalo Woman 1, 2016
ink on silk (windbox), Skull by Kevin McKenzie
274 × 107
Courtesy of the Artist

Buffalo Woman 2, 2016
ink on silk (windbox), Skull by Kevin McKenzie
274 × 107
Courtesy of the Artist

Cultural Belongings, 2016
LED firebox with transmounted chromogenic transparency
183 × 244
Collection of Rosalind and Amir Adnani

Ode to Gramsci #1 (from *Red on Red*), 2016
ink on nylon
121.9 × 152.4
Courtesy of the Artist

Ode to Gramsci #2 (from *Red on Red*), 2016
ink on linen
130 × 260
Courtesy of the Artist

Ode to Gramsci #3 (from *Red on Red*), 2017
ink on nylon
121.9 × 152.4
Courtesy of the Artist

Ode to Gramsci #4 (from *Red on Red*), 2017
ink on nylon
121.9 × 152.4
Courtesy of the Artist

The Protector, 2017
LED firebox with transmounted chromogenic transparency
243.8 × 122
Private Collection

Headdress—Jeneen, 2018
LED firebox with transmounted chromogenic transparency
152 × 102 × 18
Collection of Cathy Zuo

Lasso, 2018
LED firebox with transmounted chromogenic transparency
183 × 305
Courtesy of the Artist

NDN Ironworkers, 2018
LED firebox with transmounted chromogenic transparency
183 × 305
Courtesy of the Artist

NDN Ironworkers—Video Flipbook, 2018
single-channel video with audio
9:48 min.
Courtesy of the Artist

NDN Ironworkers Tool Still Life, 2018
chromogenic print mounted on aluminum
127 × 76.2
Courtesy of the Artist

NDN Ironworker (Warrior of...), 2018
LED firebox with transmounted chromogenic transparency
121.9 × 213.4
Courtesy of the Artist

ACKNOWLEDGEMENTS

Dana Claxton: Fringing the Cube would not have been possible without the support of the collectors, galleries and museums who have generously loaned work for the exhibition. I extend my thanks to Rosalind and Amir Adnani; Lauren Victoria Armstrong; Neil Chrystal; John Cook; Art Gallery of Greater Victoria; Robert Watson; Mary Wesik; Cathy Zuo; Westport Fuel Systems; Jennifer Winsor and the Winsor Gallery, Vancouver; Audain Art Museum, Whistler; Eiteljorg Museum of American Indians and Western Art, Indianapolis; MacKenzie Art Gallery, Regina; Moose Jaw Museum and Art Gallery, Moose Jaw; the National Gallery of Canada, Ottawa; and several lenders who have chosen to remain anonymous, for allowing their works to be included in the exhibition.

I thank all the staff at the Vancouver Art Gallery, especially Siobhan McCracken Nixon, Curatorial Assistant; Emma Conner, Curatorial Publications Assistant; Rachel Topham, Photographer; Danielle Currie, Rights and Reproductions; Ashlee Conery, Curatorial Coordinator–Interpretation; Jenny Wilson, Registrar–Exhibitions and Loans; Ken Labun and Jim Stamper, Lead Preparators; Wade Thomas, Audio Visual Technician; and Bruce Wiedrick, Manager of Curatorial Affairs for their dedicated work on the exhibition and publication. I am also very grateful for the work of Kelsey Blackwell and her staff on the design of this publication.

My profound thanks go to Dana Claxton and her assistant Pauline Petit for their gracious attention to detail and enthusiasm, which has been vital to the realization of the exhibition and publication.

—Grant Arnold, Audain Curator of British Columbia Art

I am deeply grateful to Grant Arnold for his creativity, photography, writing and for curating this exhibition; the contributing and thoughtful writers Monika Kin Gagnon and Olivia Michiko Gagnon, Jaleh Mansoor, David Garneau and Layli Long Soldier; the staff at the Vancouver Art Gallery for all their support with my curatorial selections, the catalogue and installing the exhibition. I thank all the sponsors for their generous support.

A special wopila to Siobhan McCracken Nixon for her graciousness, and to Pauline Petit who so creatively works as my studio assistant and realized I have been "fringing the cube"! I am appreciative of Daina Augaitis for the encouraging studio visit to view my yet to be produced fireboxes. And to all the private and public collections who so generously lent works—a huge wopila tanka!

I am grateful to Paul Wong, Bobbi Kozniuk, Lynne Bell, Skeena Reece, Lawrence Paul Yuxweluptun, Patricia Goodwill-Littlechild, Sam Bob, Zoe Hopkins, Sissy Goodhouse, Cowboy Smithx, Neil Eustache, Sara Diamond, Ronnie Dean Harris, Rick Erickson and Donna Partridge, Nanomi Martin, Dee Pointe, Joseph Paul, Ben Paul, Deanna and Havana Couture, Mark Nash, Andrea Tuele, Cathy Sousloff, Amir and Rosalind Adnani, Andrea Walsh, Jeneen Frei Njootli, Gary Horsnal, David Elliot, Courtenay Crane, Janice Hladki, Hugh and Debra Beard, Catherine Crowston, Marie Prince, Henri Robideau, Jennifer Winsor, Heather Smith, Ted Douglas of Etonia, SK, the late Joe Flying Bye, the late Isaac Dog Eagle, the late Grace Peigan Wood Mountain, all the Ironworkers for working with me and Peter Bob for gathering them! Everyone at ABC Colour Lab, the Department of Art History, Visual Art and Theory at the University of British Columbia, and the Social Sciences and Humanities Research Council who supported the Labour research. And many students over the years.

Michael Wesik for his generous and perfect printing of the early works. Amy Kazymerchyk for her curatorial storytelling, Glenn Alteen / grunt gallery for the deep devotion to Indigenous art. Lori Blondeau / Tribe for my first solo show with *Buffalo Bone China*, Monika Kin Gagnon for our journeys, Winston Xin for editing my films/videos for the last twenty-five years, Russell Wallace for thirty years of music, Samaya Jardey for allowing me to photograph and film her for thirty years.

CREDITS

To my family: Kim Soo Goodtrack, Ron Sr., Ron, Don, Megan, Mitchell and David Claxton, Robert Watson, Shadae Johnson and family, uncle Hartland and auntie Evelyn Goodtrack and all my cousins. My late mother Ellen (Ella) who was so cool and taught me generosity, my late grandmothers Gladys Claxton who will forever inspire me, and Pearl Goodtrack whose humility will forever be within me, my late Aunt Dr. Beatrice Medicine for bringing me into the Sundance circle. And to her son Ted Sitting Crow Garner.

I honour the spirit of mountain on the north shore
and the generous life giving sun.
Wopila pilamaya mitaukuye awasin.

I give thanks, you have honoured me, everything is related.
I raise my hands to the east—palms out.

— Dana Claxton

All images courtesy of the Artist unless noted below.

Inside front cover, 144: Don Hall © MacKenzie Art Gallery; Table of Contents, 56–57: David Barbour © Ottawa Art Gallery; 4, 124 (bottom right), 128 (right), 130 (left), 131 (right), 132 (right), 133 (right), 134 (left), 136, 137, 138 (left), 139 (right), 140, 143 (left): Maegan Hill-Carroll, Vancouver Art Gallery; 32–33: Henri Robideau; 48, 141: Pauline Petit; 62–63: Michael R. Barrick; 120, 142: Blaine Campbell; 123 (left): Steven Wasney; 124 (top): Reece Metcalfe; 124 (bottom left): Trevor Mills, Vancouver Art Gallery; 125: Sylvia E. Thome; 126-127: Merle Addison; 40–41; 68–69; 106–107; 129; 130–131 (middle): Rachel Topham, Vancouver Art Gallery; 132 (left): Donna Hagerman; 138 (right): Carole Segal; 143 (right): Vishal Marapon; 145: Nicole Pacampara

Published in conjunction with *Dana Claxton: Fringing the Cube*, an exhibition organized by the Vancouver Art Gallery, curated by Grant Arnold, Audain Curator of British Columbia Art, and presented from October 27, 2018 to February 3, 2019.

PUBLICATION SUPPORT:

VISIONARY PARTNER FOR SCHOLARSHIP AND PUBLICATIONS
THE RICHARDSON FAMILY

THE JACK AND DORIS SHADBOLT ENDOWMENT FOR RESEARCH AND PUBLICATIONS

Editor: Grant Arnold
Curatorial Assistant: Siobhan McCracken Nixon
Editing: Emma Conner
Design: Studio Blackwell, Kelsey Blackwell with Meredith Holigroski
Publication coordination: Emma Conner
Digital image preparation: Rachel Topham
Rights and reproductions: Danielle Currie
Proofreading: Michael Leyne

Printed and bound in Canada by Friesens
Distributed in the U.S. by Publishers Group West
Distributed outside of North America by Prestel Publishing

Cover Image: Dana Claxton, *Cultural Belongings*, 2016 (image flipped)

EXHIBITION SUPPORT:

MAJOR SUPPORT GENEROUSLY PROVIDED BY
CATHY ZUO

VISIONARY PARTNERS FOR PHOTOGRAPHY EXHIBITIONS
MILES, MAUREEN AND LARRY LUNN

SUPPORTING SPONSOR
Vancity

ADDITIONAL SUPPORT
BRUCE MUNRO WRIGHT

Cataloguing data is available from Library and Archives Canada

ISBN 978-1-77327-050-0 (hbk.)
ISBN: 978-1-927656-40-2 (Vancouver Art Gallery)

Measurements of artworks are given as height × width × depth.

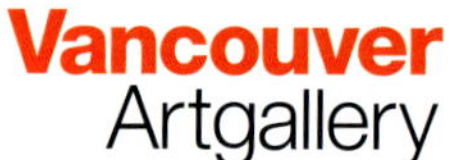

Vancouver Art Gallery
750 Hornby Street
Vancouver, BC V6Z 2H7
www.vanartgallery.bc.ca

The Vancouver Art Gallery is a not-for-profit organization supported by its members, individual donors, corporate funders, foundations, the City of Vancouver, the Province of British Columbia through the British Columbia Arts Council, and the Canada Council for the Arts.

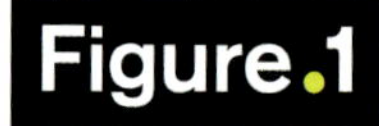

Figure 1 Publishing Inc.
Vancouver, BC Canada
www.figure1publishing.com

 OPPOSITE AND FOLLOWING: *Paris June Fourth, Fifth, & Sixth, Two Thousand & Six*, 2014 (detail)

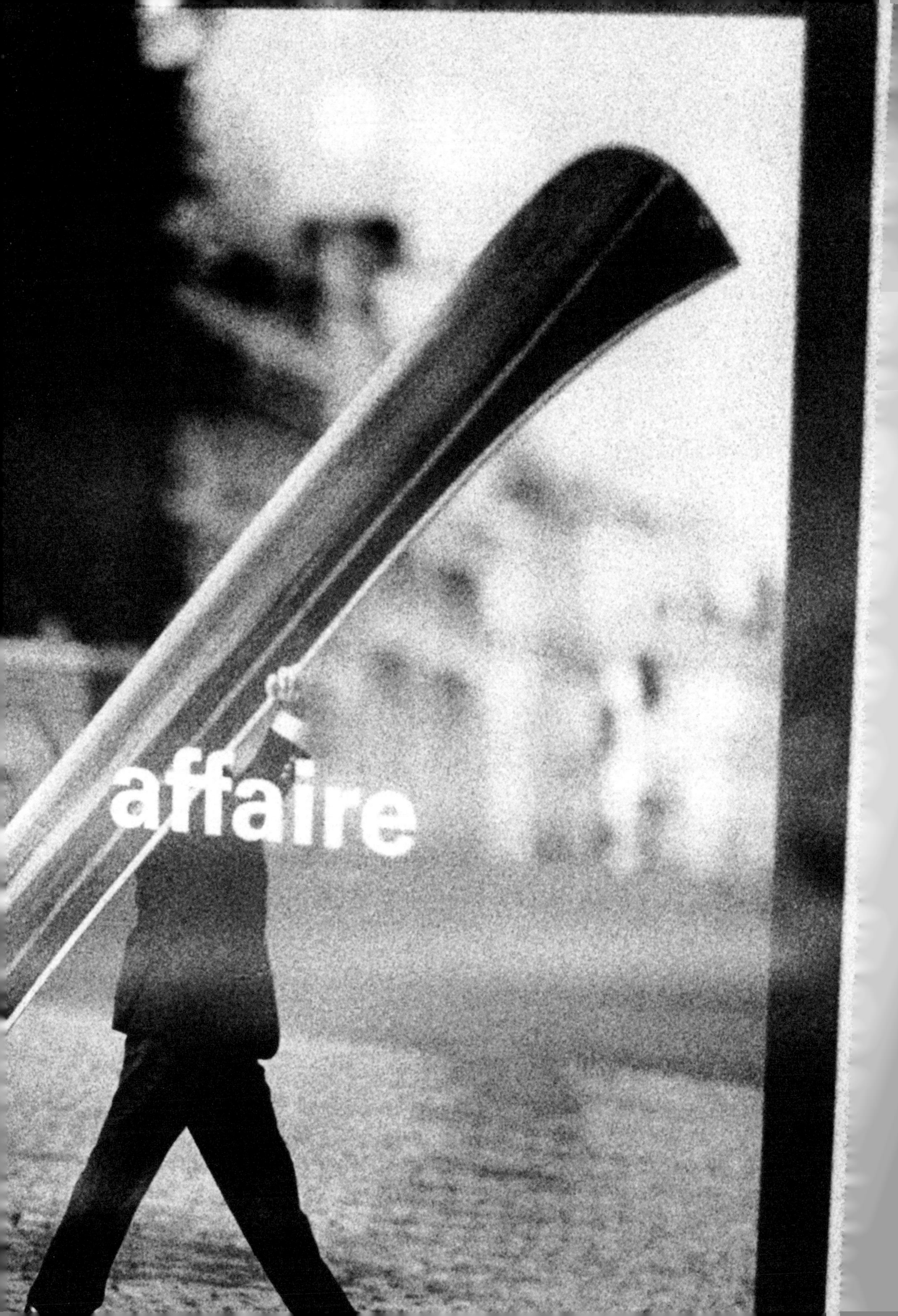

affaire

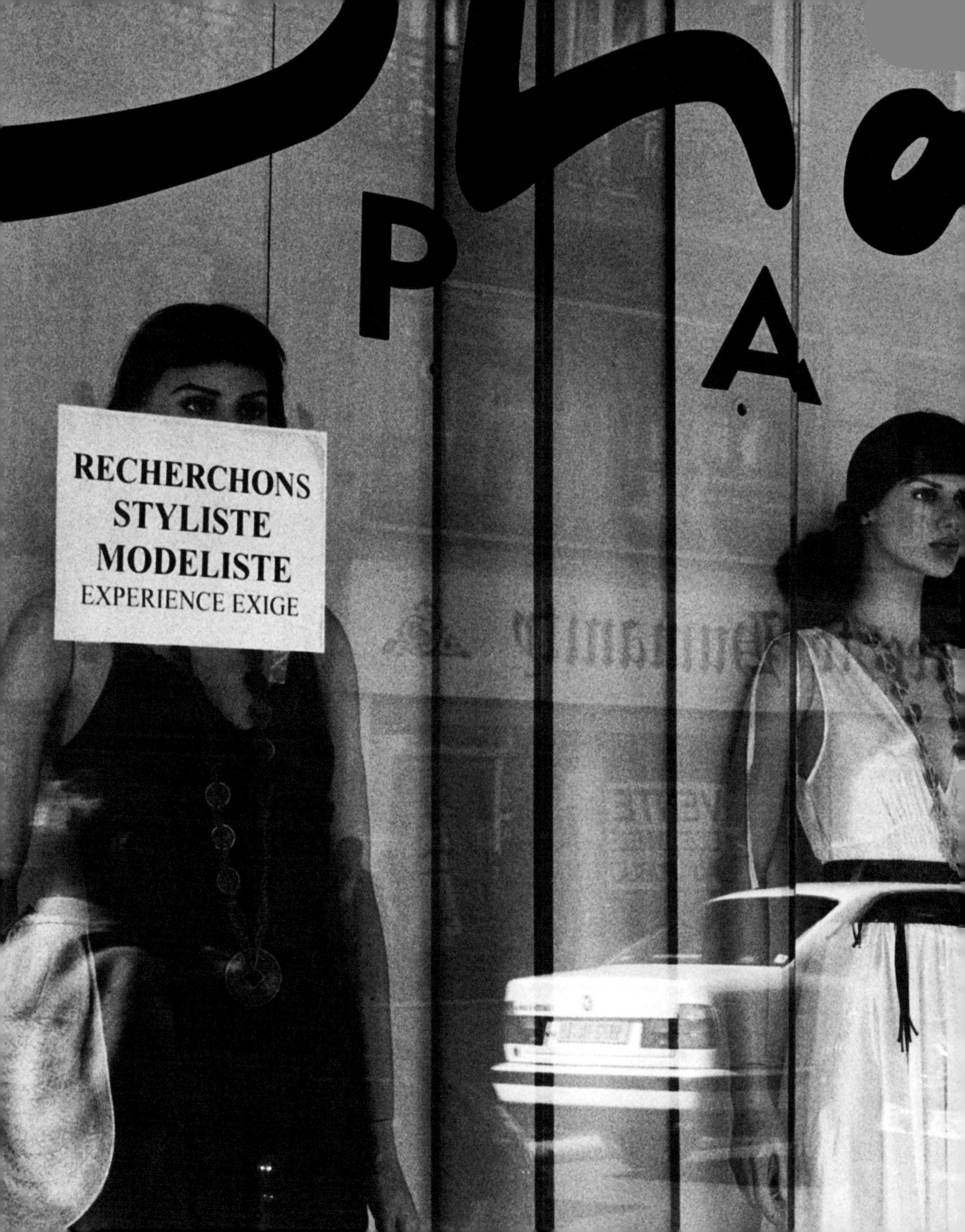
RECHERCHONS
STYLISTE
MODELISTE
EXPERIENCE EXIGE